RE-MAKING THE LIBRARY MAKERSPACE

RE-MAKING THE LIBRARY MAKERSPACE
CRITICAL THEORIES, REFLECTIONS, AND PRACTICES

Maggie Melo and Jennifer T. Nichols, Editors

LIBRARY JUICE PRESS
SACRAMENTO, CA

Copyright respective authors, 2020

Published in 2020 by Library Juice Press

Library Juice Press
PO Box 188784
Sacramento, CA 95822

http://libraryjuicepress.com/

This book is printed on acid-free paper.

Library of Congress Cataloging-in-Publication Data

Names: Melo, Maggie, editor. | Nichols, Jennifer T., editor.
Title: Re-making the library makerspace : critical theories, reflections, and practices / Maggie Melo and Jennifer T. Nichols, editors.
Description: Sacramento, CA : Library Juice Press, 2020. | Includes bibliographical references and index. | Summary: "Examines the limitations and challenges emerging from the "maker movement" emphasizing the critical work that is being done to cultivate anti-oppressive, inclusive and equitable making environments. Makerspaces in libraries are especially focused upon" Provided by publisher.
Identifiers: LCCN 2020034634 | ISBN 9781634000819 (paperback acid-free paper)
Subjects: LCSH: Makerspaces in libraries--United States. | Maker movement in education--United States. | Libraries and minorities--United States. | Libraries and women--United States. | Libraries and community--United States.
Classification: LCC Z716.37 .R4 2020 | DDC 025.50973--dc23
LC record available at https://lccn.loc.gov/2020034634

Table of Contents

Foreword – *Anne Cong-Huyen and Caitlin Pollock*   v

Introduction

Centering Voices from the Margins: Unsettling the Exceptionalist Lore of Makerspaces – *Maggie Melo and Jennifer T. Nichols*   1

Who Belongs in the Makerspace? Power and Critical Theories

1. Critical Race Theory and Makerspaces: A Practical Approach – *Jennifer Brown*   11

2. Who Belongs in the Makerspace? Experiences of Women of Color in an Academic Library Makerspace – *Anthony Sanchez, Danielle Dolan-Sanchez, and Vicki Lázaro*   27

3. Reimagining the Thirdspace through the Makerspace – *Anna Montana Cirell, Nadia Kellam, Audrey Boklage, and Brooke Coley*   47

4. From Needs Analysis to Power Analysis: A Framework to Examine & Broker Power in Makerspaces – *Brianna Marshall and Marijel (Maggie) Melo*   83

Movement, Empathy, and Inclusion in Youth Makerspaces

5. Making the Body: Physical Activity in Makerspaces – *Noah Lenstra and Heather Moorefield-Lang*   101

6. Trauma-Informed Making – *Heather Lister*   115

7. Peace Prescription: Inclusive Making in School Libraries – *Kyungwon Koh, Xun Ge, Lo Lee, Kathryn R. Lewis, Shirley Simmons, and Lee B. Nelson*   135

Counternarratives

8. Barriers to Inclusivity in Makerspaces – *DiMitri Higginbotham and Rob Rouse*   153

9. Supporting Making in Libraries Rather than Makerspaces: Rethinking the (Maker)space for Rural Libraries – *Aubrey Rogowski, Victor R. Lee, and Mimi Recker*   167

10. The Feminist Makerspace: Smashing the Patriarchy with Crafting, Mentorship, and Connection – *Meaghan Moody and Chava Spivak-Birndorf*   183

11. Interrogating What We Mean by "Making": Stories from Women Who Make in Community – *Bibhushana Poudyal, Tetyana Zhyvotovska, Estefania Castillo, Nora Rivera, Ann Shivers-McNair, Joy Robinson, and Laura Gonzales*   203

Re-Imagined Makerspaces: Policies, Procedures, and Culture

12. Makerspace Collaboration as Dialogue and Resistance – *Sanjeet Mann*   227

13. Diversity by Design: How to Create and Sustain an Inclusive Academic Library Makerspace – *Katie Musick Peery and Morgan Chivers*   247

14. Hiring, Training, Designing, and Hosting: A Case Study of an Inclusive Library Makerspace – *John T. Sherrill*   265

15. Confronting Expectations: Reflections on Impostor Syndrome in the Maker Movement – *Leanne Nay*   283

About the Contributors   301

Index   311

Foreword

Anne Cong-Huyen & Caitlin Pollock

In the first chapter of *The Maker Manifesto,* Mark Hatch writes of makerspaces that "The sharing philosophy gives a makerspace its magic. [...] Sharing makes a makerspace a community."[1] He paints a utopian vision of generous spaces that welcome people of any background and skill level as long as they are open to learning and sharing. But as the editors and contributors of this volume rightly argue, the realities of makerspaces are much more complicated and nuanced, and the stakes are higher when they take up residence in libraries.

Today, it is not a surprise to many that the maker community and its spaces have been critiqued for not being as inclusive or radical as they are purported to be by proponents. The case of Naomi Wu in 2017 brought the problematic gender, racial, and national politics of the maker community into stark relief when the community and some of its most prominent figures became embroiled in intense controversy and scrutiny. At the time, Dale Dougherty (CEO of Maker Media, publisher of *MAKE:* and host of Maker Faires worldwide) published tweets reiterating Internet conspiracy theories which speculated that Naomi Wu, a then twenty-three-year-old Chinese female from Shenzhen, China, was not who she said she was; rather, she was a "puppet that was created

---

1. Mark Hatch, *The Maker Movement Manifesto: Rules for Innovation in the New World of Crafters, Hackers, and Tinkerers* (New York, NY: McGraw-Hill 2014), Chapter 1.

to garner views and free stuff for her engineer husband."² Ultimately, Dougherty realized the error he had made by unwittingly casting aspersions on women and the Chinese and made a public apology on the *MAKE:* community website.³

Incidents like the one featuring Dougherty and Wu highlight the unspoken assumptions made within cultural texts and spaces like *MAKE:*, its Maker Faires, and makerspaces: that "makers" are assumed to inhabit certain kinds of (normative white male) bodies, hail from certain (privileged global north) nations, and make certain non-trivial techie things. It is this kind of context that led Garnet Hertz and the Concept Lab to publish their Critical Making "Maker's Bill of Rights" which ends with this pithy and biting commandment: "The term 'maker' no longer belongs to Maker Media—the organization will become irrelevant or die if it continues down a gadget oriented 'toys for boys' path."⁴

While the Maker Movement has had its own reckoning with its misogyny, racism, and a general lack of inclusivity, so too has library land. While librarianship is mostly comprised of women, the field has remained overwhelmingly white, with over eighty percent of the field in 2010 self-identified as white;⁵ this is a statistic that MIT Director of Libraries Chris Bourg referred to in a scathing blog post as the "Unbearable Whiteness of Librarianship."⁶ There has been concern and criticism that, as the Maker Movement presence in libraries grows, the gender

---

2. Nicole Kobie, "How a DIY YouTuber became the target of a sexist conspiracy theory," *The Outline*, (November 9, 2017), https://theoutline.com/post/2459/how-a-diy-youtuber-became-the-target-of-a-sexist-conspiracy-theory.

3. Dale Dougherty, "My Apology to Naomi Wu and the Make Community," *MAKE: Community* (November 19, 2017), https://makezine.com/2017/11/19/apology-to-naomi-wu/.

4. Garnet Hertz, "The Maker's Bill of Rights" (Vancouver, BC: Concept Lab, 2018), http://makermanifesto.com/.

5. American Library Association, "Diversity Counts 2009-2010 Update," (September 18, 2012), http://www.ala.org/aboutala/offices/diversity/diversitycounts/2009-2010update.

6. Chris Bourg, "The Unbearable Whiteness of Librarianship," *The Feral Librarian* blog (March 3, 2014), https://chrisbourg.wordpress.com/2014/03/03/the-unbearable-whiteness-of-librarianship/.

and racial make-up of the Maker Movement and libraries are further perpetuated and reified in library makerspaces.

As makers and librarians engage and grapple with these barriers and exclusions, the existence of library makerspaces faces accusations and criticism fueled by toxic nostalgia. In October 2019, *The Atlantic* published an article by Alia Wong, "College Students Just Want Normal Libraries," which implied that academic libraries are overreaching in their attempts to extend and grow their services.[7] While the article neglects and ignores the existence of public and special libraries, the idea that The Library should "stay the same" has dangerous implications. For libraries to remain stagnant means that they will continue to be gatekeepers to information access instead of centers of knowledge production and sharing. To maintain these perceived traditions of The Library is to uphold patterns of systemic violence towards people of color, queer and non-binary people, poor people, and many others who are often excluded from library spaces and services, regarded by many as temples of culture.

But in truth, the perceived ideal of "traditional library services" is a fallacy. During the Harlem Renaissance Regina Anderson Andrews, a Black librarian working at the 135th Street branch of New York Public Library, created workspaces for Black writers and poets that allowed them to share their work and receive feedback. She organized theatrical plays, seminars, and lectures to help acclimate Black refugees of racial violence and civil inequity arriving en masse from the South to live in New York City.[8] This is just one of many examples throughout library history to illustrate the idea that maker spaces and libraries are places of knowledge production and community formation. This is not new but is rather a longstanding tradition of libraries, particularly those serving and served by marginalized peoples.

---

7. Alia Wong, "College Students Just Want Normal Libraries," *The Atlantic*. (October 4, 2019), https://www.theatlantic.com/education/archive/2019/10/college-students-dont-want-fancy-libraries/599455/.

8. Ethelene Whitmire, *Regina Anderson Andrews: Harlem Renaissance Librarian* (Springfield, IL: University of Illinois Press, 2014), 36-37.

As two women of color librarians who knit, crochet, cross-stitch *and* who have taught at digital humanities institutes, we have felt the tensions and gaps between the so-called feminine handicrafts and the techno-utopianism of the Maker Movement and makerspaces that essentially function as start-up incubators. Such spaces are seldom inclusive of the activities that white women and BIPOC laborers and caretakers have participated in for millennia. In recent years, the rise of textile makerspaces and feminist maker labs have changed that landscape. As we build and staff these spaces in our own institutions, or carve out fugitive spaces and programs in our communities, the untapped power and potential of previously unrecognized labor is made clear. It is such a pleasure, after all this time, to see this experiential knowledge and anecdotal evidence documented in concrete and generative pieces within this present collection. These essays represent the important work being done within library makerspaces to confront the exclusionary practices that exist at the intersection of the Maker Movement and libraries while developing services and practices that are inclusive and revolutionary. To learn from the experience of such a diverse group of professionals as they critique and reflect on building their own programs brings this significance into such beautiful clarity.

Anne Cong-Huyen & Caitlin Pollock
Ann Arbor, Michigan

Bibliography

American Library Association. "Diversity Counts 2009-2010 Update." September 18, 2012. http://www.ala.org/aboutala/offices/diversity/diversitycounts/2009-2010update.

Bourg, Chris. "The Unbearable Whiteness of Librarianship." *The Feral Librarian* (blog). March 3, 2014. https://chrisbourg.wordpress.com/2014/03/03/the-unbearable-whiteness-of-librarianship/.

Dougherty, Dale. "My Apology to Naomi Wu and the Make Community." *MAKE: Community*. November 19, 2017. "https://makezine.com/2017/11/19/apology-to-naomi-wu/.

Hatch, Mark. *The Maker Movement Manifesto: Rules for Innovation in the New World of Crafters, Hackers, and Tinkerers*. New York, NY: McGraw-Hill, 2014.

Hertz, Garnet. "The Maker's Bill of Rights." 2018. http://makermanifesto.com/.

Kobie, Nicole. "How a DIY YouTuber became the target of a sexist conspiracy theory." *The Outline*, November 9, 2017. https://theoutline.com/post/2459/how-a-diy-youtuber-became-the-target-of-a-sexist-conspiracy-theory.

Whitmire, Ethelene. *Regina Anderson Andrews: Harlem Renaissance Librarian*. Springfield, IL: University of Illinois Press, 2014.

Wong, Alia. "College Students Just Want Normal Libraries." *The Atlantic*. Washington, DC: Emerson Collective, October 4, 2019. https://www.theatlantic.com/education/archive/2019/10/college-students-dont-want-fancy-libraries/599455/.

Introduction

CENTERING VOICES FROM THE MARGINS: UNSETTLING THE EXCEPTIONALIST LORE OF MAKERSPACES

Maggie Melo and Jennifer T. Nichols

Introduction

The Maker Movement is a global social phenomenon that has generated excitement around tech-centric making and learning since the mid-2000s. Founded in Silicon Valley, the Maker Movement has inspired hundreds of libraries around the world to integrate makerspaces into their own ecosystems to further support users' learning and discovery. While the affordances of the Maker Movement have been highlighted extensively over the past decade, the limitations and drawbacks of this movement have been largely overshadowed. Makerspaces, like libraries, are not inherently neutral. They are imbued with ideologies stemming from Silicon Valley that consequently dictate who makes, why making even occurs, and what is considered making. Educators and information professionals continue to grapple with the ideological underpinnings of the movement that forwards narrow conceptualizations of maker culture—a culture that is predominantly white, heteronormative, abled-bodied, male, and middle class. This edited collection centers the limitations and challenges emerging from this particular brand of "maker culture" and emphasizes the critical work that is being done to cultivate anti-oppressive, inclusive, and equitable making environments in libraries.

The Motivation and Urgency of This Collection

We first met at a campus coffee shop to talk about the possibilities for our university's first makerspace. At the time, Jen was the Fine Arts and Humanities Liaison Librarian and Maggie was a Ph.D. student with interests in digital humanities and pedagogy. We had a sense of the common technologies found in makerspaces and a general idea of the collaborative, open-concept ethos of the environment. However, it became evident that creating an interdisciplinary makerspace for both the campus and the Tucson community came with a unique set of challenges.

In retrospect, we soon realized that learning what components created a makerspace was the easy part. We together learned how to use and repair the tech, we found staff for the space, and we developed training and curriculum. The struggle for us centered on sustaining a makerspace that includes the diverse communities that we sought to support and were also simultaneously a part of. This struggle did not hinge completely on the tangible artifacts in the space, but was rooted in a deeper, ideological challenge: how could we disrupt the very sociopolitical mechanisms that fortify the values of the Maker Movement? The "maker" technologies, the privileging of open-space layouts, and the time and money needed to run and use a makerspace did not emerge from a vacuum; these features are reflective of the white, heteronormative, middle-class imagination of making. It was difficult to welcome and attract diverse user communities to a space that spatially communicates that they simply do not belong. Knowing this was a heavy burden for us. The lack of BIPOC (Black, Indigenous, people of color), first-generation, and disabled communities in the Maker conversation means that critical research and ideas are not only absent, but are routinely excluded from consideration.

For the past seven years, we've found ourselves meeting librarians, scholars, and educators doing transformative work at the margins of the Maker Movement. By transformative we mean that their labor resisted the pressures to create a tech-centered makerspace; instead, it focused on human-centered, anti-oppressive practices, which is where we, too, have chosen to situate our work and this collection. Our presentations, both to library and non-library groups, were primarily focused on the people, the communities of students and educators. This was and is contrary to the typical conference presentations and media coverage that highlight new technologies, innovative furniture, or incredible research projects that come out of makerspaces. Therefore, this collection captures narratives relegated to the margins of the Maker Movement. We wish we had these stories when we first started our own makerspace, but are thankful that this collection now exists.

Background and Key Terms

In February 2005, Dale Dougherty from O'Reilly Media released the first publication of *MAKE* magazine. This moment is often pinpointed as the beginning of the social phenomenon called the **Maker Movement**. The magazine was inspired by publications such as *Popular Mechanics* which featured DIY tutorials, and specific tech and tools.[1] The movement gained a lot of attention and spurred events across the U.S., such as Maker Faires, makerspaces, and even a national week of making in 2014.[2] Maker communities share a common interest around tech, shared knowledge and tools, and collaboration. **Maker culture** emerged as a unique strand of making arising from a common interest around technology-based DIY culture.[3] Dougherty resisted a single definition of **maker**, noting that everyone is a maker and suggesting that making is a fundamental behavior of humans.[4] In conversation with these popularized narratives are the critical interventions and reflections evident in the coming chapters. **Critical** in this collection is aptly defined by one of the authors, Anna Cirell, as the examination of "the interplay

---

1. Dale Dougherty, "The Maker Movement," *Innovations: Technology, Governance, Globalization* 7, no. 3 (July 1, 2012): 11–14, https://doi.org/10.1162/INOV_a_00135.

2. "A Nation of Makers," The White House, accessed January 23, 2020, https://obamawhitehouse.archives.gov/nation-of-makers.

3. "Maker Culture," *Wikipedia*, November 16, 2019, https://en.wikipedia.org/wiki/Maker_culture.

4. Caleb Kraft, "What Is a Maker? You Are," Make: DIY Projects and Ideas for Makers, April 1, 2016, https://makezine.com/2016/04/01/what-is-a-maker-you-are/.

of domination and subordination in society, through focusing on the distribution and (re)production of oppressive inequities." These key terms: Maker Movement, maker culture, and maker, serve as starting points for readers who are unfamiliar with these phrases. However, these terms also serve as boundary markers that will be tested, undone, and challenged in the chapters to come.

Organization

We have organized the chapters into four sections to offer readers various entries for navigating within the collection. Readers are also encouraged to read "against" the sections—categorizing the chapters does not preclude them from having multiple shared zones of overlapping themes.

This collection is comprised of four sections:

- Who Belongs in the Makerspace? Power and Critical Theories
- Movement, Empathy, and Inclusion in Youth Makerspaces
- Counternarratives
- Re-imagined Makerspaces: Policies, Procedures, and Culture

The section "Who Belongs in the Makerspace? Power and Critical Theories" is a curation of chapters that investigate systemic inequities within makerspaces. Brown examines a remarkable omission in diversity and inclusion efforts in makerspaces: discussions on race. Brown extends Critical Race Theory as a practical approach to center anti-oppressive conversations and programming in makerspaces. In the next chapter, race and gender are centralized. Sanchez et al. document a case study of the experiences of women of color in their makerspace and the problems with "representation" as the sole indicator of the success of diversity and inclusion efforts. The focus on race and gender then shifts to highlight the spatial implications of makerspaces. Cirell offers a spatial analysis of makerspaces and the importance of a third space approach that shapes "hidden culture." Marshall and Melo argue in their chapter for a shift from needs analysis to brokering power in makerspaces. They present a power analysis framework that offers an entry point to examine how power is wielded, concentrated, and systemically embedded within a makerspace.

The work and research being done in "youth makerspaces" represents a significant node in this collection. The second section, "Movement, Empathy, and Inclusion in Youth Makerspaces" provides a unique account of pedagogical approaches and departures from the Maker Movement. Lenstra and Moorefield-Lang challenge common ideas of making by extending ideas of "making the body" through physical movement. In the next chapter, Lister further broadens ideas of making by disrupting the imagined communities of makers. Lister argues that makerspace educators should adapt making to accommodate youth who have experienced trauma. In this section's last chapter, Koh et al. outline the connections between increased student empathy for one another and engagement through the co-creation of projects in their makerspace; the projects provide an environment for students to tackle bullying across various media.

In the "Counternarratives" section, marginalized perspectives on and narratives about the Maker Movement are centered. Higginbotham and Rouse disrupt the "everyone is a maker" trope by applying human-centered design methodologies to identify barriers endemic in makerspaces, while Rogowski et al. explore the possibilities of STEM-rich maker activities in public rural libraries that do not highlight the costly, high-threshold technologies often attributed to makerspaces. Moody and Spivak ask readers to imagine otherwise: what does a makerspace look like in terms of creating a space that centers feminist pedagogy and mentorship? Poudyal et al. round out this section by highlighting the power of naming "making," and the relational and collaborative making practices of women in technology.

Policies and procedures are the main focus of the last section. The daily protocols that undergird the makerspace are examined in terms of the values and beliefs stemming from the Maker Movement. In "Re-imagined Makerspaces: Policies, Procedures, and Culture," Mann identifies the need for cross-collaborations for sustainable makerspaces while refuting common portrayals of collaborations that are seen as intrinsically neoliberal. In a similar spirit, the next chapter centers on hiring practices and their impact on diverse user communities. Peery et al. introspectively examine their makerspace to devise methods to recruit, train, and attract diverse student communities. In the penultimate chapter, Sherrill investigates the importance of everyday practices and policies in makerspaces, with an emphasis on the importance of hospitality to cultivate an environment where users feel valued and a sense of belonging. The section is rounded out with discussion of the environmental features of makerspaces that could potentially and often do generate feelings of impostor syndrome. Nay's chapter on impostor syndrome provides a set of interviews on approaches to manage feelings of unbelonging in makerspaces and similar tech-centric environments.

Conclusion

It is expected that many who reach for this collection are, like us, conflicted. On the one hand there is excitement around the transformative potential of makerspaces, and on the other hand, there are endemic issues concerning equal access, racial and gender biases, and sustainability that afflict tech-centric environments like makerspaces. At the fringes of the Maker Movement are the stories of communities laboring and re-making the narratives of makerspaces by rupturing systemic structures that endorse a narrow representation of making. This collection highlights these cases and rejects the idealism surrounding makerspaces by engaging directly with these concerns. It also seeks to disrupt perceptions that makerspaces are monoliths. The strength of the collection resides in the diverse set of underrepresented voices and narratives that forward the common call to re-make makerspaces into spaces that are more accessible, human-centered, intentional, and anti-oppressive. This book is also an opportunity for librarians and scholars to get a sense of the possible directions for makerspaces—re-imagined possibilities where the intention, purpose, and community of makerspaces are clear and will lead to a future where communities and every individual feel supported and welcomed in these spaces.

Bibliography

Dougherty, Dale. "The Maker Movement." *Innovations: Technology, Governance, Globalization* 7, no. 3 (July 1, 2012): 11–14. https://doi.org/10.1162/INOV_a_00135.

Kraft, Caleb. "What Is a Maker? You Are." *Make:* DIY Projects and Ideas for Makers, April 1, 2016. https://makezine.com/2016/04/01/what-is-a-maker-you-are/.

"Maker Culture." *Wikipedia.* Accessed November 16, 2019. https://en.wikipedia.org/wiki/Maker_culture.

"A Nation of Makers." The White House. Accessed January 23, 2020. https://obamawhitehouse.archives.gov/nation-of-makers.

WHO BELONGS IN THE MAKERSPACE? POWER AND CRITICAL THEORIES

Chapter 1

CRITICAL RACE THEORY AND MAKERSPACES: A PRACTICAL APPROACH

Jennifer Brown

Making Space for Critical Reflection

Makerspaces have long been touted as egalitarian playgrounds that aid communities while bridging theory and practice. Research, though, reveals a more distressing fact: makerspaces can also replicate patriarchal structures of domination and exclusion, often at the expense of marginalized communities.

Now, I don't think this fact is completely lost on makerspace practitioners. Plenty of articles, book chapters, and conference proceedings speak to the homogeneity within makerspace communities at large; even the International Symposium on Academic Makerspaces (ISAM), one of the largest conferences in my makerspace sub-field invites themed papers on Diversity and Inclusion, singling them out for discussion before scores of conference goers. But in most of these talks and papers, race is rarely brought up as a topic worth exploring on its own. Instead, it's lumped in with other identity categories under the elusive umbrella category of "Diversity and Inclusion." Or, frankly, it often fails to be mentioned at all.

I felt this keenly while attending ISAM 2018, where I spent several days listening to diversity and equity panels that were mainly focused on gender disparity in makerspaces. I tried (and failed) not to cringe when presenters unironically touted the diversity of their user populations amid a backdrop of presentation slides featuring their all white (and mostly male) makerspace staff. What I wanted from those sessions was to explore the multifaceted nature of identity, and to unravel the vague demographic categories we devise to better explore the idea that "inclusion" can't be reached with a one-size-fits-all approach. Barring the reality that there's only so much one can cover in an hour-long panel or poster session, more must be done to probe the ways in which makerspaces are (or aren't) supporting BIPOC (Black, Indigenous, and People of Color) folks of all genders, identities, abilities, sexualities, religions, and more. I desperately want to do this work using an intersectional lens because yes, we absolutely should discuss gender disparities in makerspaces, but we must remember that gender intersects with race, ability, and so many other identities that aren't ever addressed.

To do this work requires the first step of *making space*—of giving words and room and breath to the very topics we gloss over. So I open this chapter by reflecting on my identity and selfhood within a field that has, so far, made very little space for folks like me to do so. I am a black, queer woman with particular levels of educational and socioeconomic privilege. I work as an administrator within an academic library makerspace at a liberal arts college in a diverse urban city. Throughout this chapter, I will focus on the ways in which makerspaces can meaningfully address race through race-focused pedagogy and programming.

Let's Start at the Beginning

Before we get too far ahead of ourselves, let's first explore the ways in which race hasn't factored into mainstream makerspace discussions. For starters, it's important to note that literature on the intersections between "race" and "makerspaces" is still a developing area. Much of the research focuses on how STEM departments (specifically Engineering) might use makerspaces to better retain people of color in departmental majors. This makes a lot of sense, given that STEM fields have long struggled to attract, and later support, students of color.

Still, it's helpful to know what promises the maker movement initially made with respect to diversity and inclusion. Masters mentions that "since the advent of Make [Magazine], the Maker Movement was largely publicized as and promised to be the 'democratization' of technology, science, tools, and skills needed for innovation."[1] Former President Barack Obama even "challenged U.S. mayors to support making in their communities," but with a particular focus on women and other marginalized groups.[2] However, these goals weren't ever systematically actualized for many organizations. For example, Masters cited pretty damning research that showcased just how little publication space Make Magazine dedicated to issues of inclusion—when users previously searched their website for terms like "African American" and "people of color," only a combined total of five results came back.[3] As of today (July 2019), searching for "people of color" on Make Magazine's website yields three articles, none of which focus on the experiences of people of color in makerspaces. Searching for the term "BIPOC" only returned an article on how to read ebooks on Kindle (because these letters appeared sequentially in another, larger word)…so, effectively, none.

Now, Make Magazine doesn't speak for the entire Maker Movement. This is why I also sought out research addressing the lived experiences of BIPOC makerspace users. Greene et. al. explore whether academic STEM-focused makerspaces reify the identities of the black male students who use them.[4] But their most important finding, as it relates to race and identity, is that "[…]makerspaces located at PWIs [Primarily White Institutions] were found to reflect the heteronormative culture of engineering in a way that challenged smooth navigation in and through

---

1. Adam Stark Masters and Virginia Tech, "How Making and Maker Spaces Have Contributed to Diversity & Inclusion in Engineering: A [Non-Traditional] Literature Review," n.d., 13.

2. Masters and Tech, "How Making and Maker Spaces."

3. Masters and Tech, "How Making and Maker Spaces."

4. Michael Lorenzo Greene, Nadia Kellam, and Brooke Charae Coley, "Black Men in the Making: Engaging in Maker Spaces Promotes Agency and Identity for Black Males in Engineering" The Collaborative Network for Engineering and Computing Diversity, Washington, DC: American Society for Engineering Education, April 14th-17th, https://www.asee.org/public/conferences/148/papers/24991/view.

these spaces for Black men."⁵ (It should be noted that PWIs traditionally refer to colleges and universities with long histories rooted in white-supremacist segregating practices.)—which is almost every major academic institution in the United States, with the exception of HBCUs (Historically Black Colleges and Universities), Tribal Colleges, and other institutions of higher learning founded to support BIPOC students.)

What's more, conducting this research meant visiting ten engineering makerspaces at both PWIs and HBCUs across the United States. During those visits, they met with fifty-five students, yet only fifteen of them identified as black men. Worse, only three of those black students were using makerspaces located at PWIs. While this data doesn't address how race in makerspaces is treated at large, it does provide us with a lens through which to view potential consequences that come from ignoring race and identity, particularly for makerspaces housed within institutions built on legacies of institutionally-sanctioned white supremacy.

Now, I could go on and provide you with more research, and more data—more "evidence" of race and identity being relegated to back-burner topics, or not being discussed at all, within our field. Instead, I'm going to ask you to value the lived experiences of the students discussed above, and all of the BIPOC folks willing to share their stories, without needing copious amounts of data to make them valid.

Critical Pedagogies: What, and More Importantly, *Why*?

We've established that discussions around diversity and equity in makerspaces often exclude race, so how does one center it? How does one begin to understand and embed race-conscious programming into a makerspace, especially when coming from a place of privilege?

For starters, you begin by embracing pedagogies that have transformed the way we think about makerspace inclusivity. One of the earliest movements to do this (that I know of) within makerspaces were feminist hackerspaces. Such spaces, according to Rogers, typically focused on "being inclusive [...] while also recognizing privileges that

---

5. Greene, Kellam, Coley, "Black Men in the Making," 2.

certain individuals have in society and which play out in hackerspaces."[6] This praxis is particularly powerful because of its focus on re-thinking the concept of "openness" within makerspaces. Feminist hackerspaces serving marginalized communities (in the case of Rogers' piece: women, gender non-conforming, genderqueer, and trans folks) may actually find boundaries necessary to feeling as though a makerspace is safe and inclusive for members of their community. Moreover, Rogers suggests that:

> Another reason [for boundary setting] comes from the plainly stated desire to hack in peace: that is, the refusal to tolerate everyday sexism in one's space and the desire to focus economies of attention on feminist projects and ideas without distraction.[7]

This creates a kind of closed community space where -isms are understood and treated as real, freeing marginalized folks from the need to explain what racism, sexism, homophobia, transphobia, ableism, and other oppressions are (or justify their existence), because everyone within that community has likely experienced that -ism at some point. Certainly, nobody has to pretend that those -isms don't happen in makerspaces, or were somehow magically eradicated by the space's "democratizing" tool sets.

Yet, while the work of feminist hackerspaces has transformed makerspace culture for women and queer folks, we still need to drill down even further, to better focus on race and its intersections with makerspace culture. This is where Critical Race Theory comes in.

Critical Race Theory (CRT)

Emanating from critical legal studies and radical feminism, Critical Race Theory (CRT) represents a collection of theoretical frameworks posited by scholars like Derrick Bell, Alan Freeman, Richard Delgado,

---

6. Melissa Susan Rogers, "Soft Circuitry: Methods for Queer and Trans Feminist Maker Cultures" (Ph.D., University of Maryland, College Park, 2017), https://search.proquest.com/docview/2012261232/abstract/81BA2CF702BD485DPQ/19.

7. Toupin, Sophie, "Feminist Hacker Spaces: The Synthesis of Feminist and Hacker Cultures," *Journal of Peer Production*, no.5 (2014).

Jean Stefancic, Kimberlé Williams Crenshaw, and others to address racial inequity throughout the legal system. According to Delgado and Stefancic, "many of us believed that new tactics and theories were needed to understand and come to grips with the complex interplay among race, racism, and American law,"[8] which resulted in a body of work that's grown into hundreds of articles. CRT work has primarily been about situating race alongside broader discourses, including its intersections with "economics, history, context, group-and-self-interest, and even feelings and the unconscious."[9] From its inception, CRT grew to intersect with a whole host of academic disciplines beyond legal studies.

As a makerspace practitioner, there are several themes I'm drawn to in CRT, such as counter-storytelling and interest convergence. Traditionally, counter-storytelling "is a framework that legitimizes the racial and subordinate experiences of marginalized groups"[10] by allowing them to tell stories that reflect their lived experience, and which often differ from what dominant majorities believe those lived experiences to be. Interest convergence focuses on the idea that majority groups (particularly white majorities) who oppress minority groups often do so because of a shared collective interest that benefits them. They then create narratives to justify and validate their actions, along with the oppression they've committed. Delgado and Stefancic provide an illustrative example of this very practice at work:

> Materialists [another name for CRT scholars employing interest convergence] point out that conquered nations generally demonize their subjects to feel better about exploiting them, so that, for example, planters and ranchers in Texas and at the Southwest circulated notions

---

8. Richard Delgado and Jean Stefancic, "Critical Race Theory: An Annotated Bibliography," *Virginia Law Review* 79, no. 2 (1993): 461–516, https://doi.org/10.2307/1073418.

9. "Critical Race Theory: An Introduction," accessed July 29, 2019, https://web.a.ebscohost.com/ehost/ebookviewer/ebook/bmxlYmtfXzc0MzEyX19BTg2?sid=ac0616b6-ab31-4763-9d52-dd0f41b5c1e6@sdc-v-sessmgr02&vid=0&format=EB&rid=1.

10. Payne Hiraldo, "The Role of Critical Race Theory in Higher Education," *Vermont Connection* 31, no. 1 (January 1, 2010), https://scholarworks.uvm.edu/tvc/vol31/iss1/7.

of Mexican inferiority at roughly the same period that they found it necessary to take over Mexican lands or, later, to import Mexican people for backbreaking labor.[11]

You might be wondering: okay, what does this mean within the context of makerspaces? Let's first consider that in makerspaces, the dominant group of users *and* administrators (being mostly comprised of white, cis-hetero men) have shared interests when it comes to creating the kind of atmosphere they most desire in their makerspaces. But because of the public-facing narrative around makerspaces (that they are open, accessible spaces where anyone can learn to make), those interests converge in subtle ways—they're looking to foster a community of users who think like them and who, perhaps, ignore -isms in the same way they do, so that they don't have to talk about, or think about, those -isms. This leads to marginalized folks walking into spaces and *immediately* feeling unwelcome—perhaps from the stares they receive or from the lack of support when asking questions or learning new tools. It could lead to white male students making blanket statements about how BIPOC students are "disruptive" whenever they play hip hop out loud in the makerspace (and yes, this actually happened in a makerspace I know of). Interest convergence helps articulate that dominant user groups can shape their makerspace's culture for mutual benefit in very tangible ways. If BIPOC students don't feel comfortable coming in and playing music (the way every other user would be allowed to), they may stop coming altogether. Eventually, the makerspace starts to look a whole lot more homogenous than it did before, which, I'd argue, was the intended goal and shared interest all along.

Now, consider that when confronted with the knowledge that their actions might be causing marginalized users to turn away, they create narratives that both refute this and validate their original actions. Saying things like "we can't possibly be racist, because [x] works here" (yes, I'm looking at *you*, if you're someone who's used the one BIPOC person on staff as a way to avoid your racism) or, "well, *anyone* can use our

---

11. Richard Delgado and Jean Stefancic, eds., *Critical Race Theory: An Introduction* (New York: New York University Press, 2001).

makerspace, but if [x students/community members/etc.] don't want to come, that's their problem." (Again, real stories I've heard firsthand.) Thus, the narrative of openness reifies the notion that BIPOC and other marginalized groups could feel actively excluded in their makerspace.

This is why counternarratives can be so powerful—instead of taking the theme of openness and technology as democratizing at face value, we can use CRT tenets of counter-storytelling to begin unearthing real lived experiences that BIPOC users have in our spaces, while also threading in elements of making, creativity, and identity expression.

Emergent Strategy and Speculative Futuring

Now, because I love this work so dang much, I'm going to throw in two more movements that you could use to bedrock race-conscious programming.

If you've ever seen me present, you've probably heard me talk about Emergent Strategy and Speculative Futuring. I'm bringing them back here, because they're critical to my practice in makerspaces. To keep it brief, Emergent Strategy[12] is a theory of networked principles that help individuals identify their place and role within systems. It is born out of creative traditions and mindful practices that ask us to understand the role of restorative justice within our own organizations and to work towards change as a community.

Speculative Futuring is a somewhat new concept that has made a powerful home in my heart. I first encountered this term through my colleague, Sofia Leung, who co-led a workshop called "The (Speculative) Futures of Libraries and Archives" at the Massachusetts Institute of Technology (MIT).[13] She and a number of other creatives got together and used storytelling methods that asked workshop attendees to interrogate the historical progress of libraries and archives, then speculate about where they might be headed. This involved making zines, using

---

12. "Emergent Strategy | AK Press," accessed May 3, 2018, https://www.akpress.org/emergentstrategy.html.

13. Lin Sing Lee, "The (Speculative) Futures of Libraries and Archives," MIT Events, accessed July 31, 2019, https://calendar.mit.edu/event/speculativefutures#.XUIIz9NKiCe.

story cards, and a number of other creative activities that got people into the envisioning mindset. This tradition can also be linked back to the Visionary Fiction[14] workshops based out of Detroit (associated with Adrienne Maree Brown and Walidah Imarisha) that encouraged activists to use speculative fiction as a platform to write the futures they wanted to see.

Because of this, Speculative Futuring feels like natural connective tissue for creating counternarratives—after all, writing is making. And we must first dream up what we want to see, and then concretize it by putting pen to paper.

Critical Race Pedagogies in Action

Theory is all well and good, but what does putting that work into practice mean? What does it mean to not only be cognizant of race in makerspaces, but also to recognize and value the lived experiences of BIPOC folks using your space?

For starters, I'll note my context, because the way I employ these strategies may not work for you (depending on what kind of makerspace you're in). But, for clarity's sake, I oversee day-to-day operations for a newly created (as of Fall 2018) academic makerspace called the Barnard Design Center. Our makerspace operates out of the campus library at Barnard College; because of this, we're an interdisciplinary space that isn't bound to specific departments, though we have strong ties with Barnard's artistic disciplines (such as theater, visual arts, and architecture). We have a range of prototyping tools—from sewing machines, sergers, and embroidery machines, to a laser cutter, compound miter saw, and 3D printers. Our goal has always been to connect to Barnard's curriculum by supporting making in courses, and also to support Barnard students, staff, and faculty (as well as those of its partner institution, Columbia University) to make projects they're passionate about—whether they

---

14. Walidah Imarisha, "How Science Fiction Can Re-Envision Justice," Bitch Media, accessed June 2, 2019, https://www.bitchmedia.org/article/rewriting-the-future-prison-abolition-science-fiction.

are linked to curriculum or not. The strategies and programs I discuss were all employed with this very context in mind.

I would also like to dispel any myths around expertise. You don't have to be an expert to do this work, and I certainly don't pretend to be one. While I've written about and presented on critical pedagogies for several years now, I'm still learning what this means and what it looks like in a library makerspace context, which you'll see later on when I discuss programming with CRT in mind. However, here are some of what I've found to be the most important axes of engagement when it comes to putting CRT into practice.

Recruitment and Retention of BIPOC Staff

If we acknowledge that racism can and does occur in makerspaces, then to shift that culture, we must ensure that makerspace students and professional staff alike reflect the communities we're trying to reach. In particular, the Design Center has focused on hiring diversely—bringing in folks who want to do the work and who come from a shared understanding that makerspaces often do have racist, sexist, and -ism filled histories of exclusion. Understanding that history, and acknowledging its truth, impacts the way we work together as staff to support inclusivity within our makerspace.

We make this important tenet clear, even during our student and professional hiring process, by asking interview questions like the one below:

> The Design Center is deeply committed to the Network Principles of Design Justice,[15] which include things like healing & empowering communities while seeking liberation from oppressive systems, and (for us specifically), creating an equitable, welcoming environment that also centers marginalized voices & experiences. Everyone, from myself [the interviewer] to undergrad/grad employees is committed to this. How does this align with your values and what's important to you in a workplace?

---

15. "Design Justice Network Principles," Design Justice, accessed July 31, 2019, http://designjusticenetwork.org/network-principles.

That question alone provides candidates with an opportunity to share what this perspective means to them. It also invites them to mention how they've engaged in similar community-building work previously, or to express their eagerness to do this work alongside us now. We don't care so much that they've done this work before—only that they're willing to learn with and grow alongside us while we work towards racial justice.

Although an entire book could be written on methods to better retain marginalized staff, I'll simply say here that to attract folks isn't enough. It is also necessary for administrators to make sure staff feel protected and supported in what often amounts to a busy campus gig that places a lot of demand on one's time and energy. Also be aware that, while your staff may be diverse and committed to doing the work, users may come in with completely different ideas (or be used to different makerspace atmospheres); protecting and empowering your staff, in whatever way you can, makes a whole world of difference.

Programs and Workshops (Or, Calling Myself Out + My Hopes & Dreams)
I find it's easy in makerspaces to fall into the trap of only offering workshops and programs geared around tools. Yet, if you'd like to meaningfully engage race in makerspaces, consider framing events and workshops that promote the safe sharing of counternarratives.

For example, I co-presented a panel (that was much more like a workshop) with Jenny Ferretti, Marisa Mendez-Brady, and Sofia Leung at the 2019 Joint Council for Librarians of Color Conference (JCLC) called "We Here: Community Building as Self Care." In the spirit of radical feminist hackerspaces that promote boundary-setting and space-claiming, we used our session to carve out space within the conference venue for library workers and students of color. For starters, we posted a sign on the door of our conference presentation room labeled "Do not enter this room if you don't believe the narratives of people of color," which immediately set the tone of valuing counternarratives. We then led a guided meditation around self-empowerment to get attendees into a creative frame of mind. Then, we asked users to engage with their identities as BIPOC library folk by distributing predetermined exploratory topics around the room. Printed on plain white paper in large, bold lettering, these topics included everything from discussing "impostor syndrome" to navigating "white fragility." The goal was to take the -isms and struggles all BIPOC library folk experience and encourage them to create objects of resistance or care in response; to remember that we can and will make it through, so long as we lean back on the communities that supported us. This meant that we first asked attendees to grapple with these issues emotionally; then we spent the rest of our panel time using a bevy of materials (construction paper, colored pens and pencils, coloring book pages, tarot cards and affirmation deck cards, and more) to create something personally meaningful—perhaps a custom self-care calendar drawn with pen and pencil on colored paper, or a pop-up self-empowerment collage (which a group of attendees actually made). This entire session was rooted in an ethos of care and community, and by using anti-oppressive facilitation, we acted as emotional facilitators capable of guiding folks while they worked. An activity like this could easily be applied in a makerspace context, as very little hardware or specialized tools were needed.

Though, this is where I'm going to call myself out; as I mentioned earlier, I'm still learning and still growing. Given that my role, and the Design Center, are new as of last Fall, much of the first year involved laying the staffing and organizational foundations to support an inclusive, anti-oppressive environment. This means I haven't yet practiced the critical pedagogies I care most about in Design Center programs. This coming Fall, however, I hope to lead a hands-on workshop: "Writing from the Margins: Speculating Futures & Designing Realities." Similar to the JCLC workshop I co-led, and to Sofia's MIT event, this workshop would allow attendees to develop counternarratives and to speculate futures that honor their identities and experiences in ways the present does not. Activity-wise, this might look like:

- A two-part interconnected workshop series, with the first session focused on speculating around a specific topic (e.g. futures where BIPOC have received reparations for past colonialist atrocities). This first part could be held anywhere—a classroom, for example, or perhaps in a lounge with comfy chairs and movable furniture. The activity would likely involve writing ideas down in any format (short stories, poetry, bullet point list, etc.).
- The second session would be held in the Design Center and would build off the first day's imaginings. Attendees would be guided through a makerspace activity (perhaps screen printing) and encouraged to recreate an object that represents some small part of that imagined future. Protest signs, prototypes of 3D printed gadgets (depending on how far ahead folks are speculating) and more would be welcome tools for concretizing those ideas.

Though I haven't held this session yet, I'm hopeful that grounding the workshop in identity will allow us to engage with race in a way that's rooted within the makerspace, but also reflective of how attendees imagine navigating our campus, neighborhood, and the larger world we live in.

However, other fantastic projects around race and making have already been put into play. Two recent projects, in particular, are of interest: "Critical Race Cartographies: Exploring Map-Making as Anti-Racist Praxis"[16] and "Remixing Wakanda: Envisioning Critical Afrofuturist Design Pedagogies."[17] In the former project, the scholars employed a mixture of CRT theory and "critical race spatial analysis" in two different case studies to show how "the map" provides an "innovative

---

16. Jessica T. Decuir-Gunby, Thandeka K. Chapman, and Paul Shutz, eds., *Understanding Critical Race Research Methods and Methodologies: Lessons from the Field* (New York: Routledge, 2019).

17. Michael B. Dando, Nathan Holbert, and Isabel Correa, "Remixing Wakanda: Envisioning Critical Afrofuturist Design Pedagogies," in *Proceedings of FabLearn 2019* (New York: ACM Press, 2019), 156–59, https://doi.org/10.1145/3311890.3311915.

portrait on the intersection of race and space."[18] The latter resource details an eight-week project "which brings together youth of color, artists, designers, educators, and researchers to construct a new vision for a culturally relevant and sustaining STEAM-centered learning and making framework situated in an Afrofuturist design aesthetic."[19] In each project and example, it's fantastic to see how these educators utilized both hardware and software, and the idea of "remixing" utopias to reify counternarratives.

Making (Intentional) Space for People of Color

I focused this chapter on folks of color, and specifically black folks, by contrasting my own colloquial experiences working in and using makerspaces, because I wanted to draw attention to race. Note that critical pedagogy can and *should* be used to highlight the many ways makerspaces might be failing marginalized groups at large—but we settle for broad strokes because it's easy. We need to have explicit conversations about accessibility in makerspaces for users with visible and invisible disabilities; to better explore gender disparity by promoting the counternarratives of queer, trans, and gnc folks; and to understand that race is complicated—that identities like "Blackness" represent diasporas that are expressed differently based on minute differences between ethnicities (e.g. the cultures of American-born Black folk, versus Afrolatinx folk), and that this kind of complexity rings true across the board for almost every identity category you can think of. In short, we need to be willing to wade through this with kindness and a willingness to learn; to embody the kind of openness we always talk about, but rarely practice.

But, if nothing more, I hope this chapter draws attention to the need for specifically naming race and racism as important parts of diversity and equity work in makerspaces. And I hope you find ways to incorporate critical pedagogies into your own practice, one small step at a time.

---

18. Decuir-Gunby, Chapman, and Shutz, *Understanding Critical Race Research Methods and Methodologies*.

19. Dando, Holbert, and Correa, "Remixing Wakanda."

Bibliography

"Critical Race Theory: An Introduction." Accessed July 29, 2019. https://web.a.ebscohost.com/ehost/ebookviewer/ebook/bmxlYmtfXzc0MzEyX19BTg2?sid=ac0616b6-ab31-4763-9d52-dd0f41b5c1e6@sdc-v-sessmgr02&vid=0&format=EB&rid=1.

Dando, Michael B., Nathan Holbert, and Isabel Correa. "Remixing Wakanda: Envisioning Critical Afrofuturist Design Pedagogies." In *Proceedings of FabLearn 2019*, 156–59. New York, NY, USA: ACM Press, 2019. https://doi.org/10.1145/3311890.3311915.

Decuir-Gunby, Jessica T., Thandeka K. Chapman, and Paul Shutz, eds. *Understanding Critical Race Research Methods and Methodologies: Lessons from the Field*. New York, NY: Routledge, 2019.

Delgado, Richard, and Jean Stefancic. "Critical Race Theory: An Annotated Bibliography." *Virginia Law Review* 79, no. 2 (1993): 461–516. https://doi.org/10.2307/1073418.

Delgado, Richard, and Jean Stefancic, eds. *Critical Race Theory: An Introduction*. New York: New York University Press, 2001.

"Design Justice Network Principles." Design Justice. Accessed July 31, 2019. http://designjusticenetwork.org/network-principles.

"Emergent Strategy | AK Press." Accessed May 3, 2018. https://www.akpress.org/emergentstrategy.html.

Greene, Michael Lorenzo, Nadia Kellam, and Brooke Charae Coley. "Black Men in the Making: Engaging in Maker Spaces Promotes Agency and Identity for Black Males in Engineering: American Society for Engineering Education." Washington, DC: American Society for Engineering Education, April 14th-17th. https://www.asee.org/public/conferences/148/papers/24991/view.

Hiraldo, Payne. "The Role of Critical Race Theory in Higher Education." *Vermont Connection* 31, no. 1 (January 1, 2010). https://scholarworks.uvm.edu/tvc/vol31/iss1/7.

Imarisha, Walidah. "How Science Fiction Can Re-Envision Justice." Bitch Media. Accessed June 2, 2019. https://www.bitchmedia.org/article/rewriting-the-future-prison-abolition-science-fiction.

Lee, Lin Sing. "The (Speculative) Futures of Libraries and Archives." MIT Events. Accessed July 31, 2019. https://calendar.mit.edu/event/speculativefutures#.XUIIz9NKiCe.

Masters, Adam Stark, and Virginia Tech. "How Making and Maker Spaces Have Contributed to Diversity & Inclusion in Engineering: A [Non-Traditional] Literature Review," n.d., 13.

Rogers, Melissa Susan. "Soft Circuitry: Methods for Queer and Trans Feminist Maker Cultures." Ph.D., University of Maryland, College Park, 2017. https://search.proquest.com/docview/2012261232/abstract/81BA2CF702BD485DPQ/19.

Toupin, Sophie, "Feminist Hacker Spaces: The Synthesis of Feminist and Hacker Cultures," *Journal of Peer Production*, no.5, (2014).

Chapter 2

WHO BELONGS IN THE MAKERSPACE? EXPERIENCES OF WOMEN OF COLOR IN AN ACADEMIC LIBRARY MAKERSPACE

Anthony Sanchez, Danielle Dolan-Sanchez, and Vicki Lázaro

Introduction

This chapter illustrates expectations, actual scenarios, challenges, and innovative solutions to the positioning of women of color (WOC) in a makerspace at the University of Arizona Libraries (UAL). Active from Fall 2014 to Fall 2019, the iSpace was a multidisciplinary learning community and collaborative makerspace in the Albert B. Weaver Science-Engineering Library at the University of Arizona that offered a hands-on experience in emerging technologies such as 3D printing, modeling and scanning and virtual reality headsets. A new library makerspace is slated to open in the Spring of 2020 in the UAL main library and will be rebranded as the "CATalyst Studios." The research team for this project included two UAL library faculty members and one M.S. graduate student in the UA School of Information. One of the librarians is a liaison and supports students and faculty in the College of Social and Behavioral Sciences, and the other was the Emerging Technology Librarian (now a librarian at the Pima County Public Library). Two of the researchers were involved in programming at the iSpace.

The iSpace was created with a vision of an inclusive, community-based, collaborative space in emerging technologies for students, faculty, staff, and the Tucson community. Given the University of Arizona's designation as a Land-Grant Institution and its recent status as a Hispanic Serving Institute, it was important to have programs in place that reflected its constituency. That especially included underrepresented women of color not sure of their place or excellence in science and tech environments. An emphasis on inclusion allowed for opportunities to actively incorporate and promote access for women of color into the iSpace community by putting forward workshops, tours, and student cultural center events focused on inclusivity to connect and introduce emerging technologies.

Despite inclusive programming, the lack of representation of women of color in the iSpace (as well as at other technology-focused environments on campus) was a persistent problem in the iSpace and will require attention in the next iteration of the UA makerspace. The iSpace consistently faced challenges such as gender bias against women makers and a lack of people of color represented at the faculty or staff level. The visitors to the iSpace were predominantly white, male, and science or engineering-related students. Moreover, the staff and faculty of the UAL skew predominantly white. Despite a vision and mission that aimed to address gaps in representation, the absence of people of color (particularly women) was apparent in the iSpace. This begs the question of "who belongs?" in makerspaces and what libraries are doing about it. Following this line of inquiry, we formed three research questions in which to ground our study and inform our interviews.

- How do mentorships play a part in being successful?
- How do women of color persist in male/white-dominated spaces?
- What inspires women of color about technology and making?

Interviewees included seven women of color who are (or were) faculty, graduate assistants, or staff members of the iSpace. Through these interviews and the subsequent analysis, we surfaced themes of inclusivity and discrimination affecting women actively involved in a makerspace. By looking at the environment in the iSpace made explicit by its code of conduct and the firsthand accounts of the experiences of women of color in the space, this chapter intends to explore the discrepancies between the perceived and experienced iSpace culture.

iSpace Culture

Conceived as a collaboration between various campus groups, the iSpace was considered a proof of concept project that would be used to develop the best methods for a future full-scale, multidisciplinary makerspace. In addition to extending hands-on experience in emerging technologies to students and community members, the iSpace also offered workshops and K-12 tours. Librarians and faculty members used the iSpace as a place to brainstorm new ways of bringing technology and creative thinking to the forefront of the university experience. The utilization of technology within the iSpace was central to the activities of various entities on campus such as the School of Information, the English department, and faculty in the College of Humanities.

Events such as the Women Techmakers Tucson Hackathon (now the UA Women's Hackathon), HackAZ, and Friday Tech Talks encouraged inclusive participation in technology and its use for social good. The Women's Hackathon in particular emphasized creating a safe environment for marginalized groups. As described in their event FAQs: "We welcome anyone of any skill level. We want you to be able to focus on hacking, coding, learning and having fun! Therefore, we aim to provide an inclusive space for folks across lines of race, gender, class, disability, and skill level."[1] These events explicitly state inclusivity and diversity as part of their purpose, assuming the neutrality of technology and revealing the neoliberalism inherent in the tech sphere that serves to shroud it from critical engagement.

Similarly, the iSpace Code of Conduct describes itself as a place of "inclusivity and respect." It encourages visitors to "ask questions and help each other" in the collective space, and lays out some basic tenets

---

1. "Faqs." Women Techmakers Tucson. Accessed May 1, 2019. http://womentechmakerstucson.weebly.com/faqs.html.

of thoughtful behavior within a shared space, such as "be kind to each other."[2] On the iSpace webpage, it states: "We encourage students to re-envision their research through the use of cutting-edge technologies and by collaborating with interdisciplinary experts."[3] The language associated with this official representation of the iSpace purports a model of inclusion and diversity. The realities of the day-to-day operations in the iSpace revealed discrepancies between stated inclusivity and how visitors and staff members experienced the space, as has been explored in other studies of makerspaces found in our literature review. Our study is grounded in the work of researchers who have critically engaged with issues of inclusivity, race, and gender in the realms of innovation and technology, particularly in hackerspaces and makerspaces.

Literature Review

Makerspaces, as places where ideas, people, and technology meet with the goal of creating something new, have been analyzed through critical perspectives. Questions of inclusion and access have been viewed through different lenses, yielding important observations about the pitfalls and barriers of the inclusive missions of these spaces. In his examination of the intersecting cultures of maker communities, Toombs observes that the fluctuating goals of maker communities render makerspaces vulnerable to tensions between newcomers and established members, establishing the structural exclusivity often found in tech spaces.[4] Justice and Markus take a look at gender equity within the Maker Movement, giving an overview of the beginnings of the movement in 2005 with the publication of *Make* magazine and its presentation of making and hackerspaces as the domain of "white male nerd dominance."[5] They

---

2. "Policies." The University of Arizona Libraries. Accessed May 1, 2019. http://new.library.arizona.edu/ispace/policies.

3. "Ispace." The University of Arizona Libraries. Accessed May 1, 2019. http://new.library.arizona.edu/ispace

4. Austin Toombs. "Co-nerds or Co-workers? Intersecting Cultures of Maker Communities." Paper presented at the *CHI 2016 Conference, San Jose, CA, May 7, 2016*, 1-2.

5. Sean Justice, and Sandra Markus. "Educators, Gender Equity and Making:

assert that makerspaces need to make a concerted effort to counter this narrative by inviting diverse participation.[6] Recent scholarly contributions to the area of inclusion in the science and technology fields argue for sharpening our definitions of equity, and warn against dehistoricized and depoliticized definitions of equity.[7] Looking at the value of using social justice theories to understand equity within out-of-school science learning in the forms of science television, science clubs, and makerspaces, Dawson explains that "scholars have argued that it is not enough to recruit more ethnically diverse scientists, more female scientists, or more scientists from working class backgrounds, without simultaneously changing the culture and content of scientific knowledge."[8] Examining makerspaces as "a site of struggle over issues of profound social significance," Smith makes an argument against an open innovation agenda and for the innovation democracy potential in makerspaces.[9] In our study, we attempt to incorporate their work to avoid perpetuating the status quo in discussions of equity in makerspaces.

As makerspaces are introduced into educational institutions, the issue of gender and racial representation within these spaces becomes increasingly relevant to academic study. Understanding the social and structural barriers to entry into makerspaces is key in forging new pathways to equity, moving beyond superficial gestures of inclusion. While it is well documented that women face gender bias in STEM fields,[10] researchers have also done excellent work establishing that women are

---

Opportunities and Obstacles." Paper presented at the *FabLearn Conference at Stanford University, Palo Alto, CA, September 26, 2015*, 2.

6. Justice and Markus, "Educators, Gender Equity and Making," 4.

7. Thomas M. Philip and Flávio S. Azevedo. "Everyday Science Learning and Equity: Mapping the Contested Terrain." *Science Education* 101, no. 4 (2017), 527.

8. Emily Dawson. "Social Justice and Out-of-School Science Learning: Exploring Equity in Science Television, Science Clubs and Maker Spaces." *Science Education* 101, no. 4 (2017), 540.

9. Adrian Smith. 2017. "Social Innovation, Democracy and Makerspaces." Science Policy Research Unity Working Papers Series. University of Sussex, June 2017, 1.

10. David Beede, Tiffany Julian, David Langdon, George McKittrick, Beethika Khan, and Mark Doms. "Women in STEM: A Gender Gap to Innovation. ESA Issue Brief # 04-11." (2011), 8.

underrepresented in makerspaces,[11] and that the gender bias women experience in these spaces negatively shapes the socio-technical relationships they develop.[12] In her discussion of the "privilege of being oblivious" in a tech workspace, Chua explains how women in tech are tasked with either adapting to or fixing the toxic masculine environments in which they work before being able to get into a creative, immersive flow.[13] This discussion is revealing of challenges specific to women in makerspaces, particularly women of color, who may be asked to explain or solve diversity issues within the space. Farmer emphasizes the impact of equal access to makerspaces for all ages, genders, and ethnicities,[14] while Keune, Peppler and Wohlwend explore how makerspace and other constructivist learning environments support the development of interest in STEM, particularly looking at youth-oriented makerspaces and the effects on girls who make and the value in supporting opportunities for women in STEM.[15] Important to these studies is that it be possible to attract and retain women within makerspaces, and there are many ways to do so that require grounding in the understanding of the range of challenges, from passive discouragement to active harassment.

Researchers and information professionals are also working to address the ways that makerspaces replicate hegemonic values, rhetoric, and structures. Brown, Ferretti, Leung, and Méndez-Brady write about white supremacy within libraries in *We Here: Speaking Our Truth*. They position themselves prominently as four women of color who are actively

---

11. Vanessa Bean, Nicole M. Farmer, and Barbara A. Kerr. "An Exploration of Women's Engagement in Makerspaces." *Gifted and Talented International* 30, no. 1-2 (2015): 61-67; Deborah Nagler. "A Phenomenological Study of Women's Participation in Makerspace Communities of Practice." PhD diss., New Jersey City University, 2018.

12. Marijel C. Melo. "The Shadow Rhetorics of Innovation: Maker Culture, Gender, and Technology." PhD diss., The University of Arizona, 2018, 13-15.

13. Mel Chua. "The Privilege of Being Oblivious." *ASEE Prism* 25, no. 1 (2015), 23.

14. Nicole M. Farmer. "Maker Meaning: An Exploration of the Maker Movement, Career Adaptability, and Life Satisfaction." PhD diss., University of Kansas, 2018, 5-8.

15. Anna Keune, Kylie A. Peppler, and Karen E. Wohlwend. "Recognition in Makerspaces: Supporting Opportunities for Women to "make" a STEM Career." *Computers in Human Behavior* 99, (2019), 6.

working to resist white supremacy in the library and information science profession,[16] and they offer coalition building and mentorship as a way to persist within the profession. They lay bare the historical and structural forms of racism inherent in the profession, describing the pervasive idea of libraries as neutral, democratic spaces and the "invisible whiteness" that the profession protects, stating: "Without interrogating this idea of neutrality and whiteness further, we as a profession cannot move forward in discussions of diversity and inclusion."[17] Their discussion of the assumed neutrality of libraries and the information science profession aligns with our study of a library makerspace in that the veneer of innovation and inclusive programming is not enough to ensure the success and centering of women of color. While other studies establish the importance of studying the experiences of marginalized students and show that makerspaces have the potential for benefiting these students,[18] we assert that representation and superficial attempts at inclusion are not enough. It is by excavating structural issues of sexism and racism built into the bones of information-centric spaces that we may begin to build liberatory spaces for women of color and to reframe who belongs in makerspaces.

In order to do so in this study, we build upon West-Puckett's study of makerspaces as non-traditional composing networks in which she questions who gets to make and what gets made in these spaces. She articulates a queer material rhetoric to counter the neoliberal and entrepreneurial rhetoric that must be critically considered when looking at equity and access in makerspaces. She describes the promise inherent in makerspaces as a level field for individuals to "compose new selves, new communities, and new relations as a way of ushering in more

---

16. Jennifer Brown, Jennifer Ferretti, Sofia Leung, and Marisa Méndez-Brady. "We Here: Speaking Our Truth." *Library Trends* 67, no. 1 (2018), 3-5.

17. Brown, Ferretti, Leung, and Méndez-Brady, "We Here," 5.

18. Michael L. Greene, Nadia N. Kellam, and Brooke C. Coley. 2019. "Black Men in the Making: Engaging in Maker Spaces Promotes Agency and Identity for Black Males in Engineering." Paper presented at the *2019 CoNECD-The Collaborative Network for Engineering and Computing Diversity, Crystal City, VA, April 14, 2019*, 15-16.

democratic futures."[19] We refer to Wajcman's discussion of feminist theories of technology from 2009, looking back at how technologies have the potential to reproduce patriarchy and the ways that feminist scholars have approached the reshaping of these technologies, keeping in mind that "gender is integral to the sociotechnical process: that the materiality of technology affords or inhibits the doing of particular gender power relations."[20] Toupin's analysis of feminist hackerspaces, in which "feminists debunk the myth of openness and meritocracy associated with hackerspaces culture, question the use and/or the narrowness of the term hacker and hacking in addition to foregrounding a new understanding of openness which is at the intersection of feminist and hacker culture"[21] informs our call for the application of feminist methodologies to the study of women, genderqueer, and trans individuals in makerspaces. We see a need, as Toupin asserts, to rethink the original concept of openness in tech-centric spaces in favor of an emphasis on safety. We also borrow from Kim and Sinatra's interactionist approach to investigate the experiences of women of color in the iSpace.[22] In this approach, we look at the importance of the environment (in our study, the iSpace) on science identity development. Upon observing the persistence of white patriarchal culture in the iSpace despite efforts at creating an inclusive space, we conducted our study through interviews with women of color who had firsthand experience in the iSpace in order to further understand the failures of the iSpace to follow through on its promise of inclusion.

---

19. Stephanie West-Puckett. "Materializing Makerspaces: Queerly Composing Space, Time, and (what) Matters." PhD diss., East Carolina University, 2017, 5.

20. Judy Wajcman. "Feminist Theories of Technology." *Cambridge Journal of Economics* 34, no. 1 (2010), 150.

21. Sophie Toupin. "Feminist Hackerspaces: The Synthesis of Feminist and Hacker Cultures." *Journal of Peer Production* 5 (October 2014), 1-2.

22. Ann Y. Kim and Gale M. Sinatra. "Science Identity Development: An Interactionist Approach." *International Journal of STEM Education* 5, no. 1 (2018), 5.

Methodology

Authors reviewed literature on various research methodologies including grounded theory and Indigenous research methodologies in preparation for scoping the research and writing process. This study was also evaluated by our campus Institutional Review Board in accordance with campus requirements for human research subjects. In addition to scheduling and conducting interviews, we also individually participated in transcribing interviews and coding and theming those transcripts.

Recruitment for the study first consisted of contacting the pre-identified prospective subjects to have an in-person discussion to introduce and discuss the project. At that meeting, the project and the parameters for participation were discussed and prospective subjects were invited to participate. If they were interested, the researcher followed up to initiate formal participation. Since the goal of the project was to elicit results that can be used to inform and improve library services at the University of Arizona, the project was designed to be exploratory, small-scale, and grounded in approach. This study does not purport to be statistically representative, nor are the recommendations meant to be prescriptive; rather, this chapter and its recommendations are intended to suggest areas for further investigation.

Subjects participated in a one-on-one semi-structured interview with one of the authors listed. The interviews were approximately 60-90 minutes in duration and took place in the participants' primary work spaces on the University of Arizona campus or another on-campus location as determined by the interviewer and interviewee.

Interviewees were invited to review and revise their transcribed interview and then were given the option of anonymity. The interview transcripts were analyzed thematically using grounded theory methodology, as per Strauss and Corbin.[23] As such, there were no pre-existing codes; rather, coding structures were developed in the process of reading

---

23. Juliet Corbin and Anselm Strauss. "Grounded Theory Research: Procedures, Canons, and Evaluative Criteria." *Qualitative Sociology* 13, no. 1 (1990).

through the data. Before finalizing the chapter, interviewees were invited to review and provide feedback. This process of review and dialogue reflects the underlying tenet that Indigenous research methodology is predicated on relationships maintained by mechanisms of accountability and reciprocity.[24]

Discussion

Throughout the interviews, participants noted common challenges they had experienced, either directly or indirectly, as a result of being situated in a makerspace. This included their views on female and non-white representation in makerspaces, issues of sexual harassment, impostor syndrome, patriarchy, and racism. To a lesser extent, participants also spoke about their experiences with salary or wages and retention in technology-focused spaces. In our discussion of these interviews, we will focus on descriptions of the challenges of underrepresentation, racial discrimination, and gender bias offered by our participants. We will then move on to solutions and future implications that the interviewees described.

Challenges

The lack of representation of people of color (female- or male-identified) in tech spaces and the need for sustained efforts to maximize inclusive programming were the most common areas of focus for the women interviewed. This sentiment is echoed by one former graduate assistant, who stated that "Inclusivity, as it's defined from the maker movement, is just trying to get as many people as possible in the makerspace from different genders, races, classes, orientations, abilities. It's this idea of getting all these different people in [the space]. And it's not really all that effective." Another former graduate student spoke on the importance of representation: "Before even specifying a woman of color, bringing women into these innovative spaces is really, really,

---

24. Margaret Kovach. *Indigenous Methodologies: Characteristics, Conversations, and Contexts*. Toronto, Canada: University of Toronto Press, 2009, 35.

important… Especially because there is a lack of female representation in general in these innovative spaces." She went on to express, "What draws me to and makes me very comfortable in [the iSpace] is that the people who are making decisions in this space are people or women of color…it makes it a safer space to be in because they talk about other cultural events around campus and that's a part of the conversation." These comments and others by the interviewees emphasize that seeing oneself represented in the space, particularly in leadership that includes people of color, and making connections to other diverse spaces on campus facilitates the trust-building necessary for underrepresented individuals to thrive in a makerspace.

Faced with deviations from the expected demographics of a tech-centric space, patrons often confronted women of color staff members by not accepting their help or by ignoring their presence and position despite all claims to logic. Summing up her experience on how underrepresentation affected her role in the makerspace, one graduate student recounted that "There [was] a lot of questioning in terms of what I was doing there…I'm consistently this kind of embodiment of dissonance for people, right? So, they see me in this space, and it does not compute. 'What are you doing here?'" Participants noticed that patrons experienced cognitive dissonance upon finding women of color in positions of authority not only due to race, but also gender. One graduate assistant remarked, "People who identify anywhere on the gender scale…always go to the males in our space. And sometimes in my head I'm like, 'He doesn't know anything about what you're asking him.' But I'm not going to say anything, I'm just going to wait for them to come to me…and when they do I'm going to totally disrupt what they think." She describes the frustration of being consistently ignored, while also positioning herself as a disruption to the status quo. This common thread points to the systemic challenges faced by women of color, particularly in a university where the majority of students and instructors are predominantly white.

While many libraries have leapt at the chance to provide innovative services such as a makerspace, the time spent on addressing gender discrimination and ingrained biases through conscientious hiring and training is usually inadequate. Interviewees noted instances of sexually inappropriate comments or microaggressions leveled at them or their peers in the iSpace, and recognized how male-dominated the culture surrounding making and makerspaces has become in the age of 3D printers and laser cutters. While many participants did not point to specific instances of sexual harassment, one library staff member recalled a situation of harassment targeting a student staff worker of color that required immediate attention and a change to the library's approach to staffing by strength in numbers: "It was pretty bad because we needed to create a safe working environment for her and it wasn't happening at all…That kind of actually changed our thinking about how mediated or unmediated the space needed to be…that was around the time when we added more student workers." Her words are revealing of the importance of open communication and adequate, thoughtful staffing in makerspaces. Overcoming the gender biases inherent in a white-dominant patriarchy was a common theme in our interviews. One library staff member said, "We had some students who worked in the iSpace who didn't have self-awareness about how…paternal they came across when…they want to be really helpful. It seemed subtle and familiar enough that I think people don't necessarily know how to address it…I know that the students aren't getting trained to look at that stuff themselves."

Gender bias was well-described by most of the participants, and almost all of the participants could recall instances of racist behavior directed towards them or another non-white woman. A graduate student recalled having to consistently address issues of race, generally and personally:

> When I hear individuals that work, or don't work, at the iSpace talking about some type of racial identity or issues regarding racial identity, I step in and I'm like, 'No that's not what it is.' Or, 'Actually you might want to rephrase what you're saying. Actually, we're not colored people, we're people of color.' And even that people like to be referred to as their actual racial identity. 'And no, I'm not going to

tell you what my racial identity is for the twentieth time, thank you. You know you're intentionally doing these things to make me uncomfortable.' Sometimes I have to be the person stepping in and having these conversations, instead of actually doing what I'm supposed to be doing, which is helping people use the technology that we have in this space. And I realize that these discussions and conversations are important going back to the type of community we want to build in the iSpace. But it should not be the responsibility of the only people holding those identities in that space to do that.

This feeling of the burden of being an arbiter of racial justice is worth quoting at length, as the experience was shared by other interviewees and encapsulates a major theme of the experiences of women of color in the iSpace. Another participant explained, "I feel I'm always being tasked with putting on those glasses and saying, how would it feel for a woman of color to be in this space? And [I want] everyone to ask [that question] instead of having to be the one that's always asking, and wondering if we're doing enough, or if we need to redesign, or if we thought about X." Moreover, this particular library staff member commented on how her perceived lack of authority was rooted in subtle racist overtones from her peers: "It's when…I'm challenging people. My credibility is not assumed when I'm challenging, 'Why do we do this?' Or asking any question, the defense goes up right away. And so, for me that's racial discrimination. That's them saying, 'you don't have any credibility.'" The firsthand descriptions of the effects of underrepresentation in the makerspace, sexism, and racism point to future pathways of study and considerations in creating makerspaces.

Solutions and Future Implications
Our interviews with women of color involved with the iSpace allow for an investigation of their experiences situated within the larger realm of makerspaces. Part of our motive in conducting this study is to illuminate liberatory considerations for future maker and tech centric spaces. In addition to the challenges described above, interviewees offered some pathways to creating a more inclusive and productive makerspace. One area we see for improvement is the inclusion of art and more traditionally feminine crafts in the makerspace. Multiple participants noted the

importance of including Art in STEM education discussions (STEAM). One participant said, "I think that [STEM education] needs to include the arts, especially because the maker and DIY aspect [relates to] the whole culture of art, of taking self-expression, and pushing it. There is a sense of play... a sense of experimenting." Another expressed, "I do include the A for art in STEAM, because a lot of science, technology, engineering, and math includes art and it's more enjoyable for kids... they're like, 'What, that's connected to all these other things?'" Her assessment of the importance of enjoyment and of seeing the interconnectedness between disciplines is a running theme in our study. Another participant asserted that it is through a reclaiming of makerspaces as the realm of DIY and resourcefulness that women and people of color will be centered in the spaces: "Makerspaces have been defined by... technology and being for computer savvy people, which means mostly white males and masculine spaces. And I think that having people of color come into these spaces is [allowing for] more creative ways of thinking." The participant observed that white tech-bro culture infiltrates makerspaces, but it is counterintuitive to the potential of these spaces to allow for creative expression, being able to make mistakes in a supportive environment, and finding solutions to problems that might be applied on a larger scale beyond the makerspace.

Another barrier to access is intimidation or discomfort with technology, which could be alleviated in one way by creating a strong online and social media presence of the makerspace. As one participant explained, "There are levels of making a space more inclusive and more able to provide support to newcomers. Right now we are in this intermediate space where there is someone who can help you, but in order to feel really comfortable getting that help there's a lot of digital literacy, almost like a makerspace ABCs, that you need to feel comfortable with prior to coming in and doing a project." Creating an online educational center in support of the makerspace would allow interested individuals to familiarize themselves with the space before physically entering, and the extension of the space into the digital realm would provide opportunities for staff and students to provide input and perhaps practice tech skills like web design. Materials could include examples of projects completed by visitors, staff member bios, photos of the space and tools, and more in-depth guides to the technology available.

Workshops and events geared towards marginalized groups are also important in breaking down access barriers. As a former graduate assistant explained, the iSpace "held several workshops predominantly dedicated to women, trans and also femme identified makers. In that way we really carved out space and carved out community in a tech-centric environment that is otherwise pretty male, white and affluent." She goes on to explain that "it's by design [makerspaces are] inherently racialized and also gendered." Inclusive programming is absolutely necessary in a makerspace. Beyond inclusive programming, an understanding of the bias inherent in the structure and history of makerspaces is necessary to create effective programming and outreach.

While the breadth of this study as published does not allow for an exploration of all possible challenges and solutions, further areas of interest include explorations of salary and wages, impostor syndrome, and post college life from the experiences of women of color in the makerspace. Leadership and teaching roles within the makerspace are also areas that need attention, as well as ways to train students and staff. Interviewees also offered salient points of future opportunities in studying how people of color experience tech spaces. One area is in data capture—as a participant put it: "[The experiences of] people of color and women of color in the space are so unique. It makes me think of questions like, 'What are other ways to think about what's happening in this space, beyond headcounts and seeing how many times a different station is used?'" Another participant mentioned how interesting it might be to look at the ways visitors interact with different types of makerspaces, such as those in rural areas or mobile makerspaces: "If you have a mobile unit that goes around and someone has to go into a space they've never been to, in a place that is familiar to them, I think there's a lot of potential work around that." Furthermore, a participant made the point that looking more closely at the interactions between men and women in the makerspace would be beneficial to study, suggesting that researchers be present in the makerspace so they could observe "when males or female customers just come in and go straight towards my male counterparts or my white female counterparts." Overall, the firsthand experiences of underrepresented individuals must be considered when constructing further studies of makerspaces.

Lastly, this chapter does not directly address issues affecting womxn, trans, and femme-identified people of color. Nor does it delineate between the differences of issues affecting Black, Indigenous, or other specific women of color groups. The limitations of this study are admitted with the hope that these groups and their unique challenges to using makerspaces be further investigated in future publications and research initiatives.

Conclusion

There are many approaches to improving the experiences of women of color in a makerspace. The first step is to recognize that problems of underrepresentation, sexual harassment, and racism exist for these communities. Also, it must be recognized that viewing representation as a sole factor for success is problematic. Representation alone does not create liberation from discrimination for women of color, nor does it guarantee the success of inclusive programming. A greater conversation must occur around supporting a culture of inclusion that not only provides equity of racial and gender visibility, but also pursues goals of retention and mentorship. While attempting to address issues of gender and racial discrimination, institutions must talk directly with their affected communities and derive solutions with and from the collective experiences and expertise of individuals within these communities.

Institutional bureaucracies are often ill-equipped to tackle systematic problems of oppression, and thus place the responsibilities of solving problems of equity squarely on the shoulders of people affected by the lack of it. In makerspaces, this might be avoided by adopting feminist practices into the culture of the space. Going beyond codes of conduct that maintain the status quo for behavior in these spaces, recognizing feminism as a guiding principle, and not replicating patriarchal structures from within will positively transform spaces. This stance must be overt in how it directs every action, including who is hired for positions of power, what kinds of communities are being served, and what kinds of teaching and learning happen in the makerspace.

By enacting programs that are developed for and by women, and are inclusive to multiracial communities of women, makerspaces can begin the work of developing more equitable communities of making. Ensuring safe spaces for women, while recognizing and adopting anti-racist stances, goes far to establish a baseline of conduct for any makerspace community member. Creating networks of peers that support women of color, either through mentorship or professional development, is a good start to sustain representation and ensure future generations of women of color makers.

Bibliography

Bean, Vanessa, Nicole M. Farmer, and Barbara A. Kerr. "An Exploration of Women's Engagement in Makerspaces." *Gifted and Talented International* 30, no. 1-2 (2015): 61-67. doi:10.1080/15332276.2015.1137456.

Beede, David, Tiffany Julian, David Langdon, George McKittrick, Beethika Khan, and Mark Doms. "Women in STEM: A Gender Gap to Innovation. ESA Issue Brief# 04-11." (2011).

Brown, Jennifer, Jennifer Ferretti, Sofia Leung, and Marisa Méndez-Brady. "We Here: Speaking Our Truth." *Library Trends* 67, no. 1 (2018): 1-23.

Chua, Mel. "The Privilege of Being Oblivious." *ASEE Prism* 25, no. 1 (2015): 23.

Corbin, Juliet and Anselm Strauss. "Grounded Theory Research: Procedures, Canons, and Evaluative Criteria." *Qualitative Sociology* 13, no. 1 (1990): 3-21.

Dawson, Emily. "Social Justice and Out-of-School Science Learning: Exploring Equity in Science Television, Science Clubs and Maker Spaces." *Science Education* 101, no. 4 (2017): 539-547. doi:10.1002/sce.21288.

Farmer, Nicole M. "Maker Meaning: An Exploration of the Maker Movement, Career Adaptability, and Life Satisfaction." PhD diss., University of Kansas, 2018.

"Faqs." Women Techmakers Tucson. Accessed May 1, 2019. http://womentechmakerstucson.weebly.com/faqs.html.

Greene, Michael L., Nadia N. Kellam, and Brooke C. Coley. 2019. "Black Men in the Making: Engaging in Maker Spaces Promotes Agency and Identity for Black Males in Engineering." Paper presented at the *2019 CoNECD-The Collaborative Network for Engineering and Computing Diversity, Crystal City, VA, April 14, 2019*. https://peer.asee.org/31744.

"Ispace." The University of Arizona Libraries. Accessed May 1, 2019. http://new.library.arizona.edu/ispace.

Justice, Sean and Sandra Markus. "Educators, gender equity and making: Opportunities and obstacles." Paper presented at the *FabLearn Conference at Stanford University, Palo Alto, CA, September 26, 2015*. https://www.academia.edu/16570000/Educators_Gender_Equity_and_Making_Opportunities_and_Obstacles.

Keune, Anna, Kylie A. Peppler, and Karen E. Wohlwend. "Recognition in Makerspaces: Supporting Opportunities for Women to "make" a STEM Career." *Computers in Human Behavior* 99, (2019): 1-13.

Kim, Ann Y. and Gale M. Sinatra. "Science Identity Development: An Interactionist Approach." *International Journal of STEM Education* 5, no. 1 (2018): 1-6.

Kovach, Margaret. *Indigenous Methodologies: Characteristics, Conversations, and Contexts*. Toronto, Canada: University of Toronto Press, 2009.

Melo, Marijel C. "The Shadow Rhetorics of Innovation: Maker Culture, Gender, and Technology." PhD diss., The University of Arizona, 2018.

Philip, Thomas M. and Flávio S. Azevedo. "Everyday Science Learning and Equity: Mapping the Contested Terrain." *Science Education* 101, no. 4 (2017): 526-532. doi:10.1002/sce.21286.

"Policies." The University of Arizona Libraries. Accessed May 1, 2019. http://new.library.arizona.edu/ispace/policies.

Smith, Adrian. 2017. "Social Innovation, Democracy and Makerspaces." Science Policy Research Unity Working Papers Series. University of Sussex, June 2017. http://dx.doi.org/10.2139/ssrn.2986245.

Toombs, Austin. "Co-nerds or Co-workers? Intersecting Cultures of Maker Communities." Paper presented at the *CHI 2016 Conference, San Jose, CA, May 7, 2016*. https://hci.sbg.ac.at/wp-content/uploads/2015/11/Co-Nerds_or_Co-Workers.pdf.

Toupin, Sophie. "Feminist Hackerspaces: The Synthesis of Feminist and Hacker Cultures." *Journal of Peer Production* 5 (October 2014). http://peerproduction.net/issues/issue-5-shared-machine-shops/peer-reviewed-articles/feminist-hackerspaces-the-synthesis-of-feminist-and-hacker-cultures/.

Wajcman, Judy. "Feminist Theories of Technology." *Cambridge Journal of Economics* 34, no. 1 (2010): 143-52.

West-Puckett, Stephanie. "Materializing Makerspaces: Queerly Composing Space, Time, and (What) Matters." PhD diss., East Carolina University, 2017.

Chapter 3

REIMAGINING THE THIRDSPACE THROUGH THE MAKERSPACE

Anna Montana Cirell, Nadia Kellam, Audrey Boklage, and Brooke Coley

University makerspaces are unique learning environments aimed at increasing the quantity, diversity, and competence of engineers through hands-on design projects. Makerspaces stand out from traditional engineering labs in which teachers guide students through pre-planned content around a specific aspect of engineering.[1] A makerspace honors self-directed design projects and is often defined by its maker equipment, which includes 3D printers, laser cutters, vinyl cutters, CNC machines, soldering irons, sewing machines, and even pottery kilns. Seen at this most basic level, students enter the makerspace to learn skills specific to the materials or machinery.[2] These making skills range from the highly technical (e.g., electronics, computing, coding, robotics) to the mundane required for utilizing everyday hand tools.

---

1. Dyan Branstetter, "Libraries, Makerspaces, and STEAM Labs: What's the Difference?" Education Closet, 2017, https://educationcloset.com/2017/01/10/libraries-makerspaces-steam/.

2. T. Roffey, C. Sverko, and J. Therien, "The Making of a Makerspace: Pedagogical and Physical Transformations of Teaching and Learning," *Curriculum Guide, ETEC* 510 (2016): 1-41; Clive L. Dym, Alice M. Agogino, Ozgur Eris, Daniel D. Frey, and Larry J. Leifer. "Engineering Design Thinking, Teaching, and Learning." *Journal of Engineering Education* 94, no. 1 (2005): 103-120.

Yet, when understanding the makerspace as a mindset, it becomes more than just a space with making equipment.[3] Readily-available materials combined with prototyping equipment can act as a provocation for inquiry. To this end, makerspaces have the potential to transform thinking, such that students begin to view design through more innovative or entrepreneurial lenses. A maker mindset can push students beyond the simple accumulation of skills and into the realm of design thinking. Through the process of design thinking, students can then 1) identify a design challenge, 2) ask questions that help define the challenge, and 3) iterate solutions from readily-accessible materials and machines.[4] Finally, entrepreneurial thinking can strategize ways of scaling up design solutions to real-world possibilities and/or profits.[5] As such, makerspaces promote a mindset of empowerment, wherein students combine design thinking with readily available materials and machines to design in ways that respond to real-world needs. Finding an inclusive space for empowerment is especially important for under-represented groups (URGs) in engineering, given that traditional engineering curricula do not promote URG retention.[6]

Taken together, these viewpoints (e.g., making as skills/making as a mindset) have spawned a whole makerspace movement. Making replaces a culture of consumption with one of creation, such as when students design and build a speaker system for playing music instead of buying one.[7] Additionally, making infuses critical 21st century competencies,

---

3. Jackie,Gerstein, "Maker Education and Experiential Education," 2014, https://usergeneratededucation.wordpress.com/2014/06/22/maker-education-and-experiential-education/.

4. James W. Bequette, and Marjorie Bullitt Bequette, "A Place for Art and Design Education in the STEM Conversation," *Art Education* 65, no. 2 (2012): 40-47.

5. Krishna Uppuluri, *Engineer to Entrepreneur: The First Flight* (Krishna Uppuluri, 2011).

6. Erin A. Cech, "Culture of Disengagement in Engineering Education?" *Science, Technology, & Human Values* 39, no. 1 (2014): 42-72.

7. Alberta Education, "Framework for Student Learning: Competencies for Engaged Thinkers and Ethical Citizens with an Entrepreneurial Spirit," 2011, http://education.alberta.ca/department/ipr/curriculum.aspx; Tony Wagner and Robert A. Compton. *Creating Innovators: The Making of Young People Who Will Change the World* (Simon and Schuster, 2012).

such as creative problem solving, into science, technology, engineering, and math (STEM) learning. It is therefore implicitly assumed that makerspaces will open pathways toward STEM degrees and, ultimately, STEM careers. Particularly for engineers, makerspaces help meet pressing demands of industry, which expect recent engineering graduates to possess a comprehensive set of skills involving more than mere technical competence.[8] Strong advocacy for this type of teaching and learning, along with the unwavering belief that makerspaces impart these needed skills and design mindsets, have channeled major funding towards creating more university makerspaces.

Despite the makerspace momentum and its ability to draw a sizeable portion of education's limited funding, little research has critically evaluated the makerspace promise. For example, to what extent are these makerspace mindsets and skills taken up within students' daily practices? More specifically, questions remain over whether there are differences in how readily both skills and mindsets are taken up across different university makerspaces and within engineering's URGs. These answers are important, given how URGs struggle to find belonging in engineering programs,[9] which are dominated by white males and therefore aligned with hegemonic masculinities.[10] So, if these prized makerspaces are not inclusive and by default exclusionary (such that they further constrain URGs' opportunity to learn), they will only exacerbate the invisibility of historically isolated URGs within engineering. A proactive assessment of makerspaces, while in their infancy, could generate critical insights for building a stronger foundation of inclusion and diversity into the rapidly expanding makerspace infrastructure.

However, this paper can only initiate a critical examination of makerspaces after first fleshing out a way of understanding the makerspace

---

8. Executive Office of the President, "Building a Nation of Makers: Universities and Colleges Pledge to Expand Opportunities to Make," 2014, https://www.whitehouse.gov/sites/default/files/microsites/ostp/building_a_nation_of_makers .pdf.

9. Cech, "Culture of Disengagement in Engineering Education?" 2014

10. Robert W. Connell and James W. Messerschmidt. "Hegemonic Masculinity: Rethinking the Concept." *Gender & Society* 19, no. 6 (2005): 829-859.

pedagogically and specifically through the eyes of URGs. Thus, we first provide a conceptual framework for thinking specifically about empowerment and oppression within these pedagogical spaces. We do so by looking at critical pedagogy[11] through a Thirdspace lens.[12] Through this combined conceptual framework, we can then begin to generate meaning around students' lived experiences and subsequent inclusivity within makerspaces. Accordingly, along with our theoretical perspective, we also present our Thirdspace implications through an empirical example. In doing so, we illustrate the transformational possibility of our equity-oriented research agenda.

Theoretical Approach

Historically, critical theory has been used to understand culture in a way that confronts the socio-cultural systems and ideological forces which (re)produce and constrain it. Critical theory specifically examines the interplay of domination and subordination in society by focusing on the distribution and (re)production of oppressive inequities. Under this critical approach, in order to alleviate societal ills (e.g., violence, poverty, oppression), we must first expose and untangle them. Yet, because this injustice is frequently experienced on both material and immaterial levels (i.e., physical as well as mental or emotional), efforts to ameliorate these inequities must combine material redistribution with the empowering recognition of less-dominant ways of being.[13]

---

11. Paolo, Freire, *Pedagogy of the Oppressed* (New York: Continuum, 1970).

12. Edward W. Soja, *Thirdspace: Journeys to Los Angeles and Other Real-and-Imagined Places* (Oxford: Blackwell, 1996); Edward W. Soja, *Seeking Spatial Justice* (Minneapolis, MN: University of Minnesota Press, 2010).

13. Nancy Fraser and Axel Honneth, *Redistribution or Recognition? A Political-Philosophical Exchange* (New York: Verso, 2003).

Critical pedagogy. While the significance of critical theory has been defined through diverse works,[14] Freire's[15] notion of critical pedagogy offers a particularly useful framework within education. Critical pedagogy examines power relationships in the context of pedagogy, defined broadly to include both formal and informal learning environments. Critiquing the traditional classroom as an authoritarian space, wherein the teacher has command, Freire argued for a more liberatory pedagogy. This more liberatory approach treats students as empowered and capable of identifying and redressing the injustices, inequalities, and manufactured societal myths encircling them.[16] With "humanization" as the highest goal, Freire positioned education as a central pathway to becoming "more fully human (which was a privilege of an elite but a birthright of all)."[17] Through more liberatory pedagogy, vulnerable student populations could then identify their lived oppression, define the nature of this oppression, and then act to improve it.[18] Ultimately, this approach demands even more action and engagement from students than constructivist pedagogies.[19]

Spatial lens. Yet, limiting and deficit-based models of understanding frequently erupt from framing social justice problems as solely

---

14. Michael W. Apple, *Ideology and Curriculum* (New York: Routledge, 1979); Michael W. Apple, Education and Power (New York: Routledge, 1982); Michel Foucault, *Discipline and Punish: The Birth of the Prison* (London: Allen Lane, 1975); Michel Foucault, *Power/Knowledge: Selected Interviews and Other Writings, 1972-1977* (New York: Pantheon, 1980).

15. Paolo, Freire, *Pedagogy of the Oppressed* (New York: Continuum, 1970).

16. David A. Gruenewald, "Foundations of Place: A Multidisciplinary Framework for Place-Conscious Education," *American Educational Research Journal* 40, no. 3 (2003): 619-54.

17. Freire, *Pedagogy of the Oppressed*, 88.

18. Ali Nouri and Seyed Mehdi Sajjadi, "Emancipatory Pedagogy in Practice: Aims, Principles and Curriculum Orientation." *International Journal of Critical Pedagogy* 5, no. 2 (2014).

19. William C. Rhodes, "Liberatory Pedagogy and Special Education," *Journal of Learning Disabilities* 28, no. 8 (1995): 458-467.

human-centered (i.e., putting the onus on or otherwise blaming the oppressed for their own self-made oppression). Hence, a worthwhile approach to structuring process-oriented understandings (as opposed to people-centered) lies in today's spatial turn. Though often understood differently by various scholars,[20] the work of Lefebvre[21] and Soja[22] offers an important lens. They view critical theory from a spatial lens to value the meaning and influence of inequities as they are produced and recreated through space. Casting doubt onto anthropocentricism (i.e., people-centered understandings), this spatial notion pushes ontological, epistemological, and axiological presumptions further than feminisms and post-structuralisms ever could, by simply including what they all could not: the spaces encircling and influencing us. A spatial approach, with its unparalleled ability to invite a multitude of actors and contextual factors into its field of inquiry, can then assign smaller details and/or mundane or hidden contextual occurrences greater prominence in the construction of our social reality.[16]

Thirdspace theory. Soja's Thirdspace theory further articulates process-oriented understandings of these power/knowledge distributions through his identification of first, second, and third spaces of interaction. Firstspace is the traditional *perceived* surface appearances or material outcomes (e.g., Southwest University's[23] physical campus, buildings, parking lots, manicured lawns and hedges), while Secondspace represents how the space is *conceived* (e.g., SU as the number 1 in best value, the "party school," or having a strong football team). Firstspace

---

20. Gaston Bachelard, *The Poetics of Space: The Classic Look at How We Experience Intimate Places* (Boston: Beacon Press, 1969); Mikhail M. Bahktin, *The Dialogic Imagination: Four Essays* (Austin, TX: University of Texas Press, 1981); Michel Foucault, "Des espaces autres," *Architecture, Mouvement, Continuité* (1984): 46-49; Bruno Latour, *Pandora's Hope: Essays on the Reality of Science Studies* (Cambridge, MA: Harvard University Press, 1999); Doreen Massey, *For Space* (Thousand Oaks, CA: Sage, 2005); Nigel Thrift, "Space: The Fundamental Stuff of Geography," *Key Concepts in Geography* 2 (2003): 95-107.

21. Henri Lefebvre, *The Production of Space* (Oxford: Blackwell, 1974).

22. Soja, Thirdspace, 1996; Soja, *Seeking Spatial Justice*, 2010..

23. Southwest University and details of this institution are removed/replaced with pseudonyms for blind review.

reflects the rational perspectives and interests of the dominant, or the top-down snapshot of gentrification measures throughout SU's campus malls and streets. On the other hand, Secondspace houses utopian notions of artists, the media, or scientists.[24] For instance, when singing SU's Fight Song at football games, students conceptualize a space slightly different from the mapped Firstpace of the stadium. Last, Soja introduces Thirdspace as the "in between spaces" and *lived* experiences of the marginalized "Others" deemed out of place.

While Thirdspace can be applied to the lived experiences of anyone, because Thirdspace is a radically open and less hegemonic space with unforeseen opportunity for emancipation and empowerment,[25] it holds particular importance for populations that have been historically marginalized (e.g., URGs). Extending the SU example, Thirdspace is actualized through the working practices and beliefs of PhD students[26] as they collectively mediate the Firstspace physical presence of SU's campus through the Secondspace conceptions of graduate school. Herein, viewing doctoral students' "Grad Space" as a Thirdspace would become much more than the First and Second space combined. Despite the original intentions under which the "Grad Space" was constructed on the 3rd floor of SU's McBryde building, no doctoral student actually goes there to get work done; assigned graduate student study carrels in SU's Cooper Library exist solely for that purpose. Within the McBryde "Grad Space," students enact a radically open system of lived experience, or Thirdspace, where they collectively negotiate First and Secondspace to achieve their specific goals. This means that the real work of the "Grad Space" takes place in the 15-20 minutes before class, as students gather to gossip, commiserate, and exchange short cuts for completing last minute assignments.

---

24. Homi K. Bhabha, *The Location of Culture* (New York: Routledge, 1994); Henri Lefebvre, *The Production of Space* (Oxford: Blackwell, 1974).

25. Bhabha, *The Location of Culture*, 1994; Soja, *Thirdspace*, 1996; Soja, *Seeking Spatial Justice*, 2010.

26. For our immediate purposes, we consider PhD students disempowered and low status in the context of academia.

This critical spatial lens can add to our makerspace project in various ways. Feminists, who look at gender through a spatial lens,[27] understand how the public sphere is often coded as "male," while the private sphere is coded as "female." What this tends to do is keep the good, hard work of women invisible, while showcasing men as tough pioneers "taming" the wilderness of the public sphere (and getting all the credit and glory). When women enter the public sphere (e.g., makerspace), they have the potential to take a more dominant (or at least no longer invisible) role. In leaving the home and bringing their work into male-coded spaces (i.e., engineering domains), they are actively recoding that space and rewriting the possibilities for recognition and empowerment. According to Butler,[28] women and non-binary people use their body to take up space and, in doing so, can (re)make space in the makerspace. But given this is never an easy process and lived space is neither a dystopia nor a utopia, but a hybrid "heterotopia" of the two,[29] women (as well as other minorities) will likely confront instances of both empowerment and oppression.

Purpose and Research Questions

Under this analytical backdrop, our broad purpose is to then critically explore the extent to which makerspace mindsets and skills are taken up within URG students' daily practices. More specifically, we aim to interrogate potential differences/inequities in how skills and mindsets are taken up across different university makerspaces and within engineering's URGs. Thirdspace theory will particularly serve this purpose by offering a critical spatial lens for understanding actual lived experience within and across space as well as the possibilities students and faculty may create for re-imagining a space's meaning and potential. We aim to fill pressing gaps in the literature

---

27. Hannah Arendt, *The Human Condition* (Chicago: University of Chicago Press, 1958); Judith Butler, "Bodies in Alliance and the Politics of the Street." *European Institute for Progressive Cultural Policies* 9 (2011).

28. Judith Butler, "Bodies in Alliance," 2011.

29. Michel Foucault, "Des espaces autres," 1984.

and achieve our purpose through addressing the following research questions:

1. How can a Thirdspace lens help to structure understandings of URG students' lived experiences within the makerspace?
2. How can Thirdspace implications be leveraged to empower students from URGs to re-make the makerspace for greater learning?

Methodology

Our qualitative research design explores students' lived experiences within the makerspace through URG students' interview transcripts, conversations with makerspace administrators, makerspace observations, and analytic memoing. Across this corpus, our methods of data collection outline significant interview questions, conceptual markers for observations, and general guiding themes for analytical memoing. Our analytical strategy details the coding approach taken to conceptually draw Thirdspace meaning from our data.

Context of the Research

Current practices in qualitative research take into account researchers' subjectivities as well as other relational, socio-cultural, and otherwise contextual factors pertaining to the research site[30] This discussion is needed to situate research findings, because the complexity of the research context is often what matters most. At the same time, this value is often lost upon a researcher not intimately versed in the context of the individuals and places studied.

Researcher positionality. Peshkin[31] stresses the importance of recognizing the researcher's implicit subjectivity. However, qualitative researchers should not frame their epistemology, or ways of knowing,

---

30. Peter Smagorinsky, "The Method Section as Conceptual Epicenter in Constructing Social Science Research Reports," *Written Communication* 25, no. 3 (2008): 389-411.

31. Alan Peshkin, "In Search of Subjectivity—One's Own," *Educational Researcher* 17, no. 7 (1988): 17-21.

as a weakness. Instead, Peshkin believes researchers' subjectivities can be positioned as a key strength grounding one's ability to draw necessary meaning from their work. Seen this way, while our positionality may have biased our understandings and interpretation, it also lent the needed background and epistemological lenses to make analytical sense of URGs' lived experiences within the makerspace.

Concerning our combined positionality, four researchers contributed to this paper's data collection, data analysis, and scholarly publication. However, research member one took the lead in specifying research questions, theoretically framing the paper, coding and analysis, as well as its written dissemination. She is a postdoctoral researcher in engineering education who specializes in qualitative research methods as well as theoretical aspects of space, power, and privilege. Two engineering faculty members and one postdoctoral researcher also added to this paper. These three co-authors all self-identify as makers, have PhDs in either engineering or science education, and exercise expertise in qualitative research methods and issues of diversity and inclusion.

Research site. Our study includes ten makerspaces within seven institutions across the US. Wanting a diverse set with maximum variability, or the smallest sample with the most amount of variation,[32] we selected our ten makerspaces from a variety of institutions (e.g., doctoral universities, baccalaureate colleges, prestigious liberal arts colleges, public and private institutions). Furthermore, three of these makerspaces were minority-serving institutions (e.g., Historically Black Colleges and Universities [HBCUs], Hispanic-Serving Institutions [HSIs]), which helped to ensure a diverse pool of engineering students from URGs. In all these ten university-affiliated makerspaces, we conducted observations and collected interview data.

---

32. Joseph A. Maxwell, *Qualitative Research Design: An Interactive Approach* (Thousand Oaks, CA: Sage, 2013).

Data Collection

Our data corpus grew to include interviews with sixty-seven students and seven makerspace administrators as well as ten makerspace observations and a plethora of analytic memos. Due to our inclusion criteria, each student participant was either a white woman, a woman of color, or a man of color who was enrolled in an undergraduate engineering program. While our original corpus included all seventy-four students and makerspace administrators, we critically examined only a subset of ten students and two makerspace administrators. This decision stemmed from the richness of certain students' stories as well as the amount of time spent in these students' makerspaces. Appendix A provides two tables to present our subset: one that lists out each student participant's[33] university affiliation, engineering program of study, and personal demographics and a second table stating and describing each university.

The participant interviews were intended to draw out participant's stories. Among our semi-structured interview protocol questions for URGs, this paper highlights the responses to the following: 1) What do URG's stories reveal about the culture of makerspaces? 2) How have the makerspace faculty, management and/or staff influenced you as a maker? 3) If you could give advice to the management about a way to make this makerspace a better space for you, what advice would you give? How could this makerspace be better?

Observations helped us to develop a different understanding of the context of the makerspace. During observations, researchers watched students engage in hands-on projects and attended to how these projects leveraged various aspects (e.g., machines, materials, mindsets, skills) of the makerspace. From the literature around makerspaces, observations revolved around three categories: 1) the quality of its culture for learning, 2) the meaningful organization of its space, and 3) the extent to which students' practices align with the space in a meaningful way.

---

33. Given that we did not collect demographic information on the two makerspace administrators, they are not included within Table 1.

Outside of observations, analytic memos written throughout data collection elicited the researchers' first impressions, shared personal reflection, and enabled a rich description of the context of each site. Per Saldaña's[34] suggestions, our analytical memos spanned the following topics: 1) how we personally related to participants and/or the phenomenon; 2) notable routines, rituals, rules, roles, and relationships; 3) possible networks and processes (links, connections, overlaps, flows) among the codes; and 4) patterns, categories, concepts, and assertions reflective of tentative answers to research questions.

Lastly, we interviewed makerspace administrators for a behind-the-scenes look at the overarching vision for the makerspace as well as its history. Our interview protocol for makerspace administrators included the following questions: 1) what is the history of this makerspace? 2) what is the vision for the makerspace? 3) what are your goals moving forward? and 4) what are some challenges that you have seen in trying to achieve this vision?

Analysis

To deepen understandings of students' lived experiences in the makerspace, particularly as these experiences relate to URGs, we leveraged all data. While we did explore a subset of the participants for a more granular look at the phenomena, we did not overlook the rest of the data. Or, put differently, we needed both the forest *and* the trees, as the forest helped to situate understandings of the trees. As such, our data corpus included participants' interview transcripts, interviews with makerspace administrators, makerspace observations, and analytic memos recorded directly after observations. Our coding strategy aimed to enable an analysis that could directly answer our research questions and align with our theoretical approach. As such, this analytical tack included first cycle Concept Coding and Process Coding, a second cycle of Pattern Coding, followed by various focusing strategies.[35]

---

34. Johnny Saldaña, *The Coding Manual for Qualitative Researchers* (Thousand Oaks, CA: Sage, 2016).

35. Ibid.

Coding and data reduction. For the larger project, we first generated ten codes that related to our project's research questions around identity formation, makerspaces, and URG students. Codes included "pedagogical experiences that shape identity," "road of trials in engineering," "stories of values, knowledge, skills, practices, and norms in engineering makerspaces," and "recommendations for makerspaces." Though all codes lent meaning to this particular paper's purpose (i.e., a Thirdspace understanding of URG's making experiences), we particularly focused on the last two codes relating to makerspaces. Using the Dedoose app, we separated out all excerpts attached to these two makerspace-specific codes.

After rereading these excerpts as well as revisiting administrator interviews, observational field notes, and analytic memos, our initial coding cycle used Concept Coding to organize these data under a Thirdspace framework. Given its utility in transcending the overwhelming detail of a large data corpus and scaling up towards the study's larger theoretical framing, Concept Coding adds value to cultural studies, socio-political inquiry, and critical theory.[36] Moreover, Concept Coding reflects on broader social constructs by applying more abstract or general concepts to the localized particularities of the study. We therefore chose Concept Coding, because it enabled an analysis that could directly answer our research questions and goals. Seen this way, anything relating to the makerspace equipment or the physical facility was coded as Firstspace. All notions of makerspace mindset, we coded as Secondspace. Last, a Thirdspace code represented any hint of the makerspace mindset and/or skill being taken up in students' daily practices.

Given our research questions sought a Thirdspace understanding of URGs' daily design practices, we needed to further interrogate our Thirdspace codes. Henceforth, we separated out all excerpts coded as "Thirdspace" and applied another initial cycle of Process Coding. According to Saldaña, Process Coding looks for action in the data and uses gerunds ("-ing" words) exclusively to highlight this action as a

---

36. Ibid, 111.

process unfolding dynamically across time and space. Thus, given our need for a process-oriented understanding in lieu of a human-centered one, Process Coding helped to situate URG routines and rituals as an evolving process caught up in space and time. Examples of these process codes included "shaping hidden culture," "reconciling personal with professional self," "remaking the makerspace," and "increasing belonging in this remade space."

Next was Second Cycle Analysis, which took place through Pattern Coding. We employed Pattern Coding, because we wanted to create a cohesive narrative by finding relationships between the larger ten code categories and our Thirdspace subcategories. In our case, we examined both the forest and the trees to draw out the broader theoretical meaning while still maintaining the integrity of students' unique lived experiences. This helped reveal how students were tackling challenges of belonging in engineering in relation to our broader Thirdspace categories. Providing more descriptive labels for the coded categories (e.g., expanding "Secondspace" to "Secondspace Mindset of Making") and regrouping certain categories into larger ones revealed more interesting connections between the code categories as well as the insights these connections might enable.

Lastly, our After Second Cycle Analysis sought final data reduction through several focusing strategies. In particular, we utilized Saldaña's "codeweaving" technique.[37] Codeweaving helps to weave individual components of a phenomenon together to see how they best fit together to create the larger whole. One can compare this focusing strategy to building a jigsaw puzzle, whereby a larger image is revealed. This larger image does not preclude the interplay of all its pieces, but instead provides an at-a-glance heuristic for identifying process or suggesting causality. In our case, this process forced our code categories to work together to link back to the "so what" of the original Thirdspace theory framing our study. Thus, this codeweaving focusing strategy structured

---

37. Ibid, 276.

holistic understandings and implications of how students were creating a Thirdspace within the makerspace.

Validity checks & inter-coder reliability. To ensure the reliability of our analysis, we applied several analytical checks. This checklist followed a process-oriented framework for research quality.[38] This was important, because locating appropriate validity checks throughout the research process can increase the trustworthiness of qualitative findings.[39] Various validation strategies within the data gathering phase, or what Walther et al. call "making the data," can help to mitigate threats that may compromise the researchers' ability to capture students' inter-subjective reality. An example of such a threat would be engineering students from URGs simply answering what they think the researcher wants to hear. We avoided this threat by collecting and cross-comparing information from a large corpus of data.[40] In the next phase of analysis, or "handling the data,"[41] researchers' conclusions must also be grounded in the students' accounts. In our case, inter-coder reliability helped when cross-checking the social reality investigated against our resultant findings. Combating validity threats in this way involved 1) blind coding, whereby each coder reads and analyzes transcripts blind to others' interpretation, 2) peer debriefing to reconcile, or work through, coder disagreements, and 3) revising codes for validity (i.e., ensuring that understandings are co-constructed and the process is checked for bias). As we worked through

---

38. Joachim Walther, Nicola W. Sochacka, and Nadia N. Kellam, "Quality in Interpretive Engineering Education Research: Reflections on an Example Study," *Journal of Engineering Education* 102, no. 4 (2013): 626-659.

39. Nadia Kellam and Anna Montana Cirell, "Quality Considerations in Qualitative Inquiry: Expanding Our Understandings for the Broader Dissemination of Qualitative Research," *Journal of Engineering Education* 107, no. 3 (2018): 355-361; Michael Q. Patton, *Qualitative Evaluation and Research Methods* (Thousand Oaks, CA: Sage, 2015); Joachim Walther, Nicola W. Sochacka, and Nadia N. Kellam, "Quality in Interpretive Engineering Education Research: Reflections on an example study." *Journal of Engineering Education* 102, no. 4 (2013): 626-659.

40. Norman K. Denzin, *Sociological Methods: A Sourcebook* (New York: Routledge, 1978); Joseph A. Maxwell. *Qualitative Research Design: An Interactive Approach.* (Thousand Oaks, CA: Sage, 2013).

41. Walther, Sochacka, and Kellam, "Quality in Interpretive Engineering Education Research, 2013.

these steps to understand the codes from all angles, the robustness of our findings increased.

Findings

What follows is a discussion of critical insights from the application of a Thirdspace framework, with particular attention to its potential to foreground the extent to which makerspace mindsets and skills are taken up within students' lived practices. Distinct makerspace events and students' insights will be contextualized through a spatial understanding of makerspaces, such that they exemplify Firstspace, Secondspace, and Thirdspace representations. In particular, Thirdspace representations will be explained in terms of how students from URGs can remake the makerspace for greater ownership of their learning. Given Thirdspace representations are the focus of this paper, Firstspace and Secondspace representations are only briefly discussed. Their brief inclusion is positioned as a means to structure, but not take away from, the more central, process-oriented Thirdspace understandings of students' lived experiences in the makerspace.

Firstspace Top-Down Approach to Making

Firstspace represents how the dominant/authoritative view or experience a space. An example of this would be how campus administrators think of makerspaces with an "impetus to impress"[42] concerned with who has the biggest space or the most makerspaces per campus with the most expensive high-tech machines. This view doesn't necessarily benefit the student because (as we saw among certain makerspaces) students can be discouraged from using expensive machinery and the makerspace in general through over-intensive training or keeping doors locked. We found that a major goal of this Firstspace makerspace "impetus to impress" was to dazzle and draw in prospective students and

---

42. The actual words that the administrator used were "pissing contest." Though this notion accurately reflects the Firstspace of the alpha male dominating engineering, we felt it too vulgar to include in the body of the paper.

their parents when touring the makerspace facility. Baxter,[43] a first-year computer science/engineering student at the HBCU of South Atlantic,[44] describes this experience:

> When we would go on college tours, [my mother] would always ask if they had a 3D printer, which was embarrassing sometimes. I understood her point. She wanted to make sure that I was in a competitive space. It was more so learning about 3D printers, learning about modeling, putting different components together on a computer, and see how those would fit together as they're produced into the real world.

This "impetus to impress" was further manifested through donor dollars funding certain costly makerspace equipment as well as the nearby plaques and signs honoring their contribution.

This goal is also articulated by Isabelle, a fourth-year mechanical engineering student from a public, doctoral university of South Central University, as she discusses how makerspaces are used to impress prospective students:

> I've been in the Makerspace Y[45] a few times, where a group of adults just comes in and asks me, "Oh, what are you doing?" I'm like, "I don't know, why are you here?"...It's like tours, and stuff like that. I don't know, the Makerspace Y is more of a trendy thing, but it's fun.

When designed through a Firstspace lens, makerspaces are good for drawing in prospective students but not for keeping them. Makerspaces built for tours and trends are uninviting and often empty of student makers. This sentiment is also echoed by Baxter. Even though he had toured the space with his mother, his university's makerspace is often empty due to failure to advertise the space to students. He believes this may have to do with funding: "I feel like the more people that use it, the more funding you would need for it."

---

43. All students' names are pseudonymized.

44. All institutions' names are pseudonymized.

45. All makerspace names are replaced with "Makerspace X" or "Makerspace Y" to protect the university's identity.

Secondspace Mindset of Making

Secondspace represents how the space is conceived or marketed through the utopian eyes of the artist or the media. This notion of space is represented in the makerspace through its website and how the makerspace brands itself. Isabelle echoes this Secondspace sentiment, "The Makerspace Y is definitely marketed a lot, like oh my god, the [university] has Makerspace Y. It's this really trendy, fun thing, that the engineering department just boasts about. You see it everywhere." As an example of this "seeing it everywhere," Isabelle's university broadcasts their makerspace marketing video during football games from a giant Jumbotron screen. Outside of Jumbotron TVs, one can look on any given makerspace website to see its mission statement or photos showing students making. The mission statements are also imbued into how the staff talks about the space. In the words of a manager of South Central University's makerspace, "This is not an academic place for engineers, this is a place to BECOME and BE an engineer." Within the actual makerspace, Secondspace can also be represented through the posters that the makerspace administration places on the walls. Some makerspaces had empowering images of women on the wall. The private, doctoral, New England University had only one poster in its EE/CS makerspace, and it was of an Asian female using high tech machinery. At the all-women college/makerspace at South Atlantic University, an HBCU, the only posters were of black females and others that read "The Future is Bright. The Future is Female." One makerspace manager from Middle Atlantic University, a prestigious liberal arts college, describes the importance of posters through the following quote:

> David: ...[Y]ou go into so many labs, and you see a poster of the magnetic spectrum, or the insides of a chip, or something. So we were kind of sensitive to stereotype threat, and how that might make people feel. There's a comic strip I read called Zen Pencils. The guy takes inspirational quotes (he's a Malaysian cartoonist) and turns them into these inspirational cartoons. So, we have those up around the walls, and we've been very careful to try to make the space as social as possible, and kind of a multipurpose space. Not to make it just the weird kinda smelly techy place to go... I don't know if it's working or not.

These posters and mission statements help to create a makerspace culture that can be (and often is) empowering. Yet, similar to this makerspace manager's musing of "I don't know if it's working," it may not actually represent how students view or use the space.

Thirdspace Lived Experiences in the Making

Thirdspace, on the other hand, represents the lived experience of those without authority. Oftentimes, this means the marginalized and oppressed. Yet, in terms of makerspaces, it can also represent student makers in general. As such, we present Thirdspace representations across the following process-oriented themes: shaping hidden culture, reconciling personal self with professional self, remaking the makerspace, and increasing belonging in this remade space.

Shaping hidden culture. Because makerspaces are places where students enact self-directed projects (as opposed to those led by a teacher), they are the perfect space to reflect that student-driven, or hidden, culture. Examples of student makers' Thirdspace lived experience would be what making practices students enact outside of normal business hours (e.g., weekends and late-night personal time on weekdays). Thirdspace artifacts left behind could be empty pizza boxes or half-finished electrical engineering projects temporarily abandoned on the makerspace's large reconfigurable tables. Oftentimes, the makerspace staff will see this as evidence of how students really make the space their own only when opening up the space for official business the next morning.

This idea of a hidden culture is shown in the following exchange between the makerspace manager from Middle Atlantic University and a researcher:

> Damien: [A] lot of that culture's invisible to us...I'm here Monday through Friday, eight to five, but I think a lot of the goings on happen beyond that time, so in the evenings, or on the weekends, even, I think a lot of times students are meeting in here, so maybe there are other students that are in here...but I just have no idea because I'm not here when they're meeting. And, I know that people are meeting in here, because oftentimes I'll come in, in the morning and things are left out,

> there's pizza boxes, so it's obvious that people have been in here doing stuff, but I don't necessarily see everything that happens.
> Interviewer: So, would you say the real culture emerges when you're away? With the pizza boxes?
> Damien: Potentially, yeah. There are definitely people in here during the day, as well. There's sort of a difference in atmosphere versus nine to five.

An example of how users of the makerspace may manifest a hidden culture of exclusion is expressed as Baxter discusses the challenges of hands-on group work:

> It's kind of that same isolating feeling where it's like you kind of feel excluded because none of the people look like you. It's almost like you're kind of doing it on your own. You know that when it comes time for groups ... Like I said, this isn't everybody's experience. But when it comes time to group up, people are usually gonna group with people they're comfortable with.

Reconciling personal self with professional self. The following are examples of students bringing personal interests, outside projects, and other bits of their URG identity into the space. Whit, a humanitarian engineering senior at Mountain University, discusses how a defining hands-on experience helped her to find herself and her passions within her program:

> When it came to the point where I needed to make the decision as to what kind of engineering I wanted to do, I started going through a bit of an existential crisis...I took a project course with [a professor from the humanitarian department], and that was the first time I was exposed to using engineering to help people with problems with the most basic necessities of life. Things that you don't think of.

Aaron, an engineering technology student from a Hispanic-serving institution we called Gulf University, said he used the university makerspace to fix broken appliances around his house and make up for the socio-economic challenges of being an impoverished student. Isabelle brought crocheting to her robotics design project and leveraged this feminine skill to win over the other competition. Finally, Amanda, an electrical engineering major from New England University used the makerspace to affirm her spiritual identity when making greeting cards for her Christian Fellowship. In this way, we show how bringing personal interests into the space can help URGs to test out, to incorporate, and perhaps even to reconcile, personal self with their professional engineering identity. Hence, while a student-driven makerspace can reflect the broader hidden culture being formed on a larger scale, it can also reveal the intimate, dynamic interplay between URGs' personal self and their growing engineering identity.

Remaking the makerspace. Similar to bringing in personal interests and intersecting identities into the makerspace, notions of Thirdspace can also be represented through the extent to which URG's skills and design mindset can help to remake the makerspace. This is shown through the following exchange between a researcher and Blake, an electrical engineering major from Middle Atlantic University who designed a table that is now a functional part of Makerspace X:

> Interviewer: What's your favorite thing you've made?
> Blake: I don't know. Oh, well, on the 3D printer or just in the Makerspace X?
> Interviewer: In Makerspace X.
> Blake: This time I made a cool ... it's in there, actually, like a little red ... the gaming table. Yeah. I made that last time...[I]t's really just an IKEA table, a monitor, an Arduino on the inside. I also made a printed circuit board (PCB) for it in order to power it because [you need] the connection to the Arduino and then to the screen and then to power.

Likewise, the walls and tables of this particular college's Makerspace X were completely covered with students' vinyl stickers and laser-cut *objets d'art*, including its only clock, which a student made with the laser cutter and some hand tools. Students using the makerspace would laugh, because the clock was not only hard to read, but also told the wrong time. Another instance of how much this space represented the students' lived experiences (and not that of the faculty) was how its whiteboard for organizing student tech hours hadn't been updated in months. A mechanical engineering student named Wendel shared how the space was going through a transition in leadership, and while the standards of safety are still being upheld, the student techs have their own system for keeping abreast each other's hours.

Although these grassroots examples may seem impractical or inhibiting (e.g., a clock that doesn't work), it nonetheless represents how students are remaking a space to represent their lived experiences of learning, making, and designing. Final proof of Thirdspace representations was how packed Makerspace X was. Of all makerspaces we visited, those most aligned with Thirdspace held the most makers doing the most activities. In this successful Makerspace X, located at the liberal arts Middle Atlantic University, three different classes were using the space at once to engage students in three different types of projects (vinyl cutting, bookmaking, and pillow making). The desire for more and more students to not only use the space, but make it their own is voiced by its makerspace manager:

> Damien: I just want to know how to get more people in here, and specifically people who are outside of the traditional users of makerspaces. So, at least from our space, non-engineers. That's probably my biggest question. Yeah, helping foster that, because we talk about the space being a communal space, and collaborative, and social, and there are elements of that there, but I don't think students really feel like they own it yet.

Increasing belonging in this remade space. Further, Makerspace X was attached to a lively coffeehouse, which not only attracted the makers but kept them there through breakfast, lunch, and dinner. This is important because Andrea, a female mechanical engineering major at South Central University, talks about how carving out a space of their own takes several days, not just one. "It's never about making stuff in one day...I'm not just cutting out a piece of wood, or shaving off the suction of a metal part. It's always like, I have to make this finished design." A member of our research team (and a co-author) discovered this sense of belonging in Middle Atlantic University's Makerspace X and asked a student about it: "One thing I've noticed here is that y'all are so group focused...there's a lot of 'we.' I hear a lot of 'we'..." McKenzie also mentioned a feeling of belonging, using this collective "we" when discussing her work with other students in Makerspace X:

> I don't know if you've noticed, but we're all very close knit…and especially our class we all work together and everything. It's not very competitive here, I'd say. It's not "best of the best" grade. People aren't trying to shut each other down. It's everyone will help each other with the homework, everyone will help each other with the labs…[S]o we'll talk about everything, we will give help when needed. We will ask for help.

Wallace also echoed this sense of belonging in Makerspace X, when he mentioned how:

> [We] view it as a hangout space. Me and my friends were eating lunch and we all came up here because that's just where we sit around until we have senior design. We're not really anywhere else. If I need to go find someone, I would check the Makerspace X first…There's events all the time in the Makerspace X. That idea of building community and building a space that we can call our own…

This symbolized how a remade space could better foster belonging (day after day). The want to make it a place to return to was also demonstrated through Winona's experience. As an environmental engineering major from Middle Atlantic University, she discussed the importance of learning how to make the Makerspace X a place to take ownership of your learning:

> When I went with my friend, I was like, "Oh yeah, you can just do that," and she was like, "No, I'll show you how to do it so then you can do it later." I was like, "Oh, I guess that would make more sense than just having you do it, because obviously, you're not going to be with me every time I'm down here."

Findings in Context
Here we place our findings in context of the broader literature of spacemaking. This helps us to synthesize across possibly divergent meanings, generate similar paradigmatic examples, draw out more nuanced understandings of our data, and establish more enduring implications.

To achieve this, we then pull from seemingly unconnected research around punk rockers' creativity and studies of ecological evolution.

To underscore how a makerspace can facilitate the development of engineering skills and identity, we briefly discuss how a certain performance space helped to shape punk rock. Relating makerspaces to a punk rock club can extend our findings and further illustrate the importance of how spaces impact the creative work executed within it. David Byrne lead singer of The Talking Heads and author of the 2017 book, *How Music Works*, discusses "creation in reverse," whereby "opportunity and availability are often the mothers of invention."[46] Byrne believes that the "emotional story—'something to get off my chest'—still gets told, but its form is guided by prior contextual constrictions."[47] Too often we assume that creativity comes from within the artist. However, this limited way of thinking overlooks how the context (i.e., space surrounding the artist) more often than not dictates what is painted, designed, written, sculpted, sung, and performed. As an example, New York City's East Village music club, CBGB, housed a unique space that attracted punk rock/new wave bands, such as the Ramones, Blondie, and The Talking Heads. Byrne, having performed regularly in the space, claimed he would write and perform specific music for that space. For Byrne, the specific sound architecture and intimate quarters didn't just inspire a rebel culture, but actually helped to author it. By changing the sound of popular music, CBGB became just as much a part of the unique sound and feel of punk music as the bands who performed there. That said, CBGB owes some of its credit to its owner, Hilly Krystal, who let its shape and influence evolve. This comparison helps to illustrate how makerspaces shape and are shaped by design in engineering.

This then moves us to deeply consider who is shaping the space: the students, the faculty, or both? Here, we turn to the evolutionary concept of niche construction. This notion of niche construction involves a process whereby organisms' activities and choices remake

---

46. David Byrne, How Music Works, (New York: Three Rivers Press, 2017), 16.
47. Ibid.

their environment for their own immediate gain.[48] Examples include the building of nests, burrows, and shade structures as well as biological strategies of nutrient cycling in soil systems. Though these niche alterations are often advantageous to the creator, they are not always beneficial to others. Nonetheless, niche construction diverges from a theory of evolution by natural selection where organisms adapt to an unchanging environment (rather than change it themselves). In this way, it troubles accepted notions of evolution. This applies to makerspaces in that we anticipate a paradigm shift. The guiding philosophy has shifted from telling students (and especially URG students) to adapt their needs to the makerspace (i.e., survival of the fittest) to one where they are told to adapt the makerspace to their needs so more are fit to survive.

Conclusion

This paper re-imagined makerspace inclusivity by examining how engineering design skills, mindsets, and students' design practices are caught up in space. In other words, we took a spatial approach to understanding URG students' Thirdspace experiences in the makerspace, with particular attention to how URGs may remake the makerspace to serve their specific needs. Our conclusions briefly restate our major Thirdspace findings. Next, we share implications of students remaking space in the makerspace. Last, we suggest recommendations for future research into more inclusive makerspaces.

Exploring makerspaces through the Thirdspace has helped us to show the process of URGs 1) shaping hidden culture, 2) reconciling personal self with professional self with professional engineering identity, 3) remaking the makerspace, and 4) increasing belonging in this remade space. These findings are important in light of how URGs struggle to belong within engineering spaces dominated by white males and associated norms of hegemonic masculinity. With the wealth of resources being currently channeled towards these highly prized and increasingly

---

48. John F. Odling-Smee, Kevin N. Laland, and Marcus W. Feldman, Niche Construction, *The Neglected Process in Evolution* (Princeton, NJ: Princeton University Press, 2010).

more prevalent makerspaces, a proactive evaluation of makerspaces within their early years could help to model a more inclusive foundation for better retention for all. Lastly, given how often deficit thinking accompanies a human-centered approach to social justice (i.e., blaming the oppressed for their own oppression), our spatial approach offers a more systemic solution to engineering education's most enduring systemic problems.

Implications

One makerspace located in the public, doctoral university of South Central University was re-designed with iteration in mind. The old makerspace was newly renovated to allow for rapid prototyping first and more finalized fabrication later. As such, the layout of the space and the organization of machinery allows for this linear design process. At first blush, this appears to be a foolproof solution. Yet, if the spatial design of CBGB dictated what was sung and performed, wouldn't a makerspace dictate what is designed and fabricated? Seen this way, a makerspace that attempts to dictate a linear design process may produce a standardized design product. Likewise, marketing a standard approach to design may constrain the hidden culture being shaped. Further, this approach may not be so ideal for all learners using that space. This may especially be the case for URG students who may disproportionately confront challenges when self-identifying with their design project and reconciling their personal identity with their professional one. Above all, makerspaces would do well to allow all students a bit of niche construction when remaking their space into one in which they feel they can belong. The importance of permitting students to do what works for them is echoed by David, the makerspace manager from Middle Atlantic University:

> And, if people don't have a space they can gather, it's really hard to build community. So, one of the things I came in really sensitive to, having done it before, is how do you build spaces students want to be in, and then don't have this sort of rigid, hierarchical interactions? It's like, not a lab space, and you show up for your three hours, and there's

somebody in charge of it, but really a space that you can come and go to begin to, over probably a decade, start to shift the culture...[O]ne of the things I've walked away with from NSF, and I think this is one of the differences between our space and then Lab Y, which is tied to a machine shop, old school machine shop, and Makerspace X, which is more mechanically engineering focused, is don't make rules if you're not willing to enforce them, and the fewer rules the better. So, we've been trying very much not to have this long list of rules and policies.

Recommendations for Makerspaces

From our Thirdspace findings, we draw out various best practice recommendations for more inclusive makerspaces. For makerspace staff training student techs, teach them to anticipate a proximal zone of development. Briefly described, zone of proximal development is a concept introduced by Vygotsky,[49] which calculates the right amount of instructive support, or scaffolding, provided to the learner to keep them on the edge of their understanding. Through scaffolding, techs thus find the right balance between amount of help and the amount of freedom given to the student to learn. This want was particularly echoed in our interviews with female students, who too often experience "mansplaining," where a male peer may explain a design task in a condescending manner. One female student particularly felt at home in her makerspace, because its staff had a fail forward approach to learning. Other times, females complain about the tendency for male peers to not teach them, but instead complete the task for them due to doubts over the female's ability to do it herself. For other ways to increase makerspace inclusivity, staff could hire more student techs who come from URGs. This would implicitly communicate a makerspace culture that honors diversity.

In terms of makerspace safety, staff could gauge the most workable balance between comprehensive rigor and usability. This would mean that training courses would be rigorous, while also allowing a level of accessibility and transferability. In this way, students would be less

---

49. Lev Vygotsky, *Mind in Society: The Development of Higher Psychological Processes* (Cambridge, MA: Harvard University Press, 1978).

intimidated or turned off by overly demanding training requirements. Further, allowing training modules to transfer across their various university makerspaces provides flexibility, so students can move around at end-of-semester crunch time, in the chance that time/space within their usual makerspace was limited. Additionally, when classes are scheduled within a makerspace, providing accessible training options to its students would allow a classful of students to train in time for their upcoming class. Lastly, other students have called for an online system that matches student techs to new users of the makerspace, such that new users get more extensive one-on-one attention when they need it.

These makerspace recommendations for availability and openness are summarized by Blake in the following:

> I guess availability. Damien is just always available, ready to help. You can ask him 10 questions in a row and there will be no annoying ... he's just always willing to help you in any way, shape, or form, and I guess just the setup they've made it. They've made it in a sense that you should be ... I don't wanna say self-sufficient, kind of, as in they've made tutorials that you can follow so even if they're not available, there is something that you can use, or if they aren't there, there is something you can use...[A]nd it's open 24 hours, too, so just making the space available all the time when they're not available.

Calls for Future Research

Our findings only scrape the surface and therefore invite the need for more research at the intersection of engineering education, inclusivity, and URG retention. Continuing to explore URGs lived experiences in these increasingly important engineering spaces may clarify the complex and dynamic ways in which power and identity is caught up in space. Needless to say, numerous opportunities arise for extending this work. For instance, as new questions emerge and continue to challenge us, sophisticated tools and innovative approaches are needed to provide potential answers. Future studies, which make quantitative connections from increased URG use of makerspaces to improved URG retention, may add insight into makerspace inclusivity in new and unexplored ways. Future research could also apply different data collection strategies to more thoroughly examine various factors across time (not just space). Similar to exploring how CBGB evolved along with punk rock, a longitudinal makerspace study could track the nuanced process of how students may be remaking their makerspace across time. As an example, researchers may elect to study makerspaces through ethnography and shadow students' daily making practices over time. Also, our sample of ten university makerspaces is by no means representative of the diversity of all makerspaces across the world. Additional qualitative studies of makerspaces are needed in other parts of the world where engineering programs struggle to retain URG students. Last, studies of makerspaces in the community could also yield insights into how community-run makerspaces may impact the broader community of makers and possibly create a more productive pathway for nontraditional engineering students.

Appendix A

Table 1.
Participants' Pseudonym, University Affiliation, Program of Study, and Demographics

Pseudonymn	University	Gender	Ethnicity	Major	Year
Baxter	South Atlantic	M	Black	Computer Science	1
Isabelle	South Central	F	Other-Middle Eastern	Mechanical Engineering	2
Aaron	Gulf	M	Asian	Engineering-Technology	5
Amanda	New England	F	Asian	Electrical Engineering	2
Blake	Middle Atlantic	M	African American	Electrical Engineering	3
Wendel	Middle Atlantic	M	White	Computer Engineering	4
Andrea	South Central	F	Asian	Mechanical Engineering	1
McKenzie	Middle Atlantic	F	Asian/White	Electrical Engineering	3
Winona	Middle Atlantic	F	White	Environmental Engineering	4
Whit	Mountain	F	White	Humanitarian Engineering	4

Table 2.
University Affiliation, Program of Study, and Demographics

University	Description
Middle Atlantic	Private Liberal Arts University, Primarily White Institution (PWI)
South Central	Public Doctoral University, PWI
Gulf	Public Doctoral University, Hispanic-Serving Institution (HSI)
New England	Private Doctoral University, PWI
Pacific	Public Doctoral University, Asian-American Pacific Islander-serving Institution (AANAPI)
South Atlantic	Private Historically Black Colleges and Universities (combines 2 majority-women HBCUs with mostly male HBCU)
Mountain	Public Doctoral University

Bibliography

Alberta Education, "Framework for Student Learning: Competencies for Engaged Thinkers and Ethical Citizens with an Entrepreneurial Spirit," 2011, http://education.alberta.ca/department/ipr/curriculum.aspx.

Apple, Michael W. *deology and Curriculum*. New York: Routledge, 1972.

Apple, Michael W. *Education and Power*. New York: Routledge, 1982.

Arendt, Hannah. *The Human Condition*. Chicago: University of Chicago Press, 1958.

Bachelard, Gaston. *The Poetics of Space: The Classic Look at How We Experience Intimate Places*. Boston: Beacon Press, 1969.

Bahktin, Mikhail M. *The Dialogic Imagination: Four Essays*. Austin, TX: University of Texas Press, 1981

Bequette, James W., and Marjorie Bullitt Bequette. "A Place for Art and Design Education in the STEM Conversation." *Art Education* 65, no. 2 (2012): 40-47.

Bhabha, Homi K. *The Location of Culture*. New York: Routledge, 1994.

Branstetter, Dyan, "Libraries, Makerspaces, and STEAM Labs: What's the Difference?" Education Closet, 2017. https://educationcloset.com/2017/01/10/libraries-makerspaces-steam/.

Butler, Judith. "Bodies in Alliance and the Politics of the Street."*European Institute for Progressive Cultural Policies* 9 (2011).

Byrne, David.*How Music Works*. New York: Three Rivers Press, 2017.

Cech, Erin A. "Culture of Disengagement in Engineering Education?" *Science, Technology, & Human Values* 39, no. 1 (2014): 42-72.

Connell, Robert W., and James W. Messerschmidt. "Hegemonic Masculinity: Rethinking the Concept." *Gender & Society* 19, no. 6 (2005): 829-859.

Denzin, Norman K. *Sociological Methods: A Sourcebook*. New York: Routledge, 1978.

Dym, Clive L., Alice M. Agogino, Ozgur Eris, Daniel D. Frey, and Larry J. Leifer. "Engineering Design Thinking, Teaching, and Learning." *Journal of Engineering Education* 94, no. 1 (2005): 103-120.

Executive Office of the President. "Building a Nation of Makers: Universities and Colleges Pledge to Expand Opportunities to Make." 2014/ https://www.whitehouse.gov/sites/default/files/microsites/ostp/building_a_nation_of_makers .pdf.

Fraser, Nancy, and Axel Honneth. *Redistribution or Recognition? A Political-Philosophical Exchange*. New York: Verso, 2003.

Foucault, Michel. *Discipline and Punish: The Birth of the Prison*. London: Allen Lane, 1975.

Foucault, Michel. *Power/Knowledge: Selected Interviews and Other Writings, 1972-1977*. New York: Pantheon, 1980.

Foucault, Michel. "Des espaces autres." *Architecture, Mouvement, Continuité* (1984): 46-49.

Freire, Paolo. *Pedagogy of the Oppressed*. New York: Continuum, 1970.

Gerstein, Jackie, "Maker Education and Experiential Education." 2014. https://usergenerateddeducation.wordpress.com/2014/06/22/maker-education-and-experiential-education/.

Gruenewald, David A. "Foundations of Place: A Multidisciplinary Framework for Place-Conscious Education." *American Educational Research Journal* 40, no. 3 (2003): 619-54.

Kellam, Nadia, and Anna Montana Cirell. "Quality Considerations in Qualitative Inquiry: Expanding Our Understandings for the Broader Dissemination of Qualitative Research." *Journal of Engineering Education* 107, no. 3 (2018): 355-361.

Latour, Bruno. *Pandora's Hope: Essays on the Reality of Science Studies*. Cambridge, MA: Harvard University Press, 1999.

Lefebvre, Henri. *The Production of Space*. Oxford: Blackwell, 1974.

Massey, Doreen. *For Space*. Thousand Oaks, CA: Sage, 2005.

Maxwell, Joseph A. *Qualitative Research Design: An Interactive Approach.* Thousand Oaks, CA: Sage, 2013.

Nouri, Ali, and Seyed Mehdi Sajjadi. "Emancipatory Pedagogy in Practice: Aims, Principles and Curriculum Orientation." *The International Journal of Critical Pedagogy* 5, no. 2 (2014).

Patton, Michael Q. *Qualitative Evaluation and Research Methods.* Thousand Oaks, CA: Sage, 2015.

Peshkin, Alan. "In Search of Subjectivity—One's Own." *Educational Researcher* 17, no. 7 (1988): 17-21.

Odling-Smee, F. John, Kevin N. Laland, and Marcus W. Feldman. *Niche Construction: The Neglected Process in Evolution.* Princeton, NJ: Princeton University Press, 2010.

Rhodes, William C. "Liberatory Pedagogy and Special Education." *Journal of Learning Disabilities* 28, no. 8 (1995): 458-467.

Roffey, T., C. Sverko, and J. Therien. "The Making of a Makerspace: Pedagogical and Physical Transformations of Teaching and Learning." *Curriculum Guide, ETEC* 510 (2016): 1-41.

Saldaña, Johnny. *The Coding Manual for Qualitative Researchers.* Thousand Oaks, CA: Sage, 2016.

Smagorinsky, Peter. "The Method Section as Conceptual Epicenter in Constructing Social Science Research Reports." *Written Communication* 25, no. 3 (2008): 389-411.

Soja, Edward W. *Thirdspace: Journeys to Los Angeles and Other Real-and-Imagined Places.* Oxford: Blackwell, 1996.

Soja, Edward W. *Seeking Spatial Justice.* Minneapolis, MN: University of Minnesota Press, 2010.

Thrift, Nigel. "Space: The Fundamental Stuff of Geography." *Key Concepts in Geography* 2 (2003): 95-107.

Uppuluri, Krishna, *Engineer to Entrepreneur: The First Flight.* Krishna Uppuluri, 2011.

Vygotsky, Lev. *Mind in Society: The Development of Higher Psychological Processes.* Cambridge, MA: Harvard University Press, 1978.

Wagner, Tony, and Robert A. Compton. *Creating Innovators: The Making of Young People Who Will Change the World.* New York: Simon and Schuster, 2012.

Walther, Joachim, Nicola W. Sochacka, and Nadia N. Kellam. "Quality in Interpretive Engineering Education Research: Reflections on an Example Study." *Journal of Engineering Education* 102, no. 4 (2013): 626-659.

Chapter 4

FROM NEEDS ANALYSIS TO POWER ANALYSIS: A FRAMEWORK TO EXAMINE AND BROKER POWER IN MAKERSPACES

Brianna Marshall and Marijel (Maggie) Melo[1]

This chapter presents a power analysis framework that extends an entry point to examine how power is wielded, concentrated, and systemically embedded within a makerspace. Power analyses are not novel concepts. People, especially women, LGBTQIA+, and Black, Indigenous, and People of Color (BIPOC), assess power dynamics in their lives routinely. Research shows that the marginalization of these communities is especially pronounced in tech-centric environments such as makerspaces.[2] This is baffling because makerspaces are notoriously promoted as open, collaborative environments where everyone is considered to be a maker.[3] This is where this power analysis framework intervenes: How do purportedly open and collaborative makerspaces continue to attract a narrow demographic of users, while simultaneously marginalizing

---

1. Author affiliations: Brianna Marshall, Director of Research Services, University of California Riverside Library; Marijel (Maggie) Melo, Assistant Professor, School of Information and Library Science at the University of North Carolina at Chapel Hill. These authors contributed equally to this work.

2. Anna Meyer, "Feminist Makerspaces: Making Room for Women to Create," *The Riveter* (February 14, 2018), https://www.therivetermagazine.com/feminist-makerspaces-making-room-for-women-to-create/; Jen Lewis, Barriers to Women's Involvement in Hackerspaces and Makerspaces, accessed Oct. 30, 2019, https://access-space.org/portfolio/barriers-to-womens-involvement-in-hackspaces-and-makerspaces/.

3. "Be a Maker," Maker Faire, https://makerfaire.com/be-a-maker/.

certain communities?[4] This framework provides structured, not prescriptive, guidance to support persons interested in analyzing the power dynamics within a makerspace (or, by extension, other [in]formal STEM-rich learning spaces). In particular, the analysis offers users an instrument to examine the phenomenological properties of power with a structured approach. The intention is to give language and semblance to power—an otherwise abstract entity.[5] This tool is meant to generate insights and data for the user and is comprised of open-ended questions/suggestions relevant to several domains where power resides. The following domains comprise this burgeoning framework: "people," "space and equipment," "events and programming," and "outputs"—these areas are further detailed later in the chapter. Similar to a 360° image, there isn't one place to start, because power is multi-directional and complex. Users are encouraged to begin with any domain of their choosing.

This framework was developed with practitioners and scholars in mind; specifically, for those who acknowledge that equity, diversity, and inclusion (EDI) are challenges in their makerspace but are unsure of what needs to be changed, how to identify challenges, and/or how to create pathways towards action. We're hope this framework helps users narrow these knowledge gaps. EDI work is labor intensive, and it's labor that should be shared by a community and not undertaken alone. We recommend that several people within a community conduct the power analysis framework. Each individual experience offers critical perspectives that one person alone cannot provide. A rich collection of data from multiple perspectives creates opportunities to talk about EDI

---

4. Lauren Britton, Power, Access, Status: The Discourse of Race, Gender, and Class in the Maker Movement, https://tascha.uw.edu/2015/03/power-access-status-the-discourse-of-race-gender-and-class-in-t he-maker-movement/; Shirin Vossoughi, Paula K. Hooper, and Meg Escudé, "Making Through the Lens of Culture and Power: Toward Transformative Visions for Educational Equity," *Harvard Educational Review* 86, no. 2, (June 2016): 206–32; C. Warnshius, "Where Are the Women in Makerspaces?" Make: DIY Projects and Ideas for Makers, Nov. 30, 2001, https://makezine.com/2014/09/08/where-are-the-women/.

5. Raul Pacheco-Vega, Writing Theoretical Frameworks, Analytical Frameworks and Conceptual Frameworks, 2018, http://www.raulpacheco.org/2018/09/writing-theoretical-frameworks-analytical-frameworks-and-c onceptual-frameworks/.

and power in a way that strives to mitigate silencing and resists settling on stereotypes and assumptions.

Defining Power

Power can be defined in a multitude of ways, but in this chapter, we situate our definition within the field of Library and Information Science. Our underlying premise concerning power is that library spaces are not neutral. As Meredith Farkas states, "[N]eutrality is not only unachievable, it is harmful to oppressed groups in our society. In a world that is fundamentally unequal, neutrality upholds inequality and represents indifference to the marginalization of members of our community."[6] As authors and brokers of power within our own maker communities, we recognize that our environments are ideologically charged with a host of values, attitudes, and perceptions. To put a finer point on power we draw on Emily Drabinski's article "What is Critical about Critical Librarianship?" to define power.

Drabinski, critical pedagogy librarian, describes power as a means to produce order: to facilitate "some ways of knowing and not others, representing certain ideological ways of seeing the world, and, crucially, not others."[7] We extend Drabinski's conceptualization of power as a guiding definition and seek to respond to Drabinski's call to "interrogate the works of power in structures and systems."[8]

Background

The desire to create a power analysis framework emerged during a workshop in Durham, N.C. at the Racial Equity Institute (REI). The instructor and REI co-founder, Suzanne Plihcik, asked participants to stop equating the collection of needs analyses to the achievement of

---

6. Meredith Farkas, "Never Neutral: Critical Librarianship and Technology," *American Libraries Magazine*, Jan. 3, 2017, https://americanlibrariesmagazine.org/2017/01/03/never-neutral-critlib-technology/.

7. Emily Drabinski, "What Is Critical about Critical Librarianship?" *Art Libraries Journal* 44, no. 2 (Apr. 2019): 50.

8 . Ibid, 51.

inclusion and equity. *What do women need in our makerspaces? What types of workshops would attract transgender users? What types of technologies are people of color interested in?* The problem with this mindset is that it assumes that the identification of community needs is enough to bring forth equity. However, systemic change doesn't solely focus on people, it intervenes at the structural level of the environment as well: the policies; the hiring; the training; and the arrangement of the space.

Equity doesn't emerge from the number of sewing workshops that a makerspace offers. We need to challenge the logic that sewing workshops (and other gender-coded workshops) signal a makerspace's inclusivity. We should move from needs analyses, to **power** analyses. This chapter is inspired by Suzanne's declaration, and furthers this over-arching question: How can we analyze power in makerspaces, and how can we generate data to inform approaches to become better brokers of power in makerspaces?

Authors' Positionality

Creat'R Lab - Brianna Marshall

The Creat'R Lab was founded in 2017 as a partnership between the University of California, Riverside (UCR) Library and the UCR Office of Research and Economic Development. It was envisioned as a student-driven space with a focus on innovation, entrepreneurship, and creativity. I was hired as Director of Research Services and took responsibility for overseeing the fledgling makerspace and staff just weeks after it opened. In the two years that have followed, my colleagues and I have figured out how to run a makerspace in real time, experiencing triumphs and failures large and small along the way. I am proud of our work building a maker community, onboarding dozens of new tools and equipment, developing research and instructional partnerships, and setting up a robust 3D printing service, among other successes. Despite this progress, our team has many lingering questions about how to further embed EDI values into our makerspace operations and programs.

Conversations tend to happen in fits and starts, sometimes spurred by limitations we know about and sometimes by situations that arise. How should we approach the clear gender disparity in our space? We are located in a science library; how do we ensure that non-STEM users know that they are welcome? How should we encourage low-tech and no-tech approaches to making? How can we empower makers with the knowledge and skills to share and build on their creations? How do we best support our neurodiverse makerspace users? What does a genuinely student-driven makerspace look like?

The questions go on and on. Admittedly, it has been challenging to gauge our overall progress in the day-to-day chaos and churn of managing an increasingly busy and complex space. We need a more holistic approach to thinking about EDI as a team. I also welcome the opportunity to examine my own power and positionality. I've often questioned how I should navigate my identity as a cisgender white woman in a middle manager role, and especially how I can make room to invite other perspectives to shape our makerspace. This framework is an appealing entry point for individuals and teams to move beyond pockets of conversation or anyone's gut feeling about the power dynamics in a makerspace. It is a tool for structured conversations about our own practices and assumptions, and I am eager to use it to more actively and intentionally cultivate an EDI-centered environment in the Creat'R Lab.

iSpace and Be A Maker (BeAM) Makerspaces - Maggie Melo
My first exposure to the Maker Movement started with my involvement in the launch of the iSpace at the University of Arizona in 2014. This was the university's first interdisciplinary makerspace. I helped co-found the space with two partners: InnovateUA (a student-led entrepreneurship organization) and the University of Arizona Libraries. I, at the time, represented the third partner: Digital Humanities from the English

Department. As a Ph.D. student, I was interested in learning about ways to support faculty and students who wanted to explore experiential, tech-supported learning. The launching of the iSpace was very much a grassroots endeavor, and we had a lot of creative freedom to dream up and create the space.

Early on, my optimism around the makerspace was put into check. I realized my introductory involvement with the makerspace spurred questions that I really didn't know the answers to. Many of these questions have turned into research questions that engaged closely with equity and anti-oppressive theories and frameworks. For example, I vividly remember working with colleagues to generate a tech purchase list for the makerspace. We sat in the empty makerspace to generate the list. My colleagues enthusiastically added 3D printers, micro-controllers, and an *Oculus* SDK to the list. I didn't know much about makerspaces, but I knew that they were spaces to create and learn with tech, so I said aloud: "Let's add a couple of sewing machines to the list." My colleague's response remains so clear in my mind's eye. He leaned over and said: "Don't you think having sewing machines would make men feel excluded from the space?" Many thoughts and emotions coursed through my body, but two questions stood out: "What were the narratives, values, and perceptions my colleague was subscribing to? How does a learning environment signal or communicate who belongs in a space?" Like Brianna, I wanted a framework that would allow me to formulate responses to these complicated questions. I wanted a framework that would identify the oppressive mechanisms at play which continue to marginalize communities that have been historically underrepresented in tech-centric environments like makerspaces.

As a new assistant professor at the School of Information and Library Science, I immediately began immersing myself in the BeAM Makerspace network on campus. Currently, I'm partnering with Drew Robertson, BeAM technical supervisor, to facilitate staff conversations about ways to define and explore EDI within our maker community. This chapter's power analysis framework will serve as an exploratory entryway to define and take action on many of the EDI-related challenges.

Framework

The analytical framework includes the following subsections: people, space and equipment, events and programming, and outputs. Each subsection includes an exercise, guiding questions, and concrete suggestions, all intended to help you examine power within your organizational context.

In its current state, the framework is relatively simple; it's intended to be a low-barrier-to-entry way to kickstart a broader organizational conversation. It focuses mainly on reflective, open-ended questions. Future expansions of this work will include testing the framework with different use cases to highlight gaps, pulling framework components into handouts or other formats that might increase its usefulness to practitioners, and expanding the framework's scope to delve deeper into more specific questions.

People

Exercise: Create a power flow network. Sketch out the various entities that are involved in the space, as users or in an operational or advisory capacity. Think broadly! Some affiliations may be informal.

Guiding Questions

First, situate yourself (the person[s] conducting the analysis) in the power flow. Where do you fall?

Consider the other people or organizational entities involved in administrative and operational roles in your makerspace:
- Who has provided funding for your makerspace? Consider past and current funding. How does this influence how decisions are made?
- Is the decision-making structure top down, bottom up, or lateral?
- Is there a shared governance or advisory group?

Consider day-to-day makerspace operations and staffing:
- Who, if anyone, interfaces with users in your makerspace? What kind of training has this person had?

Consider the transparency around decisionmakers and decision-making:
- Is there any documentation that notes how decisions are made?
- Is there a documented mission and vision for the space? If so, who compiled and/or updates it? Is your document current?
- Is there a strategic plan? If so, who compiled and/or updates it? Is your document current?
- What types of data are collected for, and used to support, decision-making: Scholarly research? Online forums? Surveys? User feedback?

Consider equity, diversity, and inclusivity within your makerspace:
- What demographic information do you have about your users? (major/disciplinary affiliation; year in school; ethnicity; gender, etc.)
- Based on what you know about who is using your makerspace, who *isn't* using your makerspace? Jot down some reasons why this might be and ideas for actively inviting and engaging these potential users.
- Is there a code of conduct? If so, who compiled it, who enforces it, and *what process do they* follow? Is it visible to makerspace users?
- How could users provide direct feedback regarding their experience? How could users report code-of-conduct violations?

Suggestions
- Create documentation! Transparently describe and display the who and how of decision-making, including how the space is being funded and supported. Make this visible in your space and readily available to users who want to learn more.
- Create and display an enforceable code of conduct, community agreement, or similar document. Make sure you have a process in place for enforcing it.
- Provide inroads for users who want to participate in decision-making by creating a shared governance or advisory structure whose composition reflects a diverse array of perspectives. Also consider inviting feedback in ways that are less time-intensive for users, for example by having an anonymous suggestion box.

Space and Equipment

Exercise: Take pictures of your space from a variety of angles and vantage points. Don't tidy up. Capture your space as it is on an average day. We suggest that you use these images to help you objectively reflect on the guiding questions below (as opposed to just thinking about it, which relies on your potentially fallible mental image of the space!). If you are in a hurry, observe your space and sketch out a map of where items are located.

Guiding Questions

Consider the location and accessibility of your space:[9]

- Is the makerspace located in an "agnostic" space (e.g., a library)? Or is it located in a space that is associated, either by name or location on campus, with a particular disciplinary focus?
- Have you considered the needs of users with disabilities? Does your space comply with the Americans with Disabilities Act (ADA) regulations?

Consider users' first impressions, signage, and wayfinding:

- What does the check-in or sign-in process entail? Are users stopped at the door?
- What do new users see at the threshold or window? What is their first impression? What could they infer is done in that space?
- How do new makerspace users "know" how to engage with the space?
- List the types of signs or flyers you see in your makerspace. Who created them and what do they convey to users? What is missing?

Consider the overall layout of your makerspace:

- Does it feel like an open stage? Are there sectioned-off spaces?

---

9. For many more excellent questions about makerspace accessibility, we recommend that you look to "Making a Makerspace? Guidelines for Accessibility and Universal Design." The general questions we've included in the tools and equipment section are pulled from this fantastic resource.

- Which equipment is located front and center? Highlighted?
- Which equipment takes up the most space? The least?
- List the types of projects you see displayed in your makerspace. Who created them? What types of project or creator is missing? (Note: We consider "display" to mean that they are intentionally featured in the space and are not just projects that are out because they're being worked on.).

Consider your tools and equipment:
- Are tools and equipment kept in designated areas? Can they be reached from a seated position?
- Are tools and equipment labeled with large print and braille labels? (Pro-tip: these are easily created with your 3-D printer or laser cutter!)
- Can both right- and left-handed people use tools?
- Are power cords, including those suspended from the ceiling, kept out of walkways? Are their positions easily adjustable?[10]

Do you have any other observations on how space is allocated?

Suggestions

- Learn about accessibility and universal design and apply what you have learned to your space. Strive to cultivate mixed-ability maker culture, defined as "a collaborative culture within which people with and without disabilities can co-exist and co-create as they work to maximize and develop their own skills"[11]
- Think about ways to lower the barrier to entry for new users. Use signage to make it very clear who your makerspace is open to and why. If your makerspace is only open to undergraduates, for

---

10. Ibid.

11. Meryl Alper, Making Space in the Makerspace: Building a Mixed-Ability Maker Culture, https://teethingontech.files.wordpress.com/2013/03/idc13-workshop_meryl-alper.pdf.

example, create signage that clearly conveys this. Consider having someone greet all new users to ensure that they are welcomed into the space.
- Showcase a diverse array of project types and creators in your makerspace. This signals that your makerspace values different ways of making and dispels the idea that some maker approaches (and some makers!) are inherently better than others. For example, you might highlight low-tech or no-tech creations alongside technical projects.

Events and Programming

Exercise: Review a list of events and programs associated with your makerspace over the past one to two years. If you don't have this documented yet, create a list with as much information as you can, with a particular focus on capturing what you know about the topics, instructors, and learners, as well as the variety of programs you offer (workshops, hackathons, etc.).

Guiding Questions

Consider and reflect on events that are held in or associated with your makerspace:
- Which skills and equipment are spotlighted?
- What is the format for most learning opportunities—peer learning or "sage on the stage"?
- Who is invited to facilitate or lead events? Who is doing the inviting?
- Who is consistently facilitating? Are facilitators being compensated?
- Have you offered programs that are led by, and/or actively invite participation from, specific user groups, particularly those which have been historically marginalized in makerspaces (e.g., BIPOC, women, or members of the LGBTQIA+ community)?
- How do you compensate workshop facilitators?
- What do you know about who is attending?

Suggestions
- Diversify your pool of facilitators and event types with an intention of increasing peer learning. If your core audience is undergraduate students, connect with student-led organizations. If you want to reach out to faculty, perhaps you could support a series that spotlights faculty members who are makers. This will help ensure that your makerspace is driven by your community's interests.
- Build community in your makerspace with events and workshops that welcome underrepresented communities' access to your makerspace during a designated time and day. For example, the University of Arizona, Northern Arizona University, and Arizona State University makerspaces collaborated to create a Women, Trans, Femme Night (founded by Amanda Meeks) to center ways of making and knowing that are often dismissed within the Maker Movement writ large. Don't be dismayed if attendance is low (1-2 people) at the beginning—communities and trust are developed over time!
- Consider ways you can make events even more inclusive for attendees. For example, you might ask facilitators to review the code of conduct or community values before an event starts in order to remind everyone that all are welcome.

Outputs
Exercise: Reflect on the variety of things a user might create in your makerspace. Consider why makers are creating: just for fun, to serve a specific function, for instructional or research purposes, etc. Jot down any possible creations that come to mind.

Guiding Questions:
- Does your organization claim intellectual property ownership rights when something is created in your makerspace? How are intellectual property considerations communicated to makerspace users?
- How does your makerspace invite users to share what they have created?

- How does your makerspace connect users to entrepreneurial resources?
- How does your makerspace invite users to ask questions? To seek help?

Suggestions
- Ensure that makerspace users understand the intellectual property of their creation.
- Invite users to share what they have created. For scholarly outputs, explain open licenses and point to open platforms where files can be uploaded alongside additional project data and narratives to give context for the work. For non-academic audiences, users may want to create a digital portfolio to showcase their work—this could be a useful workshop topic to offer.
- Connect with local entrepreneurial programs or begin to build expertise in-house. Regardless of the initial purpose of a user's creation—something that's just for fun, a purely functional object, or having a particular research or instructional purpose—invite users to view it as a creative output that they could build on.
- Overall, give your users a rich context for exploring how to think about and where to go next with something they have created. Advocating for sharing openly may seem to be in tension with providing entrepreneurial resources, which often has the goal of creating a business and monetizing an idea, but both are possible paths for users. We are in a position to empower users to make these choices for themselves.

Conclusion

The development of this power analysis framework is in its nascent stages. We expect that the framework will evolve in the same way our makerspaces and users continue to change. This is just the start of a larger body of work. In the past, we've informally applied the power analysis in our own makerspace, but we are eager to apply the framework as it's outlined in this chapter. We are also equally curious to hear about the framework's application in other makerspace environments.

This power analysis framework emerged from our collective desire to approach inequity from a structured, multi-perspective manner. The purpose of this chapter was both to extend this framework and to extend a small peace of mind: EDI work is hard work, and it's often easier to confront when done as a community. EDI work is messy. Users may find that the application of the framework may yield more questions than answers—this is totally okay. The open dialogue will create opportunities for conversations on power to emerge, which is no small feat. Extend the data from the framework to generate more dialogue, to ask more questions, to identify possibilities, and to take steps (no matter how big or small) towards change. Recognizing oppressive, unjust systems is one part of the equation. While it's critical to recognize the systemic mechanisms in place that produce racist, patriarchal, gendered, and neoliberal structures, the next step forward is to use this awareness to create pathways to disrupt these oppressive structures. We hope this chapter supports that initial step.

Bibliography

Alper, Meryl. Making Space in the Makerspace: Building a Mixed-Ability Maker Culture. https://teethingontech.files.wordpress.com/2013/03/idc13-workshop_meryl-alper.pdf

"Be a Maker." Maker Faire. https://makerfaire.com/be-a-maker/.

Britton, Lauren. Power, Access, Status: The Discourse of Race, Gender, and Class in the Maker Movement. https://tascha.uw.edu/2015/03/power-access-status-the-discourse-of-race-gender-and-class-in-the-maker-movement/.

Drabinski, Emily. "What Is Critical about Critical Librarianship?" *Art Libraries Journal* 44, no. 2 (Apr. 2019):49–57. doi:10.1017/alj.2019.3.

Farkas, Meredith. "Never Neutral: Critical Librarianship and Technology." *American Libraries Magazine*. Jan. 3, 2017. https://americanlibrariesmagazine.org/2017/01/03/never-neutral-critlib-technology/.

Lewis, Jen. Barriers to Women's Involvement in Hackerspaces and Makerspaces. https://access-space.org/portfolio/barriers-to-womens-involvement-in-hackspaces-and-makerspaces/.

"Making a Makerspace? Guidelines for Accessibility and Universal Design." DO-IT: Disabilities, Opportunities, Internetworking, and Technology, 2015. https://www.washington.edu/doit/making-makerspace-guidelines-accessibility-and-universal-design.

Meyer, Anna. "Feminist Makerspaces: Making Room for Women to Create." *The Riveter* (February 14, 2018). https://www.therivetermagazine.com/feminist-makerspaces-making-room-for-women-to-create/.

Pacheco-Vega, Raul. Writing Theoretical Frameworks, Analytical Frameworks and Conceptual Frameworks. http://www.raulpacheco.org/2018/09/writing-theoretical-frameworks-analytical-frameworks-and-c onceptual-frameworks/.

Vossoughi, Shirin, Paula K. Hooper, and Meg Escudé. "Making Through the Lens of Culture and Power: Toward Transformative Visions for Educational Equity." *Harvard Educational Review* 86, no. 2, (June 2016): 206–32. doi:10.17763/0017-8055.86.2.206.

Warnshius, C. "Where Are the Women in Makerspaces?" Make: DIY Projects and Ideas for Makers. Nov. 30, 2001. https://makezine.com/2014/09/08/where-are-the-women/.

MOVEMENT, EMPATHY, AND INCLUSION IN YOUTH MAKERSPACES

Chapter 5

MAKING THE BODY: PHYSICAL ACTIVITY IN MAKERSPACES

Noah Lenstra and Heather Moorefield-Lang

On September 13, 2018, the Madison Public Library published the post "Wild Rumpus: Flying" on the blog *Library Makers: Hands-On Learning for All Ages*.[1] The post featured children who, as part of a library program, made three-dimensional play spaces from which they then launched their bodies into the air. Around the same time in Connecticut, Kari Ann St. Jean, Children and Teen Services Manager for the Avon Free Public Library, started a series of storytime programs focusing on integrating yoga, movement, and stories. She writes that:

> ...by asking participants to *embody* the movement in stories and rhymes...we invent our own actions, and storytime is transformed! ...The result is an interconnected experiential set of imaginative activities that only exist in the here and now.[2]

This chapter considers these and other examples of what we are calling "making the body": maker activities that focus in whole or in part on physical activity. Most of the events discussed in this chapter con-

---

1. Madison Public Library, Wild Rumpus: Flying. *Library Makers: Hands-On Learning for All Ages,* September 13, 2018, http://librarymakers.blogspot.com/2018/09/wild-rumpus-flying.html.

2. Mary C. Fletcher, *The Creative Edge: Inspiring Art Explorations in Libraries and Beyond.* (Santa Barbara, CA: ABC Clio, 2019), 2-3. Emphasis in the original.

sist of "maker activities," which *Library Journal* defines in its survey as programs or events that foster making without, necessarily, having dedicated spaces or supplies for that purpose.[3]

The examples of making the body discussed in this chapter come from our ongoing monitoring of, and involvement in, the librarianship profession[4] and the makerspace movement.[5] Based on this monitoring, three forms of making the body in libraries are identified:

1. Making something new with your body
2. Making something used for physical activity
3. Making using large objects that require substantive movement

After introducing these three forms of making the body, this chapter concludes with a discussion of additional research needed to better understand and support this emerging trend.

Making Something New with Your Body

The U.S. Centers for Disease Control and Prevention point out that "our bodies are made to move,"[6] and one cluster of maker activities in libraries focus on making something new through the movement of the body. For instance, Gerstein argues that "kid controlled, kid directed, and kid policed"[7] dancing should be considered a type of making activity.

---

3. Jennifer A. Dixon, "Making It Happen.: *Library Journal*, June 9, 2017, https://www.libraryjournal.com/?detailStory=making-it-happen-programming.

4. Noah Lenstra, "Movement-Based Programs in US and Canadian Public Libraries: Evidence of Impacts from an Exploratory Survey," *Evidence Based Library and Information Practice* 12, no. 4 (2017): 214-232; Noah Lenstra, "The Experiences of Public Library Staff Developing Programs with Physical Activities: An Exploratory Study in North Carolina," *Library Quarterly* 88, no. 2 (2018): 142-159; Heather Moorefield-Lang, "Makers in the Library: Case Studies of 3D Printers and Maker Spaces in Library Settings," *Library Hi Tech* 32, no. 4 (2014): 583-593.

5. Moorefield-Lang, "Makers in the Library, 2014.

6. U.S. Centers for Disease Control and Prevention. (2017). *Make Your Workout Work for You.* https://www.cdc.gov/features/diabetes-physical-activity/index.html, para. 5.

7. Jackie Gerstein, "The Classroom or Library as a Makerspace," *Medium*, April 1, 2018, https://medium.com/@jackiegerstein/the-classroom-or-library-as-a-makerspace-13ced283076a, para. 1.

This idea can be seen in action at Ballyfermot Library in Dublin, Ireland, where as part of the Dublin City Council's Children's Art in Libraries (CAL) initiative, children "watch professional dancers in their local library, then respond and create their own work which they perform in front of a local audience."[8] Here, the thing being made is a new dance created by children's bodies in motion. Similarly, in India, where yoga continues to be a living tradition, yoga poses are also something that can made through maker activities, according to Bunkar, a librarian at Parul University in Gujarat.[9]

These types of activities can also build upon the library's literary role. Beth Smiley, school librarian in the Charlotte Mecklenburg Schools in North Carolina, provides her students with prompts that she asks them to "make" using their bodies. For instance, in 2016 the North Carolina Children's Book Award winner was *Giant Squid* by Candace Fleming. The students were charged with figuring how to use their bodies to make a giant squid on the floor of the library. By working together, students laid down on their backs across the library floor, creating the shape of the titular character from the book.[10]

Examples of making something new with your body can also be seen in more traditional makerspace initiatives. For instance, in an activity called Dance Mat Pacman[11] participants use a Makey Makey linked to dance pads such that the interface involves dancing. We also see examples

---

8. Samantha Derenthal, "Ballyfermot Library—Unique Dance Programme," *Echo*, November 22, 2018, http://www.echo.ie/show/article/ballyfermot-library-unique-dance-programme.

9. Anjana, R. Bunkar, "Enhancing Library Services with the Application of Makerspaces in Academic Libraries," in *Proceedings of the International Conference on Internet of Things and Current Trends in Libraries*, 2018.

10 . Beth Smiley, *The Media Center of Movement*, presentation for the North Carolina School Librarian Media Association Annual Conference, Winston Salem, NC, 2018, https://static.sched.com/hosted_files/ncslma18/76/Media%20Center%20of%20Movement.pptx.

11. Mark Shillitoe, "Make Space for Makerspaces," *Learning Freewheel: Redefining Learning Experiences*, February 19, 2016, https://learningfreewheel.wordpress.com/2016/02/19/make-space-for-makerspaces/.

of making something new with the body in TASK Parties,[12] improvisational events with a simple structure and very few rules. Participants arrive at a predetermined location where they are given a mix of props/materials and a task to complete. Once a task is done, participants can write a new task, ask for another task, or join others in the completion of their assignment.

Making Something Used for Physical Activity

Libraries can make activities, items, and experiences accessible that were possibly not accessible in the past. In other words, libraries open doors to creation experiences.[13] A second cluster of making the body activities is centered around making things used for physical activity. These activities include: 1) making, repairing, and creatively customizing things like bicycles and skateboards; 2) making mini golf courses and other large-scale games in library spaces, and 3) making StoryWalks.

In Spring 2019, the Santa Maria Public Library in California started a "Bike Kitchen" program focused on providing access to supplies and expertise needed to assemble and repair bicycles.[14] (Syed, 2019). This has become a popular program model in California libraries, with similar initiatives in Oakland[15] and in the City of San Diego.[16] (2019). The Oakland program extends the initiative beyond bike repair to include

---

12. Oliver Herring, *What is TASK?* July 11, 2008, https://oliverherringtask.wordpress.com/.

13. Amy Vecchionne, Deana Brown, Gregory Brasier, and Ann Delaney, "Encouraging a Diverse Maker Culture," in *The Makerspace Librarian's Sourcebook*, edited by Ellyssa Kroskim, (Chicago, IL: ALA Editions, 2017): 51-71.

14. Razi Syed, "Santa Maria Public Library Kicks Off Bike Kitchen Program," *Santa Maria Times*, February 25, 2019, https://santamariatimes.com/news/local/santa-maria-public-library-kicks-off-bike-kitchen-program/article_65936aa4-810d-5f71-8064-27daf1f1484b.html.

15. "Wheels of Change," *Library Journal*, March 13, 2017, https://www.libraryjournal.com/?detailStory=reginald-burnette-jr-anthony-propernick-movers-shakers-2017-innovators.

16. City of San Diego, *Learn Bicycle Repair and Maintenance*. 2019, https://www.sandiego.gov/blog/learn-bicycle-repair-and-maintenance.

bike decoration.[17] Participants are invited to customize their bicycles in creative, personal ways.

Other libraries apply this model to skateboarding. Since 2017, the Aldine Branch of the Harris County Public Library in Texas has sponsored an annual skateboarding program that takes students' love of sports and design and blends them together. Youth design and create their own skateboards and then learn how to use them at a local skatepark. This program involves collaboration between the library, the local YMCA, and the parks department.[18]

Libraries also empower people to make things used for physical activity in programs that focus on transforming the library space into a space for physical play. For instance, at the McCrae Public School Library in Guelph, Ontario, the librarian developed a learning commons exercise game which the librarian describes like this: "Today we turned the learning commons into a huge board game! We made up rules, then we made a gigantic set of dice to play."[19] Nearly everything about this game was designed and developed by the students. This exercise game shares some similarity to the Code to Move program developed by the librarian at Detroit Country Day Lower School in Bloomfield Hills, Michigan.[20] In this program, youth assemble a code out of cards that includes different physical activities. When the code is assembled, the children enact it by performing the physical activities on the cards in the order that the code specifies. Other games are less overtly focused on physical activity, but still include a lot of moving around in the library.

---

17. Oakland Public Library, Fix and Decorate Your Bike with the Scraper Bike Team. 2019, http://oaklandlibrary.org/events/martin-luther-king-jr-branch/fix-decorate-your-bike-scraper-bike-team.

18. Vagney Bradley, "Skate park program blends sport with art and design," *Chron*, July 25, 2017, https://www.chron.com/neighborhood/spring/news/article/Skate-park-program-blends-sport-with-art-and-11381575.php.

19. McCrae Public School Library, *The Learning Commons Exercise Game,* January 17, 2019. https://mccraelibrary.wordpress.com/2019/01/17/the-learning-commons-exercise-game/, para.1.

20. Kelly Hincks, "Code to Move: Mixing Coding with Brain Breaks," *KnowledgeQuest*, October 10, 2018, https://knowledgequest.aasl.org/code-to-move-mixing-coding-with-brain-breaks/.

At the Waterford Public Library in Wisconsin, librarians developed a Teen Mini Golf Program in which participants created their own golf course using supplies like foam noodles, book discards, tape, and paper rolls, and then played a couple of rounds in the library on the course they had made.[21]

Still other libraries have adapted the StoryWalk program model to include community-driven making. Briefly, a StoryWalk typically consists of a deconstructed children's book that families read together as they walk along a path. In Maryland, the Laurel Branch of the Prince George's County Library adapted this model by adding making activities to it. At this library, young patrons used TinkerCad and a Makerbot 3D printer to create their own tactile storywalk.[22] In other words, rather than walking along a StoryWalk created for them, youth made their own StoryWalk. Similarly, at the Albert Wisner Public Library in Warwick, New York, the library decided to feature artwork made by local seventh graders in its Storywalk installation as opposed to the traditional use of a published book.[23]

Making Using Large Objects that Require Substantive Movement

Finally, we see making the body in activities that require substantive movement as part of the making. For instance, a Dutch designer developed the Cycle Knitter, a contraption that knits a scarf using the energy generated from pedaling a stationary bicycle.[24] Similarly, at the Cowbridge Library in the United Kingdom, the library sponsored a paint

---

21. Dana Jensen, "Golfing Around," *The Day*, January 18, 2019, https://www.theday.com/local-news/20190118/golfing-around.

22. Prince George's County Memorial Library System, *3D, Tactile Storybook Walk, Now @ Laurel Branch Courtyard*, May 7, 2018, https://ww1.pgcmls.info/website/2690.

23. Warwick Valley Central School District, *Warwick's First Storywalk Installation Features Student Artwork*, August 13, 2018, https://www.warwickvalleyschools.com/warwicks-first-storywalk-installation-features-student-artwork/.

24. Kate Sierzputowski, "Cyclo Knitter: A Bicycle-Based Machine that Knits a Scarf in Five Minutes," *Colossal*, June 12, 2018, https://www.thisiscolossal.com/2018/06/cyclo-knitter-a-bicycle-based-machine-that-knits-a-scarf-in-five-minutes/.

spinning program in which paint poured into a drum took on different shapes based on the speed at which one pedals an attached stationary bike. Another type of bike-makerspace crossover appears in mobile miniature makerspaces attached to bicycles that can be taken around a community for pop-up maker activities.[25]

Maker activities that involve large three-dimensional objects also require substantial movement. These include making things with objects like giant legos, which have been used in library programs: public, academic, and school (e.g. Nanyang Technological University).[26] This type of activity also includes making with supplies like Rigamajigs™, a large-scale building kit used for hands-on free play and playful STEAM learning. The Madison Public Library has developed a more DIY approach to Rigamajig-like play in their ongoing Anji Play Initiative.[27] As librarians explain on the library's blog *Library Makers: Hands-On Learning for All Ages*, "Another common play pattern, especially in Anji Play is leaping, flying off of tall things, often onto a softened surface."[28] Participants in Anji Play programs are encouraged to create their own play spaces using large, heterogeneous three-dimensional objects—think of it as making your own playground at the library.

Discussion

As more and more libraries develop "making the body" activities, additional research on this emerging trend becomes necessary. In particular, additional work is needed on accessibility and how these activities connect to kinesthetic learning and to health. In addition, more theoretical work is needed about what it means to make through the body.

---

25. AlecM.NL, *Mobile Miniature Makerspace*, 2019, https://alecm.nl/portfolio/mobile-miniature-makerspace/.

26. Nanyang Technological University, Singapore, "Get Creative with Colorful Blocks at NTU Library. 2018, http://news.ntu.edu.sg/library2/2018/Pages/GetCreativewithColourfulBlocks.aspx.

27. Madison Public Library, Wild Rumpus: Flying, *Library Makers: Hands-On Learning for All Ages*, September 13, 2018, http://librarymakers.blogspot.com/2018/09/wild-rumpus-flying.html.

28. Ibid, para.1.

Regarding accessibility, there are two ways to approach this question. On the one hand, there is a need to ensure that disabled individuals have access to these types of programs to avoid inadvertently reinforcing ableist structures. On the other hand, there is some evidence that programs focused on making the body can in fact enable makerspaces to become more accessible. For example, Doris Gebel, a librarian in Virginia, found that adding physical activities to library programs for youth made those programs more accessible to individuals for whom English was not their first language: "When the second-graders attended the Wednesday session, it was at the end of a long school day and they were tired. Activities, such as Migration Hopscotch, energized them for the rest of the program. In addition, there was no language barrier during any of the activities using action and movement, and thus easier to enjoy for these second-graders."[29]

In any case, future projects could investigate how making the body activities connect with efforts to support different learning styles, including kinesthetic learning. In a curriculum plan entitled *Learning through Movement: Applying Exercise Education and Movement Activities in a Library Setting*, school librarian Deborah Yu-Yuk Jung argues that the makerspace movement creates opportunities for libraries to become more physically active spaces:

> As librarians begin to turn towards a learning commons and/or MakerSpace environment for learning, we need to provide for areas of active learning. This means not only incorporating technology and redesigning facilities for flexible grouping, social learning, and increased noise, but also providing areas for safe movement.[30]

---

[29]. Quoted in Paula Holmes, "Curiosity Creates: Innovative Library Programming for Children," *Association for Library Service to Children*, 2016, http://www.ala.org/alsc/sites/ala.org.alsc/files/content/awardsgrants/minigrants/ALSC_Curiosity_Creates_Best_Practices_Final.pdf, 3.

[30]. Deborah Yu-Yuk Jung, Learning through Movement: Applying Exercise Education and Movement Activities in a Library Setting," *Charlotte Teachers Institute*, 2015, http://charlotteteachers.org/wp-content/uploads/2016/01/DJung_unit_11-22-15.pdf, para. 1.

Part of the rationale for the makerspace movement in libraries has been to support a variety of learning styles and formats. As Jung points out, however, we have yet to fully grapple with how we learn through our bodies and through movement (i.e., kinesthetic learning) in makerspaces.

Furthermore, there are opportunities through the activities discussed in this chapter to connect makerspaces to the field of public health. Across the globe, one in four people are placed at risk due to a lack of physical activity according to the World Health Organization (WHO).[31] In response to this health crisis, the U.S. Centers for Disease Control and Prevention (CDC) states in the 2nd edition of its Physical Activity Guidelines for Americans, that Americans should be more active, moving and exercising in their own fashion and coming up with their own ways of moving.[32] By creating spaces and opportunities that encourage people to move and to think about movement in new ways, making the body activities could help address this health crisis.

Finally, additional work is needed to address more theoretical questions relating to whether something is a maker activity or not. Ultra-endurance runner Scott Jurek called his record-breaking run of the Appalachian Trail his "masterpiece," suggesting that feats of athleticism such as this constitute a type of making. Would (or should) we consider endorsing such feats, and other forms of making the body, appropriate for a library makerspace? Why or why not? Is there a boundary here? Would dance be appropriate to makerspaces while other forms of movement (i.e., sports) would not? We do not have answers to these questions, but suggest that additional inquiry is necessary to better understand the contours and dimensions of making the body in libraries.

---

31. Regina Guthold, Gretchen A. Stevens, Leanne M. Riley, and Fiona C. Bull, "Worldwide Trends in Insufficient Physical Activity from 2001 to 2016: A Pooled Analysis of 358 Population-Based Surveys with 1-9 Million Participants," *The Lancet Global Health* 6, no. 10 (2018): e1077-e1086.

32. Health.gov.*Move Your Way: What's Your Move?* (Washington, D.C.: Department of Health & Human Services, 2018), https://health.gov/paguidelines/moveyourway/materials/PAG_MYW_Adult_FS.pdf.

Conclusion

Through the use of illustrative examples, this chapter has sought to outline a new area of inquiry that could be explored in future work. At least three types of making the body activities already occur in libraries—making something new with your body, making something used for physical activity, and making using large objects that require substantive movement. Additional research is needed to better understand and support this trend.

Bibliography

AlecM.NL. *Mobile Miniature Makerspace.* 2019. https://alecm.nl/portfolio/mobile-miniature-makerspace/.

Bradley, Vagney. "Skate park program blends sport with art and design." *Chron*, July 25, 2017. https://www.chron.com/neighborhood/spring/news/article/Skate-park-program-blends-sport-with-art-and-11381575.php.

Bunkar, Anjana, R. "Enhancing Library Services with the Application of Makerspaces in Academic Libraries." In *Proceedings of the International Conference on Internet of Things and Current Trends in Libraries*, 2018. https://www.researchgate.net/profile/Chintan_Pandya7/publication/327416369_Internet_of_things_and_current_trends_in_libraries_ITCTL/links/5b8e26baa6fdcc1ddd0a1385/Internet-of-things-and-current-trends-in-libraries-ITCTL.pdf#page=113.

City of San Diego. *Learn Bicycle Repair and Maintenance.* 2019. https://www.sandiego.gov/blog/learn-bicycle-repair-and-maintenance.

Dixon, Jennifer A. "Making It Happen.: *Library Journal*, June 9, 2017. https://www.libraryjournal.com/?detailStory=making-it-happen-programming.

Derenthal, Samantha. "Ballyfermot Library—Unique Dance Programme." *Echo*, November 22, 2018. http://www.echo.ie/show/article/ballyfermot-library-unique-dance-programme.

Fletcher, Mary C. *The Creative Edge: Inspiring Art Explorations in Libraries and Beyond.* Santa Barbara, CA: ABC Clio, 2019.

Gerstein, Jackie. "The Classroom or Library as a Makerspace." *Medium*, April 1, 2018. https://medium.com/@jackiegerstein/the-classroom-or-library-as-a-makerspace-13ced283076a.

Guthold, Regina, Gretchen A. Stevens, Leanne M. Riley, and Fiona C. Bull. "Worldwide Trends in Insufficient Physical Activity from 2001 to 2016: A Pooled Analysis of 358 Population-Based Surveys with 1-9 Million Participants." *The Lancet Global Health* 6, no. 10 (2018): e1077-e1086.

Health.gov. (2019). *Move Your Way: What's Your Move?* Washington, D.C.: Department of Health & Human Services. https://health.gov/paguidelines/moveyourway/materials/PAG_MYW_Adult_FS.pdf.

Herring, Oliver. *What is TASK?* July 11, 2008. https://oliverherringtask.wordpress.com/.

Hincks, Kelly. "Code to Move: Mixing Coding with Brain Breaks." *Knowledge-Quest*, October 10, 2018. https://knowledgequest.aasl.org/code-to-move-mixing-coding-with-brain-breaks/.

Holmes, Paula. "Curiosity Creates: Innovative Library Programming for Children." *Association for Library Service to Children*. 2016. http://www.ala.org/alsc/sites/ala.org.alsc/files/content/awardsgrants/minigrants/ALSC_Curiosity_Creates_Best_Practices_Final.pdf.

Jensen, Dana. "Golfing Around." *The Day*, January 18, 2019. https://www.theday.com/local-news/20190118/golfing-around.

Jung, Deborah Yu-Yuk. Learning through Movement: Applying Exercise Education and Movement Activities in a Library Setting." *Charlotte Teachers Institute*, 2015. http://charlotteteachers.org/wp-content/uploads/2016/01/DJung_unit_11-22-15.pdf.

Lenstra, Noah. "Movement-Based Programs in US and Canadian Public Libraries: Evidence of Impacts from an Exploratory Survey." *Evidence Based Library and Information Practice* 12, no. 4 (2017): 214-232. https://doi.org/10.18438/B8166D.

Lenstra, Noah. "The Experiences of Public Library Staff Developing Programs with Physical Activities: An Exploratory Study in North Carolina." *Library Quarterly* 88, no. 2 (2018): 142-159. https://doi.org/10.1086/696580.

Madison Public Library. Wild Rumpus: Flying. *Library Makers: Hands-On Learning for All Ages,* September 13, 2018. http://librarymakers.blogspot.com/2018/09/wild-rumpus-flying.html.

McCrae Public School Library. *The Learning Commons Exercise Game.* January 17, 2019. https://mccraelibrary.wordpress.com/2019/01/17/the-learning-commons-exercise-game/.

Moorefield-Lang, Heather. "Makers in the Library: Case Studies of 3D Printers and Maker Spaces in Library Settings." *Library Hi Tech* 32, no. 4 (2014): 583-593. https://doi.org/10.1108/LHT-06-2014-0056.

Moorefield-Lang, Heather. "Lessons Learned: Intentional Implementation of Second Makerspaces." *Reference Services Review* 47, no. 1 (2019): 37-47. https://doi.org/10.1108/RSR-07-2018-0058.

Nanyang Technological University, Singapore. "Get Creative with Colorful Blocks at NTU Library. 2018. http://news.ntu.edu.sg/library2/2018/Pages/GetCreativewithColourfulBlocks.aspx.

Oakland Public Library. *Fix and Decorate Your Bike with the Scraper Bike Team.* 2019. http://oaklandlibrary.org/events/martin-luther-king-jr-branch/fix-decorate-your-bike-scraper-bike-team.

Prince George's County Memorial Library System. *3D, Tactile Storybook Walk, Now @ Laurel Branch Courtyard.* May 7, 2018. https://ww1.pgcmls.info/website/2690.

Shillitoe, Mark. "Make Space for Makerspaces." *Learning Freewheel: Redefining Learning Experiences,* February 19, 2016. https://learningfreewheel.wordpress.com/2016/02/19/make-space-for-makerspaces/.

Smiley, Beth. *The Media Center of Movement.* Presentation for the North Carolina School Librarian Media Association Annual Conference. Winston Salem, NC, 2018. https://static.sched.com/hosted_files/ncslma18/76/Media%20Center%20of%20Movement.pptx.

Sierzputowski, Kate. "Cyclo Knitter: A Bicycle-Based Machine that Knits a Scarf in Five Minutes." *Colossal,* June 12, 2018. https://www.thisiscolossal.com/2018/06/cyclo-knitter-a-bicycle-based-machine-that-knits-a-scarf-in-five-minutes/.

Syed, Razi. "Santa Maria Public Library Kicks Off Bike Kitchen Program." *Santa Maria Times*, February 25, 2019. https://santamariatimes.com/news/local/santa-maria-public-library-kicks-off-bike-kitchen-program/article_65936aa4-810d-5f71-8064-27daf1f1484b.html.

U.S. Centers for Disease Control and Prevention. (2017). *Make Your Workout Work for You*. https://www.cdc.gov/features/diabetes-physical-activity/index.html.

Vecchionne, Amy, Deana Brown, Gregory Brasier, and Ann Delaney. "Encouraging a Diverse Maker Culture." In *The Makerspace Librarian's Sourcebook*, edited by Ellyssa Kroskim, 51-71. Chicago, IL: ALA Editions, 2017.

Warwick Valley Central School District. *Warwick's First Storywalk Installation Features Student Artwork*. August 13, 2018. https://www.warwickvalleyschools.com/warwicks-first-storywalk-installation-features-student-artwork/.

"Wheels of Change." *Library Journal*, March 13, 2017. https://www.libraryjournal.com/?detailStory=reginald-burnette-jr-anthony-proper-nick-movers-shakers-2017-innovators.

Chapter 6

TRAUMA-INFORMED MAKING

Heather Lister

Many educators are familiar with the Adverse Childhood Experiences Survey (ACE) from which trauma-informed education has evolved. Just as this information plays a role in designing responsive classroom instruction, it also plays a large role in designing (or re-designing) a makerspace. When traumatic life experiences can manifest themselves as disruptive, unwanted, or even unsafe behaviors, how can educators respond in a way that addresses the underlying cause, as opposed to just responding to the behavior? In a 2012 study, Dr. Chris Blodgett and his research team found that the more trauma a school-aged child has experienced, the more likely he or she is to experience issues in behavior, attendance, coursework, and overall health. Making is about trying new things and taking risks, and with risks comes the potential for failure. The Maker Movement celebrates failure as a part of the creative process, as it gets us one step closer to the intended result. Making is an iterative process and success on the first attempt is rarely expected. So, while the maker culture champions failure, it is important for educators to recognize the impact of failure on students who have experienced high levels of trauma. Situations that may seem like nothing more than a creative struggle can be an emotional and physical trigger for some students. Students who have high ACE scores or who have experienced high levels of trauma, have a different reaction in the brain when exposed to stressors because of the impaired development of coping skills. Not only can this stress prompt an undesirable response, but it can also chemically trigger further damage to a child's developing brain.

In this chapter, we will explore how educators can create a makerspace inclusive to students with trauma. We will also explore how educators can strategically and intentionally design makerspace programming with an optimal level of challenge and manageable conflict, as is recommended for youths who have experienced trauma. Carrying over best practices from trauma-informed classrooms, we will discuss how to use a strengths-based approach to develop programming that allows students to exercise initiative responsibility, has integrity, and gives a sense of accomplishment. This practice can not only be more inclusive for students who have experienced trauma but can also aid in developing their social and emotional skills. Last, we will also discuss how to effectively respond when student trauma manifests as negative or harmful behavior.

In 1998, a groundbreaking study, commonly referred to as the ACE Study, was conducted by Dr. Robert Anda and Dr. Vincent Felitti in collaboration with the Centers for Disease Control and the Department of Preventive Medicine at Kaiser Permanente in California. The goal of the study was to observe the relationship between adverse childhood experiences, referred to as ACEs, and subsequent mental and physical health as adults. The original ACE's comprised:

- Substance abuse in the home
- Parental separation or divorce
- Mental illness in the home
- Witnessing domestic violence
- Suicidal household member
- Death of a parent or loved one
- Parental incarceration
- Experience of abuse or neglect

It is important to note that this is not an exhaustive list of traumatic experiences. Witnessing a school shooting or surviving a natural disaster are inarguably traumatic experiences but were not included in the original study.

The ACE Study concluded that childhood trauma is far more prevalent than projected. While it was assumed that trauma would be more prevalent in areas of poverty, the study revealed that trauma does not discriminate by demography and was spread across all races, religions, socio-economic statuses, and family systems.[1] Trauma is everywhere. Unfortunately, the prevalence of childhood traumatic experiences has only increased since the initial study. According to the 2017 National Survey of Children's Health, nearly one in four children have experienced at least one adverse childhood experience and nearly one in five children have experienced two or more.[2]

Since the original study, hundreds of additional studies have been administered researching the short- and long-term effects of ACEs. High ACE scores have been linked to poor attendance, behavior problems, and poor cognitive and social development. In addition to academic issues, those with high ACE scores are also more likely to be overweight or an alcoholic, smoke, attempt suicide, and die prematurely.

While the initial ACE Study focused on the long-term effects of childhood trauma, a more recent study conducted by Dr. Chris Blodgett at Washington State University investigated the more immediate impacts of adverse childhood experiences in children ages 5-11. **Figure 1**, from *Fostering Resilient Learners*, shows the correlation between the number of ACEs and struggles with school.

Further research has shown that exposure to violence leads to:
- Decreased IQ and reading ability[3]

---

1. Vincent J. Felitti et al., "Relationship of Childhood Abuse and Household Dysfunction to Many of the Leading Causes of Death in Adults: The Adverse Childhood Experiences (ACE) Study," *American Journal of Preventive Medicine* 56, no. 6 (June 2019): 774–86, https://doi.org/10.1016/j.amepre.2019.04.001.

2. Child and Adolescent Health Measurement Initiative, 2017 National Survey of Children's Health (NSCH) data query, Data Resource Center for Child and Adolescent Health supported by Cooperative Agreement U59MC27866 from the U.S. Department of Health and Human Services, Health Resources and Services Administration's Maternal and Child Health Bureau (HRSA MCHB), www.childhealthdata.org. CAHMI: www.cahmi.org.

3. V. Delaney-Black, C. Covington, S.J. Ondersma, B. Nordstrom-Klee, T. Templin, J. Ager, J. Janisse, and R.J. Sokol, "Violence Exposure, Trauma, and IQ and/or Reading

- Lower grade-point average[4]
- Higher absenteeism[5]
- Decreased rate of high school graduation[6]
- Significant deficits in attention, abstract reasoning, long-term memory for verbal information, decreased IQ, and decreased reading ability[7]

	Attendance	Behavior	Coursework
3+ ACEs	4.9	6.1	2.9
2 ACEs	2.6	4.3	2.5
1 ACE	2.2	2.4	1.5
No known ACE	1.0	1.0	1.0

Figure. 1 Correlation between Number of ACEs and Struggles in School, adapted from *Fostering Resilient Learners*[8]

Deficits Among Urban Children," *Archives of Pediatric and Adolescent Medicine*, 156 (2002): 280-285.

4. H. Hurt, E. Malmud, N.L. Brodsky, J. Giannetta, "Exposure to Violence: Psychological and Academic Correlates in Child Witnesses," *Archives of Pediatrics & Adolescent Medicine* 155 (2001): 1351-1356.

5. S. Beers, and M. DeBellis, "Neuropsychological Function in Children with Maltreatment Related Posttraumatic Stress Disorder," *American Journal of Psychiatry* 159 (2002): 483–486.

6. J. Grogger, "Local Violence and Educational Attainment," *Journal of Human Resources* 32 (1997): 659–682.

7. J. Grogger, "Local Violence and Educational Attainment."

8. Kristin Souers and Pete Hall, *Fostering Resilient Learners: Strategies for Creating a Trauma-Sensitive Classroom*.(Alexandria, VA: ASCD, 2016).

It is critical to remember that trauma refers to the *response* to an event, not the event itself. No two individuals respond to a situation in exactly the same way. While these studies have identified the correlation between childhood trauma and academic and health challenges, we are now able to neurologically identify why this correlation exists.

To illustrate what is happening in the brain of a child suffering from trauma, imagine you are building a house equipped with smoke detectors and fire sprinklers. In the event of a fire, the smoke detector would trigger the fire sprinkler, which should do its job and put out the fire by emitting water. For children suffering from the effects of trauma, the smoke alarm may set off the sprinklers too often, even when there is no fire. Eventually, due to the continued water damage from the fire sprinkler, it becomes incredibly difficult to continue building because you are focused on preserving the structure from further damage.

The smoke detector represents the amygdala, the area in the brain that recognizes a potential threat, and the fire sprinkler represents the prefrontal cortex of the brain. The water represents cortisol, the hormone humans naturally release to trigger a fight, flight, or freeze response in times of stress. However, for children who have lived in extended periods of extreme stress, the elevated levels of hormones became toxic and disrupt the development of their brains. Instead of being able to focus on building the house, the child is constantly in a state of crisis response. With a damaged flow between the amygdala and prefrontal cortex, children may have difficulty regulating their emotions, demonstrating appropriate behavior, and paying attention, which ultimately makes school and learning increasingly complex.

Not only does this damage compromise executive functioning skills, but these crisis responses can manifest as undesirable (and sometimes dangerous) behavior. A study showed that children with four or more ACEs were thirty-two times more likely to have learning and behavioral problems than their peers with no ACEs.[9] The National Child Traumatic Stress Network has identified behaviors that may be observed in children who have suffered a traumatic experience, as seen in **Figure 2.**

---

9. N.J. Burke, J.L. Hellman, B.G. Scott, C.F. Weems, V.G. Carrion, "The Impact of Adverse Childhood Experiences on an Urban Pediatric Population," *Child Abuse & Neglect* 35 (2011): 408-413.

Elementary School	Middle School	High School

• Anxiety, fear, and worry about self and others (more clingy with parents or teacher)
• Increased distress (whiny, irritable, moody)
• Changes in behavior
   ○ Increase in activity level
   ○ Decreased attention and/or concentration
   ○ Withdrawal from others or activities
   ○ Angry outbursts and/or aggression
   ○ Absenteeism
• Distrust of others
• Change in ability to interpret and respond to social cues
• Increased somatic complaints (e.g., headaches, stomach aches, overreaction to minor bumps and bruises)
• Changes in school performance
• Recreating the event (e.g., repeatedly talking about, "playing" out, or drawing the event)
• Over- or under-reacting to bells, physical contact, doors slamming, sirens, lighting, sudden movements
	• Anxiety, fear, and worry about safety of self and others
	• Worry about recurrence or consequences of violence
	• Changes in behavior:
	   ○ Decreased attention and/or concentration
	   ○ Increase in activity level
	   ○ Change in academic performance
	   ○ Irritability with friends, teachers, events
	   ○ Angry outbursts and/or aggression
	   ○ Withdrawal from others or activities
	   ○ Absenteeism
	• Increased somatic complaints (e.g., headaches, stomach aches, chest pains)
	• Discomfort with feelings (such as troubling thoughts of revenge)
	• Repeated discussion of events and focus on specific details of what happened
	• Over- or under-reacting to bells, physical contact, doors slamming, sirens, lighting, sudden movements
		• Anxiety, fear, and worry about safety of self and others
		• Worry about recurrence or consequences of violence
		• Changes in behavior:
		   ○ Withdrawal from others or activities
		   ○ Irritability with friends, teachers, events
		   ○ Angry outbursts and/or aggression
		   ○ Change in academic performance
		   ○ Decreased attention and/or concentration
		   ○ Increase in activity level
		   ○ Absenteeism
		• Increase in impulsivity, risk-taking behavior
		• Discomfort with feelings (such as troubling thoughts of revenge)
		• Increased risk for substance abuse
		• Discussion of events and reviewing of details
		• Negative impact on issues of trust and perceptions of others
		• Over- or under-reacting to bells, physical contact, doors slamming, sirens, lighting, sudden movements

• Statements and questions about death and dying • Difficulty with authority, redirection, or criticism • Re-experiencing the trauma (e.g., nightmares or disturbing memories during the day) • Hyperarousal (e.g., sleep disturbance, tendency to be easily startled) • Avoidance behaviors (e.g., resisting going to places that remind them of the event) • Emotional numbing (e.g., seeming to have no feeling about the event)	• Re-experiencing the trauma (e.g., nightmares or disturbing memories during the day) • Hyperarousal (e.g., sleep disturbance, tendency to be easily startled) • Avoidance behaviors (e.g., resisting going to places that remind them of the event) • Emotional numbing (e.g., seeming to have no feeling about the event)	• Repetitive thoughts and comments about death or dying (including suicidal thoughts, writing, art, or notebook covers about viol or morbid topics, internet searches) • Heightened difficulty with authority, redirection, or criticism • Re-experiencing the traum: (e.g., nightmares or disturb memories during the day) • Hyperarousal (e.g., sleep disturbance, tendency to be easily startled) • Avoidance behaviors (e.g., resisting going to places th: remind them of the event) • Emotional numbing (e.g., seeming to have no feeling about the event)

Figure 2. Common Behaviors of Students with Trauma[10]

Regardless of the response, it is important to remember that every behavior is an expression of a need. The four prevalent areas of need are emotional, relational, physical, and control.[11] Often, the person is unaware of the specific need they have because the behaviors they exhibit are their body's natural reactions to those needs. Since they can't articulate what they need, they show it through certain behaviors or actions.

While we continue to learn more about the ways that trauma and chronic stress impact the development of the brain, we are also learning

---

10. National Child Traumatic Stress Network Schools Committee, Child Trauma Toolkit for Educators (Los Angeles, CA & Durham, NC: National Center for Child Traumatic Stress, 2008).

11. Kristin Souers, and Peter A Hall, *Relationship, Responsibility, and Regulation: Trauma-Invested Practices for Fostering Resilient Learners* (Alexandria, VA.: ASCD, 2019).

more about the incredible neuroplasticity of the brain. Neuroplasticity refers to the brain's ability to adapt and "rewire" itself. While there isn't a magic age, ongoing research has shown that the brain is much more malleable at a younger age; however, the brain will continue to change throughout adulthood.[12]

This information is critical for anyone working with youth. We now know that with the right supports and systems, we can impact a child's ability to "rewire" and repair brain functioning. This science allows us to address the cause of the issues, rather than simply responding to the behavior. With millions of children impacted by trauma, this is promising news for all those who work with children.

What does this mean for maker educators?

While the connection may not seem obvious, many studies have shown the connection between creative expression and healing after trauma. Creative expression is a way for individuals to communicate their feelings when they do not have the words or capacity to communicate them otherwise. Psychiatrist Bruce Perry found that areas of the brain can be reshaped and reorganized through activities that include touch and movement.[13] A study from Drexel University found that the simple act of art-making, regardless of skill level, reduced the levels of cortisol in the brain.[14]

---

12. Maura McInerney and Amy McKlindon, "Unlocking the Door to Learning: Trauma-Informed Classrooms & Transformational Schools," Education Law Center, 2014, https://www.elc-pa.org/wp-content/uploads/2015/06/Trauma-Informed-in-Schools-Classrooms-FINAL-December2014-2.pdf.

13. Heidi Durham, "How Art Can Help Children Overcome Trauma," *Education Week*, February 20, 2019, https://www.edweek.org/ew/articles/2016/12/14/how-art-can-help-children-overcome-trauma.html.

14. Girija Kaimal, Kendra Ray, and Juan Muniz, "Reduction of Cortisol Levels and Participants' Responses Following Art Making," *Art Therapy* 33, no. 2 (2016): 74–80, https://doi.org/10.1080/07421656.2016.1166832.

While every makerspace is unique, the Maker Movement fosters:
- **Sense of independence.** Makers are given voice and choice in the problems they are tackling, the resources they use, and the overall plan.
- **Confidence building.** Makers can learn new skills by taking classes or experimenting with the guidance of an expert. They can also gain confidence by teaching others skills they possess.
- **Relationship building.** Makers are surrounded by other like-minded creators and learn to collaborate.
- **Resilience building.** Makers are provided with a safe area to fail—without grades, judgement, or outside expectations on their creations.

Makerspaces are uniquely positioned to help foster skills like collaboration, empathy, and problem-solving. However, with nearly one-third of all children in U.S. public schools having significantly impaired cortical functioning because of trauma, it is imperative that educators of all types are aware of users with challenges in this environment. There is a deep complexity in designing a space that is both open and flexible, yet designed with the intention to support students that have compromised emotional regulation abilities and behavioral problems.

Research suggests that schools and other learning communities can support these students in four ways:[15]
1. People
2. Places
3. Practice
4. Plan

We're going to take a closer look at these four factors and how educators can adjust our practices in a library makerspace.

---

15. Advancement Project, "Restorative Practices: Fostering Healthy Relationships & Promoting Positive Discipline in Schools," March 2014, http://schottfoundation.org/sites/default/files/restorative-practices-guide.pdf.

People

When a child's brain is constantly in a state of survival mode, they rarely enter thrive mode. It is only when the child feels safe that their constant state of crisis can rest and they can enter thrive mode and begin learning and working to reshape their brain. In 2008, John Hattie conducted the largest meta-analyses of the key factors that impact student achievement.[16] One of the most effective indicators was teacher-student relationships. Positive teacher-student relationships allow students to feel safe. With safety, students are more likely to take risks and less likely to be afraid of the repercussions in the event of an error, for they recognize that it is a part of the learning process. The feeling of safety is only achieved through nourishing relationships. The best thing about this is that it requires no advanced degrees, no special certifications, and no unique skills. This is not to say that fostering safe relationships for students is easy.

How does one foster a positive teacher-student relationship, particularly with the most challenging students? While there are many strategies in addition to those discussed in this chapter, in short, people (not just children) need to feel loved. The Grant Study identified that men who felt loved and cared for by someone in their childhood—even feeling loved by one other individual—made fifty percent more money and were more likely to feel satisfied with their lives in adulthood.[17] Feeling loved reduces stress hormones and quiets the amygdala (the smoke detector). Love doesn't just calm brains, "it changes them, and maybe faster and better than anything else."[18] Psychologist Louis Cozolino argues that the greatest contributor to neuroplasticity is love.[19] For a child living with trauma, each loving experience moves them closer to a state of

---

16. J. Hattie, *Visible Learning: A Synthesis of Over 800 Meta-Analyses Relating to Achievement* (London: Routledge, 2009).

17. Meg Jay, *Supernormal: The Untold Story of Adversity and Resilience* (New York: Grand Central Publishing, 2019), 289.

18. Jay, *Supernormal: The Untold Story of Adversity and Resilience*, 294.

19. Louis J Cozolino, *The Neuroscience of Human Relationships: Attachment and the Developing Social Brain* (New York: W.W. Norton & Company, 2014), 243.

normalcy. These positive, loving experiences are reparative. Researcher Barbara Fredrickson calls this the "undoing effect."[20]

This is not to say that every interaction with your patrons needs to be overly affectionate. Fredrickson uses the term love to describe joy, gratitude, contentment, interest, hope, pride, amusement, inspiration, and awe.

I would encourage you to reflect upon your current relationships with your makers.
- How well do you know them? Do you know their names?
- What efforts have you made to get to know them?
- Have your interactions been initiated by you or the maker?
- Are the interactions question and response in nature, or a conversation?
- What percentage of your job duties are dedicated to establishing and maintaining relationships?
- Is everyone greeted upon arrival?
- How do you think your patrons would describe their relationship with you?

There is no checklist to follow for creating and maintaining positive relationships, but being aware of the current status of your relationships is the first step in determining how to actively work on cultivating them.

Keeping in mind that makerspaces are collaborative in nature, we also want an environment conducive to meaningful person-person or maker-maker relationships. Depending on the structure of your makerspace, supporting these relationships may be too far beyond our sphere of influence to control. As librarians, however, we are natural dot-connectors. Sometimes we connect people to books, people to tools, or in this case, people to people. As a maker-librarian, we have a 10,000-foot view of the happenings in the space. We know what individuals are working on and what interests and skills are available through the social capital of the members. The maker-librarian serves as the bridge, with the ability

---

20. Barbara L. Fredrickson, "The Role of Positive Emotions in Positive Psychology: The Broaden-and-Build Theory of Positive Emotions," *American Psychologist* 56, no. 3 (2001): 218-226.

to bring individuals or groups together to work towards a common goal. However, in addition to matchmaking makers for their skills and interest, we can also matchmake based on our users' social and emotional skills. For example, one strategy is to pair individuals living with trauma, violence and chronic stress with partners who have already developed strong empathy skills.[21]

Places

While we know that emotional intelligence, self-discipline, and resilience are neurological functions, it is not our job to figure out which neurons need to be connected to create such skills. Instead, our job is to create an *environment* that supports the development of those skills. When someone enters your makerspace, what is the first thing they see, hear, and smell? How does it make someone feel? Often, we spend so much time thinking about the contents of the makerspace that we tend to overlook the space as a whole. A makerspace should not just be a place where people can build and tinker, it should be a place where students *feel* they can thrive, feel as though they belong, *feel* valued, and *feel* safe.

When considering the products and materials you have in your space, are there certain materials that have a more prominent location? If the main floor of your makerspace is full of computers and microcontrollers for robot-making and low-tech materials are stored in bins in a back closet, it can send an unintended message to its users about what is valued. It is important to consider not only the availability of materials but their location as well.

While a makerspace is a place of construction, it can also serve as a place of exhibition. If you're lacking physical space to display creations, consider developing an online gallery or continuously posting on social media. It is important to not only praise the final product, but also to celebrate the creator(s). For a student who has a reputation for being the

---

21. L.R. Weibler, "Development Differences in Response to Trauma," in *Supporting and Educating Traumatized Students: A Guide for School-Based Professionals*, ed. Eric Rossen and Robert Hill, (New York: Oxford University Press, 2013), 39-47.

"bad kid," this can slowly help change the narrative. Now, the student is "the kid that made...."

Makerspaces are indeed places of collaboration, but it is also important to recognize that there may be situations where private space is necessary. Students that do not yet have the ability to regulate emotion may need a safe-space to de-escalate. Students may also need a place separate from the temptations of the makerspace to concentrate on a task.

Here are some things to consider when reflecting on the "space."

- Is the space accessible to patrons who may have family obligations? (i.e. a patron may have to take care of a younger sibling during a time when the makerspace is open)
- Does the space marginalize any gender, race, religion, sexual orientation or socioeconomic status?
- What assumptions are we making in the programming we offer? (i.e. are we assuming our patrons have devices and internet at home?)
- Does the space have different areas for independent and group work?

In libraries, we work to eliminate physical, emotional, and intellectual barriers, and the same efforts should be made in the library makerspace. By working in trauma-informed practices, we gain a new perspective into our spaces.

Practice

When I was first introduced to the Maker Movement, I was greatly interested in the idea of championing failure, as it was quite different than what I was doing in the classroom. I had spent several years as a school librarian, and each year would get the same projects over and over again. My students always wanted to see an example from years past and were crippled when they received a score that was anything less than perfect. I had few risk-takers or out-of-the-box thinkers. Or if they were risk-takers, they didn't see the classroom as a place for risk-taking. As the years progressed and I became more aware of the implications for creating a society without innovators and risk takers, I began taking baby steps into the Maker Movement. I established some rules and created a schedule, but I tried to keep the space as open and flexible as possible, and allow students to have as much voice and choice as possible in their projects and creations.

However, there were situations where I felt I had to "shut it down" because of what I had deemed willful disobedience. If a student refused to clean up his or her mess, I might no longer permit them to use those materials. If a student was acting in a manner that was dangerous or disruptive to others, I might have asked them to leave the space entirely. I thought I was doing the right thing by addressing the "issue" immediately with what I felt was a logical consequence based on the behavior displayed. Unfortunately, for students of trauma, consequences can be viewed as punishment and can actually increase the potential for re-traumatization.[22] Further, I wasn't actually helping the student. Punitive consequences are a short-term fix. Students don't learn anything from the punishment, and I wasn't learning anything about the cause of their behavior. By focusing on the behavior and not the cause, I was no closer to helping the student identify their need and in turn, I was no closer to helping them meet that need.

This does not mean you should abandon consequences or ignore negative behavior. There will certainly be situations where you will need to intervene. When the time comes—and it will—try to look at the behavior as a call for help and an opportunity for learning. The first action is to ensure everyone's safety. Once you confirm that everyone is physically safe, you can begin to ensure everyone's emotional safety (including your own). De-escalation and re-direction are your first line of response. Note that it will be next to impossible to de-escalate a screaming child if you are screaming back at them. Knowing that the learner is currently in a state of fight, flight, or freeze, your goal is to help them regain normalcy by helping them feel safe. Regardless of whether a physical fight has happened or someone has simply cut in line, nothing

---

22. McInerney and McKlindon, "Unlocking the Door to Learning: Trauma-Informed Classrooms & Transformational Schools."

you say and no punishments you assign will "sink in" when the child is in a state of crisis. Having the child take a walk, do some breathing, or simply sit quietly can help them de-escalate.

Once the child has de-escalated, you can then resort to one of several restorative practices. In restorative practices, the goal is to help the learner recognize their feelings and take responsibility for their actions. By having a conversation, the person not only feels cared for but feels respected and "heard". These practices help model appropriate coping techniques, communication skills, and conflict resolution.[23]

While it may take a great deal of time and patience, over 50% of the behavioral issues are from 5% of the student population; slowly but surely, we can help the child meet their needs and remedy the misalignments in their brains. It is important for us to make the assumption that every person is doing the best they can, working from where they are emotionally, intellectually, and developmentally.

Plan

In addition to changing our perspective and reactions when *responding* to behavior, there are also measures we can take to prevent certain behaviors.

Certain situations or environments may be a trigger for students. While it isn't possible to prevent every scenario that *may* be a trigger, we can go into each situation being aware that it may be a trigger. Knowing that some tools and skills in the makerspace can be challenging to master, we can identify when to offer additional support and guidance, allowing students to work within their zone of proximal development. While we want to teach students that failure is a part of learning, we also need to be aware of the mindset of the learners coming to us. We've all been in situations where it seems like everything is going wrong. Just when we think it can't get any worse, something simple, like a pencil breaking or a dead cell phone, can throw us past our breaking point. Normally, a

---

23. Advancement Project, "Restorative Practices: Fostering Healthy Relationships & Promoting Positive Discipline in Schools,"

broken pencil or a dead cell phone wouldn't be more than an inconvenience, but on one of *those days* it can send us spiraling. Imagine working with a learner who is in that state of mind constantly. Now compound that with the knowledge that this learner doesn't know how to regulate their emotions once they have passed the breaking point—it's a recipe for disaster. The stringing in a 3D print or having to wait to use a certain tool could be that "straw." Prediction is the best tool for prevention.

Another measure to prevent negative behaviors is to ensure a balance in the autonomy and independence that makerspaces provide, with a set of norms and procedures. When I first opened our library makerspace, I took a laissez-faire approach and only intervened when absolutely necessary. I allowed the students to choose what projects they worked on, what resources they used, and if and with whom they collaborated. I wanted to give students as much agency as possible. Developing a sense of agency is critical in helping children feel responsible for their actions. When this sense of agency is developed, they are more likely to take ownership of the decisions they make and the consequences associated with those choices.[24]

Here are some ways to help develop a sense of agency:
- Provide opportunities for leadership roles, even if in minuscule tasks. Examples: Designating a person to change the 3D printer filament, designating someone as the Scratch expert.
- Provide as many opportunities for choice as possible. Examples: What skill to learn, what tools to use, what product to create.
- Provide as many opportunities to "figure it out" as possible. Examples: Unboxing a new product. Navigating a new software independently.

By loosening the reins, we communicate a sense of trust that deepens the relationships that we know are so crucial for children of trauma.

This does not mean that the makerspace should be a free-for-all. In fact, too much ambiguity can cause anxiety. The absence of any guidance, direction, or control can translate into a feeling of being

---

24. Gordon Neufeld and Gabor Mate, *Hold on to Your Kids : Why Parents Need to Matter More than Peers* (New York: Ballantine Books, 2014).

unsafe. Research has found that children who grow up in homes without adequate boundaries had less impulse control, poorer self-regulation, and were more self-centered and less socially competent.[25] This doesn't mean that you need to dictate every move and action in the makerspace. However, creating a set of routines and regular practices can help establish a predictable rhythm. Groups large and small work best with rules and procedures in place, as long as they are developed with the people who will be using them in mind.[26] However, don't create rules and procedures just for the sake of creating rules and procedures. When developing rules and procedures, create them with safety, communication, and fairness in mind. These rules and procedures will be just as helpful to your patrons as to the makerspace staff.

Maker educators need to remember that trauma is everywhere. Whether your makerspace is located in a rural, suburban, wealthy, or poor neighborhood, trauma doesn't discriminate. Unfortunately, people don't come to us with a trauma history card or a label indicating that they're suffering, so knowing who needs additional support and who doesn't is challenging. Fortunately, these practices are good for *all learners*, not just those who suffer from the impact of childhood trauma. Maker educators are there to support the development of the *whole* maker, not just the hard skills associated with being a maker. Being a good maker also requires executive functioning skills, problem solving skills, and communication skills. As the "greatest unrecognized public health crisis," the prevalence of trauma is on the rise.[27] While we can't change the past, we can help learners build their future.

---

25. Shauna L Shapiro, *Mindful Discipline: A Loving Approach to Setting Limits & Raising an Emotionally Intelligent Child* (Oakland, CA: New Harbinger Publications, Inc, 2014), 140.

26. Dominique Smith, Douglas Fisher, and Nancy Frey, *Better than Carrots or Sticks: Restorative Practices for Positive Classroom Management* (Alexandria, VA: ASCD, 2015), 43.

27. Elizabeth Chuck and Marshall Crook, "From Aromatherapy to Anger Management: How Schools Are Addressing the 'crisis' of Childhood Trauma," NBC News, April 7, 2019, https://www.nbcnews.com/news/us-news/aromatherapy-anger-management-how-schools-are-addressing-crisis-childhood-trauma-n1006076?fbclid=IwAR0Cw90sqvyGdvlWIg9u6TG5LKyWoW0UJdtutBIv_atVrISOZVihPZdlRZU.

Bibliography

Advancement Project. "Restorative Practices: Fostering Healthy Relationships & Promoting Positive Discipline in Schools." March 2014. http://schottfoundation.org/sites/default/files/restorative-practices-guide.pdf.

Blodgett, Christopher, and Joyce Dorado. "A Selected Review of Trauma-Informed School Practice and Alignment with Educational Practice." Washington State University, 2012. https://s3.wp.wsu.edu/uploads/sites/2101/2015/02/CLEAR-Trauma-Informed-Schools-White-Paper.pdf.

Burke, N.J., J.L. Hellman, B.G. Scott, C.F. Weems, and V.G. Carrion. (2011). "The Impact of Adverse Childhood Experiences on an Urban Pediatric Population." *Child Abuse & Neglect* 35 (2011): 408-413.

Child and Adolescent Health Measurement Initiative. 2017 National Survey of Children's Health (NSCH) data query. Data Resource Center for Child and Adolescent Health supported by Cooperative Agreement U59MC27866 from the U.S. Department of Health and Human Services, Health Resources and Services Administration's Maternal and Child Health Bureau (HRSA MCHB). www.childhealthdata.org. CAHMI: www.cahmi.org.

Chuck, Elizabeth, and Marshall Crook. "From Aromatherapy to Anger Management: How Schools Are Addressing the 'crisis' of Childhood Trauma." NBC News, May 20, 2019. https://www.nbcnews.com/news/us-news/aromatherapy-anger-management-how-schools-are-addressing-crisis-childhood-trauma-n1006076?fbclid=IwAR0Cw90sqvyGdvlWIg9u6TG5LKyWoW0UJdtutBIv_atVrISOZVihPZdlRZU.

Cozolino, Louis J. *The Neuroscience of Human Relationships: Attachment and the Developing Social Brain.* New York: W.W. Norton & Company, 2014.

Delaney-Black, V., C. Covington, S.J. Ondersma, B. Nordstrom-Klee, T. Templin, J. Ager, J. Janisse, and R.J. Sokol. "Violence Exposure, Trauma, and IQ and/or Reading Deficits Among Urban Children." *Archives of Pediatric and Adolescent Medicine* 156 (2002): 280-285.

Durham, Heidi. "How Art Can Help Children Overcome Trauma." *Education Week*, February 20, 2019. https://www.edweek.org/ew/articles/2016/12/14/how-art-can-help-children-overcome-trauma.html.

Felitti, Vincent J., Robert F. Anda, Dale Nordenberg, David F. Williamson, Alison M. Spitz, Valerie Edwards, Mary P. Koss, and James S. Marks. "Relationship of Childhood Abuse and Household Dysfunction to Many of the Leading Causes of Death in Adults: The Adverse Childhood Experiences (ACE) Study." American Journal of Preventive Medicine 56, no. 6 (June 2019): 774–86. https://doi.org/10.1016/j.amepre.2019.04.001.

Fredrickson, Barbara L., "The Role of Positive Emotions in Positive Psychology: The Broaden-and-Build Theory of Positive Emotions," *American Psychologist* 56, no. 3 (2001): 218-226.

Grogger, J. "Local Violence and Educational Attainment." *Journal of Human Resources* 32 (1997): 659–682.

Hattie, J. Visible Learning, *A Synthesis of Over 800 Meta-Analyses Relating to Achievement*. London: Routledge, 2009.

Hurt, H., E. Malmud, N.L. Brodsky, and J. Giannetta. "Exposure to Violence: Psychological and Academic Correlates in Child Witnesses." *Archives of Pediatrics & Adolescent Medicine* 155 (2001): 1351-1356.

Jay, Meg. Supernormal: *The Untold Story of Adversity and Resilience*. New York: Grand Central Publishing, 2019.

Kaimal, Girija, Kendra Ray, and Juan Muniz. "Reduction of Cortisol Levels and Participants' Responses Following Art Making." *Art Therapy* 33, no. 2 (2016): 74–80. https://doi.org/10.1080/07421656.2016.1166832.

McInerney Maura, and Amy McKlindon. "Unlocking the Door to Learning: Trauma-Informed Classrooms & Transformational Schools." Education Law Center, 2014. https://www.elc-pa.org/wp-content/uploads/2015/06/Trauma-Informed-in-Schools-Classrooms-FINAL-December2014-2.pdf.

National Child Traumatic Stress Network Schools Committee. Child Trauma Toolkit for Educators. Los Angeles, CA & Durham, NC: National Center for Child Traumatic Stress, 2008.

Neufeld, Gordon, and Gabor Mate. *Hold on to Your Kids: Why Parents Need to Matter More than Peers.* New York: Ballantine Books, 2014.

Shapiro, Shauna L. *Mindful Discipline: A Loving Approach to Setting Limits & Raising an Emotionally Intelligent Child.* Oakland, CA: New Harbinger Publications, Inc, 2014.

Smith, Dominique, Douglas Fisher, and Nancy Frey. *Better than Carrots or Sticks: Restorative Practices for Positive Classroom Management.* Alexandria, VA: ASCD, 2015.

Souers, Kristin, and Pete Hall. *Fostering Resilient Learners: Strategies for Creating a Trauma-Sensitive Classroom.* Alexandria, VA: ASCD, 2016.

Souers, Kristin, and Peter A Hall. *Relationship, Responsibility, and Regulation: Trauma-Invested Practices for Fostering Resilient Learners.* Alexandria, VA.: ASCD, 2019.

Weibler, L. R. "Development Differences in Response to Trauma." In *Supporting and Educating Traumatized Students: A Guide for School-Based Professionals*, edited by Eric Rossen and Robert Hill, 39-47. New York: Oxford University Press, 2013.

COUNTERNARRATIVES

Chapter 7

PEACE PRESCRIPTION: INCLUSIVE MAKING IN SCHOOL LIBRARIES

Kyungwon Koh, Xun Ge, Lo Lee, Kathryn R. Lewis, Shirley Simmons, and Lee B. Nelson

Introduction

The maker movement, whose roots lie in informal environments such as Hackerspaces,[1] came to the K-12 education sphere and school libraries in the U.S. in the 2010s[2] as practitioners and researchers found the educational value of making and identified a makerspace as a learning

---

1. Sarah R. Davies, *Hackerspaces: Making the Maker Movement* (Malden, MA: Polity Press, 2017).

2. Paulo Blikstein, "Digital Fabrication and 'Making' in Education: The Democratization of Invention," in *FabLabs: Of Machines, Makers and Inventors*, ed. Julia Walter-Herrmann and Corinne Büching (Wetzlar, Germany: Transcript-Verlag, 2013), 1-21; Edward P. Clapp, Jessica Ross, Jennifer Oxman Ryan, and Shari Tishman, *Maker-Centered Learning: Empowering Young People to Shape Their Worlds*. (San Francisco, CA: Jossey-Bass, 2017); Dale Dougherty, "Makerspaces in Education and DARPA," last modified April 4, 2012, https://makezine.com/2012/04/04/makerspaces-in-education-and-darpa/; Dale Dougherty, "Learning by Making: American Kids Should be Building Rockets and Robots, Not Taking Standardized Tests," last modified June 4, 2012, http://www.slate.com/articles/technology/future_tense/2012/06/maker_faire_and_science_education_american_kidsshould_be_building_rockets_and_robots_not_taking_standardized_tests_.html; Benjamin Herold, "The 'Maker' Movement Is Coming to K-12: Can Schools Get It Right?," last modified June 6, 2016, https://www.edweek.org/ew/articles/2016/06/09/the-maker-movement-is-coming-to-k-12.html

environment.³ However, implementing maker learning was a daunting task in the high-accountability, formal school context, with the demands of the curriculum and standardized tests.⁴ Strategically and philosophically, school libraries are ideal places to bridge creative, self-directed learning and curriculum-based learning, and they can play a significant role in the maker movement in education. With a mission of empowering learners and transforming teaching and learning,⁵ an increasing number of school libraries are now embracing maker-learning approaches. All makerspaces are different, and school librarians strive to create their own makerspace or programs that meet the particular needs of their community.⁶ Some school librarians transform their physical library space into a makerspace, while others offer maker activities in different times and spaces, such as afterschool programs, morning or lunch hour activities, or during the regular classroom hours, tying activities to the standard-based curriculum and addressing a range of subjects including STEM (Science, Technology, Engineering, and Math), arts and crafts, music, and more.⁷

---

3. Kylie Peppler, Erica Halverson, and Yasmin B. Kafai, *Makeology: Makerspaces as Learning Environments. Vol. 1* (New York: Routledge, 2016); Lee Martin, "The Promise of the Maker Movement for Education," *Journal of Pre-College Engineering Education Research (J-PEER)* 5, no. 1 (2015): 4; Sylvia Libow Martinez and Gary S. Stager, *Invent to Learn: Making, Tinkering, and Engineering in the Classroom* (Torrance, CA: Constructing Modern Knowledge Press, 2013).

4. Erika Halverson and Kimberly Sheridan, "The Maker Movement in Education," *Harvard Educational Review* 84, no. 4 (2014): 495-504; Herold, "The 'Maker' Movement Is Coming to K-12."

5. American Association of School Librarians, *National School Library Standards for Learners, School Librarians, and School Libraries* (Chicago, IL: American Library Association, 2018).

6. Leslie Preddy, *School Library Makerspaces: Grades 6-12* (Santa Barbara, CA: Libraries Unlimited, 2013).

7. Sheila F. Baker and Bonnie Alexander, "A Major Making Undertaking: A New Librarian Transforms A Middle School Library into a Makerspace Aligned to High School Career Endorsements," *Knowledge Quest* 46, no. 5 (2018): 64-69; Megan Blakemore, "Problem Scoping Design Thinking and Close Reading: Makerspaces in the School Library," *Knowledge Quest* 46, no. 4 (2018): 66-69; Heather Moorefield-Lang, *School Library Makerspaces in Action* (Santa Barbara, CA: Libraries Unlimited, 2018).

The Inquiry-Based Maker Unit: Peace Prescription

The study was conducted at Leon Middle School,[8] a public middle school in a mid-size suburban community in the south-central region of the U.S. As a Title I school, approximately 53.16% of the students receive free or reduced-price lunches. The student population demographics include: 64% White, 13% two or more races, 10% Hispanic, 8% Black, 4% American Indian/Alaska Native, 2% Asian, and an increasing number of English as a Second Language (ESL) students.[9]

In Spring 2018, Ms. Brown's 7th grade English Language Arts class implemented an inquiry-based maker unit in collaboration with the middle school librarian and the gifted resource coordinator. The unit centered around Guided Inquiry Design (GID)—a specific type of guided inquiry framework in which students select, formulate, and pursue their own inquiry questions within the subject curriculum.[10] The educators innovated the inquiry instruction by integrating maker mindsets and approaches with the intent of increasing student interest, learning, and engagement. The unit lasted for four weeks and the class met five days a week for fifty minutes, either in the classroom or in the school library. The school librarian provided expertise in maker tools and activities and the inquiry learning process, and she supported student learning activities throughout the unit. Thirteen out of nineteen students in the class agreed to participate in the study by submitting signed parent consent forms and child assent forms. Data sources included participant observation, interviews with the students, teacher, and school librarian, and artifact analyses of student journals, maker products, and teaching materials.

The title of the unit, Peace Prescription, came from the poem of the same title by Mattie J. T. Stepanek, a poet and a peacemaker who was

---

8. All names in this chapter, including the school, teacher, and student names, are pseudonyms.

9. National Center for Education Statistics, "Search for Public Schools," 2019, https://nces.ed.gov/.

10. Carol Collier Kuhlthau, Leslie K Maniotes, and Ann K Caspari, *Guided Inquiry Design: A Framework for Inquiry in Your School* (Santa Barbara, CA: Libraries Unlimited, 2012).

born in 1990 and died in 2004 at the age of thirteen.[11] Throughout the unit, students engaged in various inquiry and maker activities on anti-bullying that were carefully planned and guided by the teacher and the school librarian. The unit began with a powerful opening session that sparked student interest in the topic, which involved watching a short video on the effect of bullying narrated from the victim's perspective, titled To This Day Project by Shane Koyczan.[12] Students showed strong emotional engagement in the video and the topic. Several of them reflected in their journals that the video was "powerful" and "very strong." Some students described how upset or uncomfortable they were when watching the video: "I could feel his pain."; "This made me feel sad and hurt for everyone that is going through this [bullying]."; "I felt a lot while watching this video. I almost started crying because I relate so much to the words he said." Subsequently, students acted out two role-play scenarios on bullying in schools. Each student assumed different roles, such as bully, victim, bystander, and teacher. Students not only showed empathy for the victims in the scenarios, "I kind of felt emotional, and I could tell his feelings were really hurt," but also for the bullies, "He is a bully that probably has a hard time at home ... maybe he has a rough life." To further explore the topic, students watched different videos and read articles on bullying curated by the school librarian.

Once the students were acquainted with and deeply immersed in the topic, each student came up with their own inquiry question that they wanted to investigate regarding bullying. Students formulated a range of questions such as: "What causes a bully to become a bully and how does it affect their future?"; "How can stereotyping affect bullying and what can you do to break out of it?"; "What is the cause of bullying, and how does it affect a teen's everyday life?"; "How can sexual harassment lead to depression or suicide?"; "How has technology affected bullying?";

---

11. Mattie J. T. Stepanek Foundation, "The Mattie J. T. Stepanek Foundation," 2019, http://www.mattieonline.com.

12. Shane Koyczan, *To This Day Project - Shane Koyczan*, 2013, https://www.youtube.com/watch?v=ltun92DfnPY.

and more. Students appreciated that they were able to select an inquiry question that related to their own interests or personal experiences or that otherwise resonated with them: "What motivated me to do it [the anti-bullying project] is I have a friend who has been sexually harassed and we both have depression, so I have a lot of personal connections with that." Students conducted research to answer their inquiry questions using various sources including books, articles, personal interviews, and online resources from the Internet.

While the activities described above were performed as well in other 7th grade English Language Arts classes, the students in those regular inquiry units usually created more text-based products such as posters, brochures, or essays. In the case described here, students could select any kind of maker projects to demonstrate their learning and inquiry. The students were somewhat familiar with different maker tools from a previous semester in which they had a Flex hour in the school library makerspace—a less-structured time for students to explore and tinker in the makerspace with the guidance of a school librarian. While the students had already experienced multiple inquiry units in the school year for different subjects, and they were familiar with the Guided Inquiry Design process, this was their second unit that integrated making into inquiry.

To help students experience the full potential of making, Ms. Brown and her class had a brainstorming and discussion session on the nature of making. Ms. Brown asked, "Why do people make things?" The class discussed different motivations and inspirations for making, such as "want/desire" (making for their own enjoyment) and "need/problem solving" for either the self or for other people. Ms. Brown also shared her experience of making by showing a picture of a homemade outside couch that her family had needed. Then they brainstormed potential tools and technologies they might use. In their first inquiry-based maker unit early in the academic year, the educators and researchers observed that some students tended to select a type of maker project that they were already familiar with rather than trying something they had not done before that could be more innovative or challenging. This tendency to make a "safe choice" was due to students' concerns about their grade. This time, Ms. Brown assured students that the grade criteria for this project included the "process," not just the completeness of the final product, so students felt safer in experimenting with new types of projects. Ms. Brown and the school librarian were intentional in encouraging students to think outside the box. They challenged students to come up with a unique way to demonstrate their inquiry learning and to avoid some of the more frequently-used types of projects, such as posters or Google Slides. The educators also provided a form, called a Makerspace Project Proposal, which guided the planning of maker projects with several helpful questions and prompts, such as:

- Describe your idea
- What do you need to know before you start? How will you find this information?
- What do you need to know how to do before you start? How will you learn?
- Makerspace tools needed; Other tools or materials: Where will you get them?
- Are you working alone? If not, list team members
- What can your teachers do to support you?
- Draw a sketch or diagram of your product
- How much time will you need?
- Provide a breakdown of how you will use your time; What will you do if you don't finish in this amount of time?
- What do you hope to learn by creating your product?
- How will you share your product?

With the educators' intentional guidance and the relevance of the topic, both educators and students felt a difference in student learning experiences in this unit. Students produced various creative and interactive projects, including artistic and informative crafts, role playing with student-created dolls and bullying scenarios, digital media presentations, animations, an interactive box that represented a social media platform, board games, and more. The student learning processes and products clearly showed their cognitive and emotional engagement through making in this difficult, yet relevant, social issue. During the exit interviews, students reported: "I liked this unit a lot. I think that it was a good unit because it raised awareness. I think that it inspired people to be kinder to each other."; "I liked the topic we were given. I liked that the topic was more of a realistic topic ... I really did enjoy this project, and it opened up a lot of my classmates' eyes."

At the end of the unit, students reported that, among the various learning activities, they enjoyed making a project and sharing projects with each other the most. Student favorite activities were: sharing projects (35%), making projects (30%), gathering information (15%), evaluating/reflecting (10%), identifying an inquiry question (5%), and the opening video and role playing (5%). Students appreciated viewing other people's projects, saying, "I really like the Share part, because you can see all the different creativity that everybody has and see their cool projects." A student said: "I like Create [referring to the hands-on phase in which they worked on a maker project]; with makerspace you can do whatever you want within the topic." Student interview data also revealed that the incorporation of the maker learning enhanced student choice and ownership over their learning. Students said: "I think that we [students] had a lot of control [over our own learning]. Because she [the teacher] said that we don't do things that we do normally, so I think she wanted us to have different projects from everyone else because our brains think differently, and so whenever we had different projects and we don't really have ones that are that similar, then I think that we definitely have ownership over it."; "I like [the] makerspace because that's where I could be the most creative."; "That's where you could use more tools and do a lot more things."

Student Maker Artifacts Analyses

In order to investigate if students had developed competencies related to inclusion and diversity in the inquiry-based maker unit, the researchers analyzed selected student projects according to the AASL National School Library Standards.[13] We focused on one of the standard areas,

---

13. American Association of School Librarians, *National School Library Standards for Learners, School Librarians, and School Libraries.*

Include: "an understanding of and commitment to inclusiveness and respect for diversity in the learning community." The learner competencies for Include (**Table 1**) look for evidence in which learners contribute to a balanced perspective and demonstrate empathy, equity, and tolerance for diverse ideas. Maker artifacts from selected students were analyzed looking for qualitative evidence that addresses each domain and competency. We also referenced student inquiry journals to complement the analysis of the final artifacts. This section will present three student cases.

Kate

Kate's inquiry question was, "How has technology affected bullying?" and she researched cyberbullying throughout the unit. Kate used cardboard boxes to represent an Instagram interface (**Figure 1**):

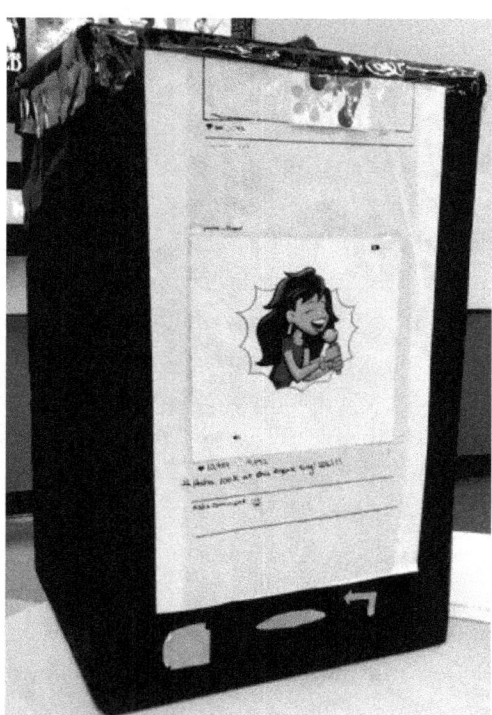

Figure 1. Kate's Maker Product

Table 1. The Include Area from National School Library Standards

INCLUDE	
Key commitment: Demonstrate an understanding of and commitment to inclusiveness and respect for diversity in the learning community	
Domain	Learner Domain and Competencies
A. Think	Learners contribute a balanced perspective when participating in a learning community by: 1. Articulating an awareness of the contributions of a range of learners. 2. Adopting a discerning stance toward points of view and opinions expressed in information resources and learning products. 3. Describing their understanding of cultural relevancy and placement within the global learning community.
B. Create	Learners adjust their awareness of the global learning community by: 1. Interacting with learners who reflect a range of perspectives. 2. Evaluating a variety of perspectives during learning activities. 3. Representing diverse perspectives during learning activities.
C. Share	Learners exhibit empathy with and tolerance for diverse ideas by: 1. Engaging in informed conversation and active debate. 2. Contributing to discussions in which multiple viewpoints on a topic are expressed.
D. Grow	Learners demonstrate empathy and equity in knowledge building within the global learning community by: 1. Seeking interactions with a range of learners. 2. Demonstrating interest in other perspectives during learning activities. 3. Reflecting on their own place within the global learning community.

> I took a box and I made it look like the front of the box was an Instagram account and somebody was making a post of someone who was getting bullied. What I did was I set up outside, in front of Ms. Brown's room and asked a question, what would you do in this situation, and on a piece of paper I would have people write what they would do in the situation, like if they would report them, block them, or like if they would be the hero.

Her maker project addressed several competencies for Include, particularly in the domains of Create, Share, and Grow. By creating a mock-up social media box and inviting people to respond, Kate interacted with learners with diverse perspectives (Create 1 & 3). She engaged other students in informed conversations and active debates based on a real-world scenario about bullying in social media (Share 1 & 2). This interactive project demonstrated her interest in learning other people's perspectives, and the mock-up demonstration raised awareness on the impact of cyberbullying (Grow 1 & 2).

Trisha

Trisha decided to pursue the inquiry question, "How can stereotypes affect bullying and what can you do to break out of it?" She created an animated video on stereotypes, labels, and bullying in schools. Trisha explained her project and motivation for it, saying: "I made an animation for my project ... It was about bullying and basically how stereotypes and labels can affect people. I know my friends always joke around [using certain labels and stereotypes] ... but I know for some people, it might actually hurt them when you call them something [a label]." In her video, she used her own voice and original drawings to share her story:

> We all know what cliques are—groups that basically protect you and have similar interests as you. However, what people don't know is that some people don't have a clique. Some people just have a few friends they hang out with. I'm one of those people. But see, kids have a habit of categorizing things that don't belong in groups. Like me, I've heard all the names- emo, edgy, goth, nerd, dork... they don't care who I am. They just want to see my label.

In her project she adopted a critical stance arguing that we are all different and we must not hurt each other by labeling or categorizing people (Think 1 & 2). By creating and sharing the video, she reflected on her own situation, demonstrated empathy and equity in knowledge-building (Grow 3), and contributed to the discussion on labeling (Share 2).

Labels (School project original animation)

Figure 2. Trisha's Maker Product

Jill

Jill's inquiry question was, "Why do teens shield themselves from society, and how does it affect their everyday life?" She conducted research on the effect of bullying in teens' everyday life and made a video blog to show everyday experiences of teens suffering from bullying in schools. Jill explained her project:

> My project [inquiry question] was: why do teens shield themselves from society like outcasts, and how does it affect their immediate life? I did a vlog and what it showed was bullying through a kid's eyes. Adults don't always know what goes on. They can picture what's going on, but they don't know how kids feel. So, I vlogged a day at school just to show adults what goes on inside the walls of middle school and what bullying looks like through our perspective, just so they have more detailed thought of what bullying is.

The maker project met her desire to speak out on bullying in teens' everyday life from their own voice and perspective. She interviewed several students in her school to document teens' lived experiences in schools. Her project sought interactions with a range of learners demonstrating interest in others' perspectives (Grow 1, 2) and represented diverse viewpoints (Create 3, Share 2).

In addition to the analyses of maker artifacts that we have presented above for the purpose and the scope of this chapter, analyses of student journals for recording all learning activities throughout the unit (e.g., their responses to readings, videos, role playing, research experiences, and more) revealed that students were meeting many competencies across the AASL standards areas.

Implications and Conclusions

The case study presented in this chapter shows how public-school educators and students co-create and redefine making—for their own learning as well as for social justice. The unit featured student creativity, intentional learning and guidance, relevancy to youth life, increased student ownership and choice, and raising awareness to make the world a better place through making.

Table 2. Maker Artifact Analysis

Students	Maker Products	AASL National School Library Standards
Kate	Mockup Instagram	Create 1 & 3, Share 1 & 2, Grow 1 & 2
Trisha	Animation	Think 1 & 2, Share 2, Grow 3
Jill	Video blog	Grow 1 & 2, Create 3, Share 2

School libraries in the U.S. have practiced anti-bullying movements by taking various approaches—from developing anti-bullying curriculums, collections, and bibliographies, to outreach to various stakeholders, such as parents and community members.[14] The case study suggests that the maker approach can further enhance efforts to make the school and the world a safer and more welcoming place for all. In this unit, students engaged in hands-on projects to demonstrate their learning on a social issue, share with peers, and voice the injustices they encounter. The examinations of maker artifacts revealed that students are fulfilling many of the AASL Standards in the area of Include and beyond. The artifact analysis approach can be replicated in relation to other standards and competencies in order to assess student learning outcomes through making. The study shows that maker pedagogy can be effective in increasing student empathy and engagement in social issues. Students in this unit felt great empathy with people involved in bullying and expressed their willingness to take actions to counter bullying, both in school and online. Our findings concur with previous successful cases on making and anti-bullying in which youth developed an anti-bullying app that crowdsourced "bully hot zones" in the community, and in which youth designed an alarm hat, backpack, and jackets to call for help when bullying occurs.[15]

---

14. Beverly Goldberg, "How Libraries Help Kids Stand Up to Bullying," *American Libraries* 45, no. 9/10 (September 2014): 15–16; American Association of School Librarians, "2011 School Libraries Count! AASL's National Longitudinal Survey of School Libraries," 2011, http://www.ala.org/aasl/sites/ala.org.aasl/files/content/advocacy/research/docs/AASL-SLC-2011-FINALweb.pdf; Daniel Callison, "Resources and Research on Bullying," School Library Monthly 30, no. 1 (2013): 20–23; American Association of School Librarians, *Empowering Learners: Guidelines for School Library Media Programs* (Chicago, IL: American Association of School Librarians, 2009); Shannon M. Oltmann, "'They Kind of Rely on the Library': School Librarians Serving LGBT Students," *Journal of Research on Libraries & Young Adults* 7, no. 3 (December 2016): 1–21.

15. Janette Hughes et al., "Addressing Bullying through Critical Making," *British Journal of Educational Technology* 50, no. 1 (2019): 309–25, https://doi.org/10.1111/bjet.12714; Angela Calabrese Barton and Edna Tan, "A Longitudinal Study of Equity-Oriented STEM-Rich Making Among Youth From Historically Marginalized Communities," *American Educational Research Journal* 55, no. 4 (August 1, 2018): 761–800, https://doi.org/10.3102/0002831218758668.

While various learning pedagogies and mindsets can be applied to makerspaces, such as inquiry-based, project-based, tinkering, and design thinking approaches,[16] the researchers and educators in this project strived to develop a maker learning model that works in the standards-based K-12 curriculum in a formal school setting. The maker approach was integrated into diverse learning activities that meet the curriculum needs, and intentional guidance was provided by educators throughout the unit. Students from different backgrounds came up with a project that addresses their own inquiry question and learning. The educators did not impose a particular technology or tool, so the learning environment accommodated different student interests and expertise. Emphasis was on maker mindsets—such as creative minds, problem-solving, and risk-taking and innovation rather than making a safe choice to get a good grade—as well as learning outcomes, including the intentional use of technology to deepen inquiry.

For successful maker learning in schools, the role of school librarian is critical. In collaboration with other educators, school librarians can provide expertise in technologies, maker pedagogies, and learning processes. While makerspaces and maker programs are available in different out-of-school settings, a significant portion of K-12 students may not take advantage of those informal learning opportunities. Carefully designed and scaffolded maker learning in school libraries will not only bridge creative and self-directed learning and curriculum-based formal learning, but also ensure all students from diverse backgrounds can benefit from the maker pedagogy, including those typically underrepresented in STEAM (Science, Technology, Engineering, Art, and Math) or who may not currently self-identify as makers.

Acknowledgement

The study presented in this chapter is part of a three-year, design-based research project on making and school libraries. The project was made possible by the 2016 Institute of Museum and Library Services (IMLS) National Leadership Grant for Libraries (LG-81-16-0151) with

---

16. Maker Ed, "Youth MakerSpace Playbook," 2015, http://tinyurl.com/makery-outhplay. 41-46.

partnerships between Norman Public Schools, the University of Oklahoma, and the University of Illinois at Urbana-Champaign.

Bibliography

American Association of School Librarians. *Empowering Learners: Guidelines for School Library Media Programs.* Chicago, IL: American Association of School Librarians, 2009.

American Association of School Librarians. "2011 School Libraries Count! AASL's National Longitudinal Survey of School Libraries." Accessed May 1, 2019. http://www.ala.org/aasl/sites/ala.org.aasl/files/content/advocacy/research/docs/AASL-SLC-2011-FINAL-web.pdf.

American Association of School Librarians. *National School Library Standards for Learners, School Librarians, and School Libraries.* Chicago, IL: American Library Association, 2018.

Baker, Sheila F., and Bonnie Alexander. "A Major Making Undertaking: A New Librarian Transforms a Middle School Library into a Makerspace Aligned to High School Career Endorsements." *Knowledge Quest* 46, no. 5 (2018): 64-69.

Blakemore, Megan. "Problem Scoping Design Thinking and Close Reading: Makerspaces in the School Library." *Knowledge Quest* 46, no. 4 (2018): 66-69.

Blikstein, Paulo. "Digital Fabrication and 'Making' in Education: The Democratization of Invention." In *FabLabs: Of Machines, Makers and Inventors*, edited by Julia Walter-Herrmann and Corinne Büching, 1-21. Wetzlar, Germany: Transcript-Verlag, 2013.

Calabrese Barton, Angela and Edna Tan. "A Longitudinal Study of Equity-Oriented STEM-Rich Making Among Youth from Historically Marginalized Communities." *American Educational Research Journal* 55, no. 4 (2018): 761-800.

Callison, Daniel. "Resources and Research on Bullying." *School Library Monthly* 30, no. 1 (2013): 20-23.

Clapp, Edward P., Jessica Ross, Jennifer Oxman Ryan, and Shari Tishman. *Maker-Centered Learning: Empowering Young People to Shape Their Worlds*. San Francisco, CA: Jossey-Bass, 2017.

Davies, Sarah R.. *Hackerspaces: Making the Maker Movement*. Malden, MA: Polity Press, 2017.

Dougherty, Dale. "Learning by Making: American Kids Should be Building Rockets and Robots, Not Taking Standardized Tests." Last modified June 4, 2012. http://www.slate.com/articles/technology/future_tense/2012/06/maker_faire_and_science_education_american_kids_should_be_building_rockets_and_robots_not_taking_standardized_tests_.html.

Dougherty, Dale. "Makerspaces in Education and DARPA." Last modified April 4, 2012. https://makezine.com/2012/04/04/makerspaces-in-education-and-darpa/.

Goldberg, Beverly. "How Libraries Help Kids Stand Up to Bullying." *American Libraries* 45, no. 9/10 (2014): 15-16.

Halverson, Erika, and Kimberly Sheridan. "The Maker Movement in Education." *Harvard Educational Review* 84, no. 4 (2014): 495-504.

Herold, Benjamin. "The 'Maker' Movement Is Coming to K-12: Can Schools Get It Right?." Last modified June 6, 2016. https://www.edweek.org/ew/articles/2016/06/09/the-maker-movement-is-coming-to-k-12.html.

Hughes, Janette, Laura Morrison, Ami Mamolo, Jennifer Laffier and Suzanne de Castell. "Addressing Bullying through Critical Making." *British Journal of Educational Technology* 50, no. 1 (2019): 309-325.

Koyczan, Shane. "To This Day Project - Shane Koyczan." Accessed May 6, 2019. https://www.youtube.com/watch?v=ltun92DfnPY.

Kuhlthau, Carol C., Leslie K. Maniotes, and Ann K. Caspari. *Guided Inquiry: Learning in the 21st Century*. Santa Barbara, CA: Libraries Unlimited, 2015.

Maker Ed. "Youth MakerSpace Playbook." Last modified 2015, http://tinyurl.com/makeryouthplay. 41-46.

Martin, Lee. "The Promise of the Maker Movement for Education," *Journal of Pre-College Engineering Education Research (J-PEER)* 5, no. 1 (2015): 4.

Martinez, Sylvia Libow and Gary S. Stager. *Invent to Learn: Making, Tinkering, and Engineering in the Classroom.* Torrance, CA: Constructing Modern Knowledge Press: 2013.

Mattie J. T. Stepanek Foundation, "The Mattie J. T. Stepanek Foundation," 2019, http://www.mattieonline.com.

Moorefield-Lang Heather, *School Library Makerspaces in Action.* Santa Barbara, CA: Libraries Unlimited: 2018.

Moorefield-Lang, Heather and Vanessa Kitzie. "Makerspaces for All: Serving LGBTQ Makers in School Libraries," *Knowledge Quest* 47, no. 1 (2018): 46-50.

National Center for Education Statistics. "Search for Public Schools." Last modified 2019, https://nces.ed.gov/.

Oltmann, Shannon M. ""They Kind of Rely on the Library": School Librarians Serving LGBT Students." *Journal of Research on Libraries & Young Adults* 7, no. 3 (2016): 1-21.

Peppler, Kylie, Erica Halverson, and Yasmin B. Kafai. *Makeology: Makerspaces as Learning Environments. Vol. 1.* New York: Routledge, 2016.

Preddy, Leslie. *School Library Makerspaces: Grades 6-12.* Santa Barbara, CA: Libraries Unlimited, 2013.

Chapter 8

BARRIERS TO INCLUSIVITY IN MAKERSPACES

DiMitri Higginbotham and Rob Rouse

The Maker Movement has given rise to community makerspaces across the country and around the globe. Community makerspaces are physical places organized and run to support their members in collaborating, making with a wide variety of tools and materials, and sharing the results of their efforts. As the Maker Movement has continued to grow and as community makerspaces have become more and more popular, institutions have increasingly recognized them as places to experiment, create, and iterate.[1] In addition, researchers have recognized makerspaces as places in which people have unique opportunities to learn through co-participation in a variety of making and non-making activities.[2]

The primary activity that occurs in any makerspace is making. Egalitarian views of making frame it as accessible to all, encompassing a wide range of physical and digital activities, and a vehicle for the democratization of fabrication tools and skills.[3] Under this view, all people have

---

1. T.W. Barrett, M.C. Pizzico, B. Levy, R.L. Nagel, J.S. Linsey, K.G. Talley, C.R. Forest, and W.C. Newstetter, *A Review of University Maker Spaces* (Paper, 122nd American Society for Engineering Education Annual Conference & Exposition, Seattle, WA, 2015); J.J. Burke, *Makerspaces: A Practical Guide for Librarians* (Lanham, MD: Rowman & Littlefield, 2014).

2. E.R. Halverson, and K.M. Sheridan, "The Maker Movement in Education," *Harvard Educational Review* 84 (2014): 495-504.

3. Chris Anderson, *Makers: The New Industrial Revolution* (New York: Random House, 2012).

the opportunity to create artifacts, build skills, and express themselves through making. The egalitarian view of making is the dominant view of making held throughout community makerspaces in the United States. However, in contrast, Buechley[4] reported that community makerspaces tend to attract users who are male, white, and upper middle class, demonstrating that even when makerspaces are founded on egalitarian views of making, this does not guarantee they will become inclusive places.

Recently, makerspaces have moved beyond community venues and into formal institutions such as libraries, museums, universities, and K-12 schools. As these types of makerspaces multiply nationwide, so do concerns about inclusivity, the purposeful effort to promote and maintain access to makerspaces for individuals from historically marginalized or underrepresented groups.[5] Of special concern is the inclusivity of makerspaces in K-12 schools. Schools with makerspaces can limit inclusivity by inadvertently preventing certain populations of students from accessing the makerspace. For example, we have observed that under pressure from high-stakes assessments, teachers in some schools are encouraged to keep students from attending makerspaces in favor of remediation (i.e., doing additional work in a deficient subject area). As a result, struggling students do not have the opportunity to use the makerspace. Similarly, when teachers employ their makerspaces exclusively for after-school activities or clubs, only a small and specific population of students gains access to the makerspace.

In order to create inclusive makerspaces in which all participants have opportunities to engage in making, it is crucially important to identify barriers that may, intentionally or unintentionally, prevent different populations from using them. In this chapter, we report using the principles of human-centered design (HCD) to identify some of these barriers (e.g., cost, access, and culture) to inclusivity in makerspaces through interviewing a number of makerspace directors.

---

4. L. Buechley, "Closing address," *FabLearn*, Palo Alto, CA: Stanford University, 2013, http://edstream.stanford.edu/Video/Play/883b61dd951d4d3f90abeec65eead2911d.

5. K.M. Steele, M. Cakmal, and B. Blaser, "Accessible Making: Designing a Makerspace for Accessibility," *International Journal of Designs for Learning* 9 (2018): 114-21

Human-Centered Design

HCD is a collection of attitudes and methods useful for solving complex real-world problems.[6] Human-centered designers work in teams and rely on mindsets such as empathy, iteration, and learning from failure to carry them through the design process. When confronted with ambiguity or uncertainty, designers remain optimistic that there is a solution and fall back on using a variety of HCD methods to make progress towards reaching that solution. Using a variety of methods encourages designers to develop a first-hand understanding of the human needs and behaviors related to a system. In addition, it allows designers to repeatedly draw on their collective creativity to reframe questions as well as make and test prototypes.

Typically, HCD unfolds in three phases: inspiration, ideation, and implementation.[7] During the inspiration phase, designers frame the challenge, complete relevant research, and collect information through interviews. Next, in the ideation phase, designers share what they learned in the inspiration phase, identify themes in the data, brainstorm ideas related to design opportunities, and create and test a number of low-resolution prototypes. Finally, in the implementation phase, designers work to bring solutions into the real world by establishing partnerships, performing continued piloting and iteration, and building a business model.

Using HCD in the World

Businesses and non-profits use HCD to generate innovative products, processes, and services that meet the needs of an ever-changing populace. The story of Doug Dietz is perhaps the quintessential HCD success story. Doug, an industrial designer for GE Healthcare who developed medical imaging systems, used HCD to reimagine the MRI experience for pediatric patients. While visiting a hospital to inspect an MRI machine he designed, Doug was taken aback when he discovered that

---

6. IDEO, *The Field Guide to Human-Centered Design: Design Kit.*, IDEO.org, 2015.

7. IDEO, *Field Guide*, 11.

for the majority of pediatric patients, the prospect of undergoing an MRI produced so much anxiety that they needed to be sedated for the procedure. To improve the MRI experience for pediatric patients, Doug assembled a team and spent time interviewing children at a daycare and learning what it was like to be a pediatric patient. Based on what he learned, Doug and his team redesigned the MRI experience by decorating the MRI room and equipment with pirate-themed decals and inviting patients to play the lead role in an adventure story in which the MRI technicians dressed as characters and followed a script. Implementing these changes resulted in a large reduction in the number of children who were sedated for the MRI, turning a potentially terrifying experience into an experience in which children were eager to participate.[8]

Using HCD To Study Inclusivity in Makerspaces
In our investigation of barriers to inclusivity in makerspaces, we used HCD for several reasons. First, HCD helped us approach our work from an unbiased and non-judgmental position. This allowed us to empathize with makerspace directors while also seeking to learn more about a sensitive topic. Second, HCD allowed us to be flexible with how we collected information from makerspace directors and gave us the freedom to dig deeper into a subset of that information. Third, HCD allowed us to look for trends and patterns in the data we collected while also keeping in mind practical aspirations. That is, HCD kept us grounded in the data and forced us to consider real circumstances when designing.

Method

Participants
Participants included seven individuals (four men and three women) who directed makerspaces at various locations across a metroplex. Of the directors, two worked at university makerspaces, one located in a

---

[8]. See T. Kelley, and D. Kelley, *Creative Confidence: Unleashing the Creative Potential Within Us All* (New York: Crown Business, 2013) for a more detailed account of Doug's use of HCD.

public university's library and the other located in a private university's engineering school; two worked in PreK-12 makerspaces, one located in a public all-girls PreK-8 school and the other located in a private coeducational PreK-12 school; one worked at a museum makerspace; one worked at a makerspace housed in a public library; and one was the president of a community makerspace. Participants were selected based on their availability and willingness to engage in interviews.

HCD Techniques

We used five HCD techniques to explore the topic of inclusivity in makerspaces. The techniques we used were recognized as best practices in HCD[9] or were developed in collaboration with other human-centered designers as new techniques that might yield insights specific to the context (makerspaces) and the topic (inclusivity) under investigation. In the subsections below we define the individual techniques and explain our rationale for using each technique.

Exploratory research. Designers use exploratory research to get better acquainted with the broader context surrounding a specific topic. Doing exploratory research often entails reviewing relevant literature and visiting appropriate Internet sites. We used exploratory research to learn more about the current state of thinking related to inclusivity and equity in makerspaces. Specifically, we searched the Internet to find publications related to equity, diversity, and inclusivity in makerspaces. After identifying a number of publications, we read them and developed an annotated bibliography. Throughout this process, the first and second author met regularly to discuss the results of the exploratory research and how it might inform our next steps.

Interview. Designers use interviews to learn about the people and organizations with whom they engage. Interview guides, or pre-planned lists of questions, provide a framework for designers to facilitate in-depth on-topic discussions with interviewees. Importantly, designers take great care to craft non-judgmental questions that demonstrate their

---

9. IDEO, *Field Guide*, 29-69.

knowledge in a specific area. As a result, interviewees feel comfortable sharing personal and technical information.

Based on what we learned through our exploratory research, we crafted our interview guide to elicit information about how makerspace directors perceived the: (a) Maker Movement, (b) role of their makerspace, (c) demographics of their patrons, and (d) future of maker education. Our interview guide consisted of eight questions. Examples of questions include: What is the role of your makerspace? Do you think about the demographics of your patrons? and What is your vision for the future of this space? (See **Table 1** for a complete list of interview guide questions.) Interviews occurred after the guided tour and before the card sort and ideal makerspace sketch. Participating in these activities lasted for roughly two hours.

Guided tour. Designers embark on guided tours to learn about people's habits and values by immersing themselves in that person's home or work environment. Guided tours are excellent ways to build rapport with interviewees as well as to collect notes and photographs that help preserve key pieces of information related to the space and how it is arranged. We used guided tours to learn more about the makerspace's size, membership, and hours of operation as well as its tools, procedures, and culture. Guided tours lasted anywhere from fifteen minutes to an hour.

Card Sort. A card sort is an activity that designers use to discover what is most important to a person or a group of people. To perform a card sort, the designer first creates a unique deck consisting of cards labeled with a single word or image. Next, the designer asks the interviewee to organize the cards in the deck based on how she sees fit. Afterward, the interviewee explains her reasoning and the designer records notes and insights. The deck we developed for use with makerspace directors included eight cards labeled with one of the following concrete or abstract concepts related to the Maker Movement, makerspaces, or maker education: high-tech tools, low-tech tools, craftsmanship, education, community outreach, hobbies, soft-skills and creative expression. These eight topics were chosen for variety and the

Number	Question	Follow-up question(s)
1	Tell me about your past and what brought you to be a makerspace director.	
2	What is the role of your makerspace?	
3	What do you feel about the maker movement?	How does your space fit into the maker movement?
4	Does your space offer workshops or one-on-one sessions for skill building?	Who facilitates this? Do you assess skills after workshops?
5	Do you think about the demographics of your patrons?	Do you feel the need to reach out to marginalized groups in making and STEM?
6	What is the role of a makerspace in education?	
7	What is your vision for the future of this space?	
8	What is your vision for the future of makerspaces and maker education?	

Table 1. Interview Guide Questions

ability to elicit conversation among participants and the interviewer. Card sorts typically lasted twenty minutes and occurred after the guided tour.

Ideal makerspace sketch. We created this technique as a way for makerspace directors to point out perceived deficiencies in their current makerspace and elicit outside-of-the-box solutions to existing makerspace problems. We began the ideal makerspace sketch by giving the director a blank sheet of paper. Next, we asked the director to sketch what his ideal makerspace would look like if he had unlimited money, materials, and space. When finished with the task, we asked follow up questions about the sketch and recorded notes and insights. The ideal makerspace sketch typically lasted ten minutes and occurred after the card sort.

Download and Synthesis

After using the techniques described above to collect information from each of the makerspace directors we interviewed, we shifted our focus to sharing the information with fellow designers using a process called downloading. During a download, designers begin by filling out sticky notes and sticking them to a sheet of paper or an oversized board to capture and display relevant chunks of information from each interview.

Next, designers present the information to outside designers who were not a part of the interview. During this process, the outside designers ask questions in an attempt to better understand the system under study, and the designers add additional sticky notes to the board in response to these questions. We participated in a download with a small group of outside designers after completing every other interview. In this case, the outside designers were seven students enrolled in a masters-level HCD program.

After the download, designers seek to synthesize their findings from across the different interviews they have completed. Synthesis allows designers to identify patterns and themes. Designers do this by moving around sticky notes, grouping and sorting them into categories. During this process, relationships and patterns emerge that represent opportunities for design. We used the post-download information from the seven interviews we completed to find themes and develop insights related to inclusivity in makerspaces. We report these themes in the next section.

Findings

Although we visited a wide variety of makerspaces and spoke with a diverse group of makerspace directors, we found that almost all of them shared a similar set of values around making and maker education. For example, the large majority of directors we interviewed agreed that the democratization of knowledge and information were key tenets of the Maker Movement and should represent core values of any makerspace. In addition, we found that directors of formal and informal makerspaces alike agreed that makerspace staff should facilitate users' learning of new skills and competencies through the use of low- and high-tech tools.

Makerspace directors adopted a variety of assessment methods. Several directors reported collecting tool and device usage data across users, while some directors reported administering user-satisfaction surveys. Similarly, several directors reported sending out questionnaires meant to judge users' current skills and future interests. Directors who reported performing these types of assessments also reported using the data gleaned from these assessments to make purchases and offer additional training to users in an effort to improve the makerspace. Directors who did not report performing assessments were less likely to be able to tell who used the makerspace, how often, and to what purpose.

Finally, we identified three barriers to inclusivity in makerspaces: cost, access, and culture. As mentioned previously, these barriers seemed to prevent makerspaces from being inclusive. It is important to note that these barriers were largely known to makerspace directors. We describe each of the barriers to inclusivity in the subsections below.

Cost as a Barrier to Inclusivity
Making can be expensive. These expenses are split between two parties: the makerspace and the user. The makerspace must purchase and maintain tools and machines as well as hire and train staff. As a result of these expenses, some makerspaces cover the cost of operating the makerspace by collecting dues from users. Thus, some users are on the hook to pay fees and purchase their own supplies (e.g., raw materials, software) to fully take advantage of the makerspace. These users also tend to invest a significant amount of time learning how to operate software and machines in the makerspace. Under these circumstances, the majority of users are those who have the money and time to work in the makerspace.

A number of directors recognized that the cost of belonging to a makerspace might prevent individuals of low socioeconomic status from gaining access to the makerspace. Fortunately, several of these same directors had actively worked to introduce programs to reduce cost as a barrier for these potential users. For example, one director explained offering a reduced price for students while another explained offering to reduce the cost of membership if the user agreed to teach a class related to tool, machine, or software in the makerspace; encouraging users to learn skills quickly in order to share their knowledge and reduce their own membership fee. Several directors also reported attempting to offset the cost of makerspace membership by applying for grants and sponsorships from companies and corporations.

Access as a Barrier to Inclusivity

Makerspaces can be difficult to physically access. For example, although some academic makerspaces (i.e., makerspaces found on college campuses) are located in common areas where they are visible to the general population of students, others are located in out-of-the-way locations, affiliated with certain departments or schools, or visible only to a subset of the student population. This difference impacts the population of students who enter the makerspace. Notably, makerspaces located in common areas tend to draw a more diverse group of users (i.e., users who identify with a variety of majors or departments). Makerspaces located away from common areas have a more homogeneous population of users who are more likely to be affiliated with the school or department in which the makerspace is located.

Community makerspaces can be difficult to access as well. Community makerspaces that depend on monthly dues generated by members may not be located near the city center. Although this practical decision may help the organization lease more affordable space, it can prevent a subset of potential users from accessing the makerspace. Unless an individual has easy access to reliable transportation, he or she may find it difficult to travel to the makerspace.

In K-12 makerspaces, accessibility is related to programming rather than proximity. That is, students in different academic tracks may have limited access to a makerspace. For example, a student on an advanced placement track or a remedial track may not have room in his or her schedule to take a class that makes use of the makerspace, as these classes may fall outside of the courses required for their track. In addition, for K-12 schools that have a makerspace, it is difficult to program students into the space because of the limited footprint and resources of the makerspace, but also because makerspaces are typically staffed by a small number of teachers, which inherently limits their capacity for working with large numbers of students.

Most directors were keenly aware of the difficulties people had accessing their makerspace. However, unlike cost as a barrier, access as a barrier is a more difficult problem to solve as it would be incredibly difficult (or sometimes impossible) to move a makerspace from one location to another or to program all students into a class that uses the makerspace. For directors of academic makerspaces and community makerspaces, one solution to this problem was to perform outreach to populations who may not have access to a makerspace. Outreach ranged from holding open workshops at the makerspace to traveling to other venues near and far with the goal of introducing people to the value of making and the Maker Movement.

Culture as a Barrier to Inclusivity
The culture of a makerspace (i.e., the manifestations of the mindsets and practices valued by the members of the makerspace) can either be inviting or intimidating. Makerspaces with an inviting culture sought to remove barriers that could hinder people from walking in the door. For example, academic and community makerspaces promoted easy entry by welcoming outsiders into the makerspace during regularly scheduled times. In addition, makerspaces with an inviting culture had a heterogeneous curriculum that changed in response to the needs and wants of their users. Many makerspace directors reported offering classes or workshops for beginners to learn new skills or operate existing machinery. Leading workshops was a point of pride for many makerspace members and they considered it a way to give back to the makerspace and propagate the values of the Maker Movement. In contrast to makerspaces with an inviting culture, some makerspaces had an intimidating culture. These makerspaces were perceived to be closed off and had few opportunities for potential users to enter the makerspace. In addition, there were few formal opportunities for novices to learn from more knowledgeable members.

Makerspace directors who wished to create an inclusive culture reported focusing on hiring a more diverse staff. Several of the directors we interviewed had gone to great lengths to recruit staff that reflected even more diversity than was present in the makerspace community. Their rationale was that having a diverse staff allowed potential users of all races and cultures to see themselves working and learning in the makerspace. In addition to hiring a diverse staff, directors also emphasized hiring a staff with disparate skills. For example, hiring teachers and artists as well as engineers and technicians was viewed as a way of creating a more inclusive culture. Their rationale was that a staff with varied experiences and specialties would be more adept at facilitating an array of workshops and helping a greater variety of people.

Discussion

The rising popularity of makerspaces has positioned them as innovative learning environments in which individuals of varied backgrounds can come together to work and share ideas. However, we believe the potential of makerspaces as learning environments is limited by their ability to attract and retain a diverse group of users. In this chapter, we described using HDC to identify barriers to inclusivity in makerspaces. We found that although directors operated makerspaces based on a similar set of values, issues related to cost, access, and culture limited users' access to makerspaces.

Reflections and Next Steps

Because lack of money commonly prevents people from participating in all types of events and activities, we were not surprised to discover that cost presented a barrier to inclusivity in makerspaces. However, we were surprised to find that most directors were aware of cost as a barrier and had a plan (or several plans in some cases) to reduce cost for those who were interested in joining the makerspace. These cost-saving tactics, such as seeking sponsorship from various businesses, represent concrete ways of removing cost as a barrier for populations of individuals who have the desire, but not the funds, to be a part of a makerspace.

Finding solutions to the significantly more complex issues of access and culture is potentially more difficult than finding a solution to the issue of cost. Self-promotion appears to be one method of increasing access to makerspaces while concurrently transforming a makerspace's culture from intimidating to inviting. For example, hosting community events, reaching out to the media, and arranging opportunities for potential users to experience what the makerspace has to offer are ways that directors have successfully positioned makerspaces as inviting places where people from all walks of life are welcome to work and learn. Interestingly, although we are especially concerned with inclusivity in K-12 school makerspaces, it seems that those makerspaces are the least able to make changes that would reduce access as a barrier.

Although some makerspace directors reported using assessments to drive makerspace improvements, none of these assessments focused on collecting information related to the issues of cost, access, or culture. We reasoned that this is because many makerspace directors were uncomfortable discussing and addressing these sometimes-taboo issues. Thus, for each of these issues, it seems that thoughtful and targeted assessment could offer invaluable data for directors who seek to make their makerspaces more inclusive. In the future, and following with the tenets of the ideation and implementation phases of HCD, we plan to create an array of measures to learn more about how assessment can provide inclusivity-related information to makerspace directors. With the help of a select group of directors, we plan to prototype the measures we create by distributing them to the members of several different types of makerspaces.

Bibliography

Anderson, Chris. *Makers: The New Industrial Revolution.* New York: Random House, 2012.

Barrett, T. W., M.C. Pizzico, B. Levy, R.L. Nagel, J.S. Linsey, K.G. Talley, C.R. Forest, and W.C. Newstetter. *A Review of University Maker Spaces.* Paper presented at the 122nd American Society for Engineering Education Annual Conference & Exposition, Seattle, WA, 2015.

Buechley, L. "Closing address." *FabLearn*, Palo Alto, CA: Stanford University, 2013. http://edstream.stanford.edu/Video/Play/883b61dd951d4d3f90abeec65eead2911d.

Burke, J.J. *Makerspaces: A Practical Guide for Librarians* Lanham, MD: Rowman & Littlefield, 2014

Halverson, E.R., and K.M. Sheridan. "The Maker Movement in Education" *Harvard Educational Review* 84 (2014): 495-504

IDEO. *The Field Guide to Human-Centered Design: Design Kit.*, IDEO.org, 2015.

Kelley, T., and D. Kelley. *Creative Confidence: Unleashing the Creative Potential Within Us All.* New York: Crown Business, 2013.

Steele, K. M., M. Cakmak, and B. Blaser. "Accessible Making: Designing a Makerspace for Accessibility." *International Journal of Designs for Learning* 9 (2018): 114-21.

Chapter 9

SUPPORTING MAKING IN LIBRARIES RATHER THAN MAKERSPACES: RETHINKING THE (MAKER)SPACE FOR RURAL LIBRARIES

Aubrey Rogowski, Victor R. Lee, and Mimi Recker

Introduction

Popular media has typically depicted making as integrally involving digital fabrication equipment such as 3D printers and laser cutters or other costly equipment—all housed within a dedicated "makerspace." Such makerspaces often are associated with high threshold activities such as robotics or programmable microcontrollers such as the Arduino. Often, access to these makerspaces requires having a paid membership or paying an entrance fee in order to be able to use the space and its equipment.[1] These fees can be a barrier to lower income users; for example, a recent study found that the median salary of those using these types of spaces is over $100,000 per year.[2] Moreover, makerspaces have catered to stereotypical male interests such as robotics and metalworking. For example, one review revealed the dominant image of makers as upper middle class, middle-aged white men, conveying the message that making is a masculine hobby reserved for privileged

---

1. Andrew Schrock, "Education in Disguise: Culture of a Hacker and Maker Space," *InterActions: UCLA Journal of Education and Information Studies* 10, no. 1 (2014).

2. Angela Calabrese Barton and Edna Tan, "A Longitudinal Study of Equity-Oriented STEM-Rich Making among Youth from Historically Marginalized Communities," *American Educational Research Journal* 55, no. 4 (2018): 761-800.

people with exclusive access to these technologies and spaces.[3] This typical depiction of a makerspace continues to promote and reinforce the underrepresentation of women, girls, and minorities in Science, Technology, Engineering and Mathematics (STEM) fields and unfairly determines who can be a "maker" and what is considered "making."[4]

Increasingly, libraries are joining the making trend by establishing makerspaces that provide access to these tools within dedicated spaces.[5] These trends have spanned all kinds of library types (from school to public) and settings (urban, suburban, and rural). While making brings with it a number of desirable qualities, such as the opportunity to democratize access to digital and fabrication technologies,[6] we should be cautious about duplicating and uncritically importing traditional makerspace models into library spaces. Instead, libraries should be promoting maker activities that avoid gender bias and promote inclusivity and accessibility for all, regardless of social status or income.

In this chapter, we describe parts of a three-year collaborative research study in which we partnered with librarians in small-town and rural libraries to implement STEM-rich maker activities for their youth patrons.[7] We focus on how librarians can adapt the traditional makerspace model to provide inclusive, low-cost, and sustainable maker programming in their libraries.

---

3. Leah Buechley, "A Critical Look at Making," Keynote address presented at the Annual FabLearn Conference, Stanford, CA, October 2013.

4. Calabrese Barton and Tan, "A Longitudinal Study of Equity-Oriented STEM-Rich Making."

5. Leslie B. Preddy, *School Library Makerspaces: Grades 6-12*. (Santa Barbara, CA: ABC-CLIO, 2013).

6. Paulo Blikstein, "Digital Fabrication and 'Making' in Education: The Democratization of Invention, in *FabLabs: Of Machines, Makers, and Inventors*, eds. J. Walter-Herrmann and C. Buching (Bielefeld, DE: Transcript Publishers, 2013).

7. Victor R. Lee, Mimi Recker, and Abigail L. Phillips, "Conjecture Mapping the Library: Iterative Refinements Toward Supporting Maker Learning Activities in Small Community Spaces," in *Proceedings of the International Conference of the Learning Sciences* (2018): 320-327.

Makerspaces vs. Making in the Library

Because of a lack of resources and space, we have observed that most rural libraries are limited in their ability to create and sustain their own library-based makerspaces. Often, only libraries in the most affluent areas are able to offer these types of resources to their patrons.[8] In addition, many librarians do not have the skills, knowledge, or expertise to build and run these types of spaces.[9] Each device, whether it is a 3D printer, laser cutter, or CNC machine, has its own interface and requirements for basic operation. Some require the use of custom software too, further increasing the overhead and cost for a lone librarian managing a rural library. Moreover, these technologies also have safety requirements and can require training to be used safely. However, these are the tools and equipment that many expect to see in a full-fledged makerspace.

Instead, we argue that the typical makerspace model with a shop-like room filled with fabrication equipment is neither affordable, sustainable, practical, nor desirable for most rural and small-town public libraries. Instead, libraries can offer access to maker activities rather than offering access to a makerspace. Making is not defined by the use of a specific set of tools, such as a 3D printer. Rather, making can be defined a set of practices where makers are creating and testing artifacts. Making can take place in a variety of spaces, and the sense that it requires a designated makerspace can perpetuate patterns of exclusion that are associated with makerspace patronage. By duplicating the traditional makerspace model, libraries may inadvertently perpetuate making as an exclusionary activity. This can result in excluding youth who may have non-traditional maker interests.[10]

---

8. Linda W. Braun, Maureen L. Harman, Sandra Hughes-Hassell, and Kafi Kumasi, "The Future of Library Services for and with Teens: A Call to Action." *Young Adult Library Services* (2014).

9. Heather Moorefield-Lang, "Change in the Making: Makerspaces and the Ever-Changing Landscape of Libraries," *TechTrends* 59, no. 3 (2015): 107-112.

10. Mega Subramaniam, Ligaya Scaff, Saba Kawas, Kelly M. Hoffman, and Katie Davis, "Using Technology to Support Equity and Inclusion in Youth Library Programming: Current Practices and Future Opportunities," *Library Quarterly* 88 no. 4 (2018): 315-331.

The few rural libraries that we have known to implement the more traditional makerspace model in our work have been less successful in attracting significant patron usage. In one library, we noted that their dedicated makerspace often sits empty, rarely used but for a few male patrons who already know about making and are keen to have access to a dedicated space. From our visits to these libraries, the makerspaces were typically separate rooms located away from the rest of the library collection and gave the impression that permission was needed to enter them, even when the door was propped open. The rationale for this was to keep the noise from the makerspace from permeating the rest of the library and to secure equipment in a space that could be closed off if necessary. However, this sequestration runs the risk of limiting access when the librarian's goal is to provide more diverse services.

An alternative to the creation of a separate makerspace, as we describe below, is to focus on offering maker programming in already existing library spaces. Existing spaces can include tables set out among book collections, study areas, or rooms that the library already has access to by virtue of being a civic establishment. We have found that programs held in such reconfigurable spaces in more common areas of a library with a variety of low threshold and affordable activities were highly attended by youth patrons.[11] By taking this approach of (re-) using existing space, rural libraries can cultivate flexible learning spaces that allow youth to experiment, explore, and create.[12]

Reconfigurable and Reusable (Maker)spaces and Making

As part of a three-year collaborative research study, we partnered with librarians in small-town and rural libraries to implement STEM-rich

---

11. Victor R. Lee, Whitney Lewis, Kristin A. Searle, Mimi Recker, Jennifer Hansen, and Abigail L. Phillips, "Supporting Interactive Youth Maker Programs in Public and School Libraries: Design Hypotheses and First Implementations," in *Proceedings of the 2017 Conference on Interaction Design and Children*, (2017): 310-315.

12. Beth Filar Williams and Michelle Folkman, "Librarians as Makers," *Journal of Library Administration* 57, no. 1 (2017): 17-35.

maker activities for their youth patrons.[13] This work led to the development of several approaches for how these libraries can leverage their existing spaces, rather than creating separate makerspaces, to provide access to STEM-rich making activities for youth in ways that are accessible, affordable, and inclusive.

The work revealed that many rural libraries have access to large tables or meeting rooms that can easily be reconfigured to promote and facilitate making activities. We also found that youth making can be supported without the overhead of costly fabrication technologies housed within a dedicated makerspace.[14] For instance, a 3D printer is often seen as iconic of making but, in our view, it is an expensive technology that is not a requirement for meaningful making to take place.

As described next, we also identified several STEM-rich maker activities that provided youth with opportunities to participate in fun, creative, and quick experiences while learning STEM concepts. In these activities, youth found ways to create artifacts using these affordable tools in ways that were driven by their own interests and experiences. The materials used in the activities came at a lower financial cost to libraries with limited budgets. The activities also challenged the traditional image of who makes, and why.

Makey Makey

The Makey Makey is a device that allows youth patrons to turn various conductive objects such as a fork or lemon into a keyboard, controller, or touch pad. It can then be used to operate a variety of computer programs and applications as well as to play games.[15] Librarians used Makey Makeys in youth programs in several ways. Youth patrons explored concepts of

---

13. Victor R. Lee, Mimi Recker, Abigail L. Phillips, and Aubrey Rogowski, "An Asset-Based Framework for Youth Maker Development in Libraries," (poster presented at the American Education Research Association, New York, NY, April 2018).

14. Victor R. Lee and Mimi Recker, "Paper Circuits: A Tangible, Low Threshold, Low Cost Entry to Computational Thinking," *TechTrends* 62, no. 2 (2018): 197-203.

15. Mitchel Resnick and Eric Rosenbaum, "Designing for Tinkerability," In *Design, Make, Play" Growing the Next Generation of STEM Innovators*, eds. Margaret Honey and David E. Kanter (New York: Routledge, 2013), 163-181.

conductivity while developing a game controller to use in a computer-based video game. Additionally, they used different conductive objects to represent the different keys on the piano. They were then able to use those "keys" or conductive objects to "play the piano" using a piano simulator on the Makey Makey website.

Squishy Circuits

Squishy circuits are a hands-on way for youth patrons to learn about a variety of basic electrical circuits using Play-Doh (which is conductive), LED lights, and a 9V or coin cell battery. Through creative play, youth patrons can build a series or parallel circuit in various ways. When implemented in a rural library, youth patrons used circuitry to create a variety of artifacts that reflected their interests, from lit up hot dogs to chickens (see **Figure 1**).

Paper Circuits

Similar to squishy circuits, paper circuits allow youth patrons to create various light-up paper crafts by using copper tape, LED lights, and coin cell batteries to create a complete circuit. In a few library activities, youth patrons created Valentine's Day and other holiday cards to gift to one another. Youth also created pop culture representations including Star Wars light sabers, Captain America shields, and Pokémon balls.[16]

E-Textiles

Building upon the concepts learned with squishy circuits and paper circuits, youth patrons use conductive thread to sew LED lights into various fabric crafts. A battery holder with connection points is sewn into the fabric to hold a coin cell battery.[17] For example, one librarian implemented this program near the Halloween holiday, and youth patrons created different masquerade masks. Other program ideas

---

16. Lee and Recker, "Paper Circuits," 197-203.

17. Leah Buechly, Kylie Peppler, Michael Eisenberg, and Yasmin Kafai, T*extile Messages: Dispatches from the World of E-Textiles and Education. New Literacies and Digital Epistemologies* (New York: Peter Lang Publishing Group, 2013).

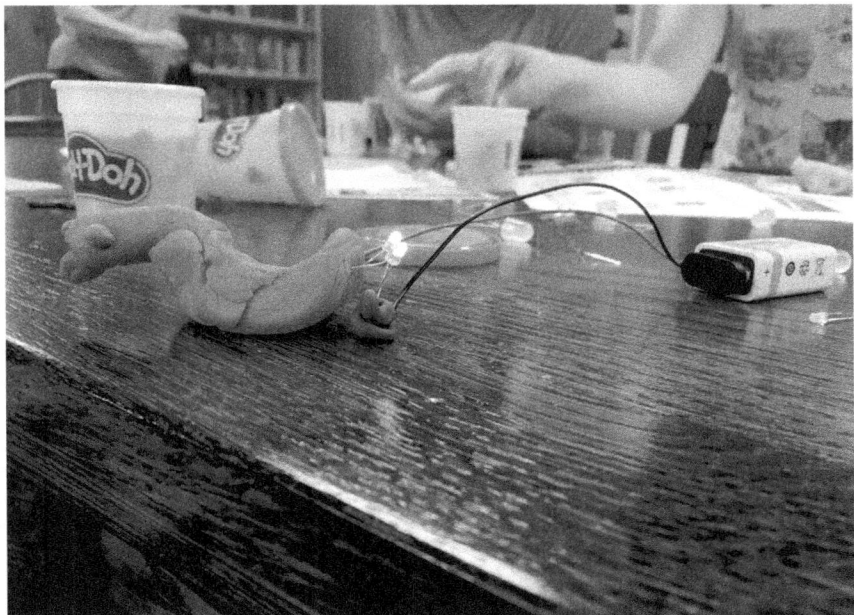

Figure 1: Youth squishy circuit creation of a chicken created during a rural library maker program

include creating light up backpack badges or bracelets in ways that enable youth patrons to express their individuality and creativity.

K'Nex

Using plastic rods, connectors, blocks, wheels, and other building components, youth patrons can design and construct various structures and models in ways that encourage the exploration of engineering concepts. Librarians can provide youth patrons the opportunity to collaborate and build freely or provide themed kits available for purchase through K'Nex. One librarian with whom we worked provided youth patrons with various kits that allowed them to build several rides often found in theme parks including a roller coaster with a motor, a carousel, and a swing. These then went on display on the library bookshelves.

Blutracks

The Blutrack racing system is a flexible, bendable racetrack that includes ramps. Youth patrons can learn about physics concepts while building loops and jumps. The track is easy to set up and take down in a library space. One librarian found that the aisles in libraries can provide the right amount of space for the track. Librarians can provide youth the opportunity to weigh the cars and test out the speeds with various weights and judge the performance of cars on different designed loops and jumps. Librarians can also provide a space for youth to record their best times and participate in friendly competition with other youth patrons.

Examples of Use of Space in Rural and Small-Town Libraries

The key point that we make in this chapter is that libraries can and should use the spaces already at their disposal rather than trying to establish a dedicated makerspace. For example, one of our partnering libraries was located in a small town with a population of just over 500 people. The library was located in one large room of the town's city hall. The library's space was minimal and was primarily utilized in such a way as to maximize the space for its growing book collection. There was little open space for youth activities. However, across the hall from the library was an empty classroom often used by the volunteer fire department for training purposes and occasional library events. After setting up folding tables and chairs, the librarian reconfigured the space for STEM-rich making. The librarian kept the door propped open for youth to see that a program was in progress and that they were welcome to pop in as they were visiting the library. In this space, youth were able to participate in Squishy Circuits and Makey Makey activities. Laptop computers for the Makey Makey were brought over from across the hall for the program. After the program, the folding tables and chairs were put away and the room was once again available for other uses.

Another partnering library in a town of 7,000 people was concerned about the lack of space and rising noise level in their small library during youth programming. To address this concern, an adjacent city building was often used to host youth maker programming when larger numbers of youth patrons were expected to attend. This space, located next to the library (which was in the city hall complex as well), used to be utilized as the city's dance hall and provided ample room for youth to create and loudly engage with one another while not disrupting other patrons utilizing the limited library space next door. Various maker activities were held in this space including paper circuits and stop-motion animation production. The youth even built marshmallow shooters and had a shootout in that space.

Other times, maker programming was held in the dedicated teen space in the library. Located in a small corner of the library, this space consisted of a counter of computers against the wall and a few small, round tables, as well as a small TV and some beanbag chairs for the youth to play video games. It was in this space that Makey Makey activities were conducted using the area computers. Another activity held in the teen space was unable to be contained there. Youth were working in groups with Snap Circuit kits and various groups of teens were trying to get the motorized fan they were building to fly. In their search for more space, a group of youths ended up settling on the ground in the book aisles to fly their fan. The aisles provided some personal space where patrons could be separate from the group but still in close proximity.

A third rural library we partnered with tackled the space issue in a more unique way. While they would occasionally offer programs outside or in an adjacent classroom, the library would also schedule youth programming after regular library hours. This was done as a way to provide space and avoid conflicts related to noise level. The youth had the library to themselves and could utilize the space without concerns about being too noisy. The library had moveable bookshelves that were pushed together and out of the way to provide more space during youth programming. Coffee tables, couches, and chairs were also pushed out of the way to provide more space for the various youth activities. During one program, youth used the Makey Makey and copper tape to create a *Dance Dance Revolution* mat and projected the computer onto a large screen on the wall of the library. Youth congregated in the space to both participate and observe (see **Figure 2**).

Figure 2: Bookshelves and other furniture moved to create space for youth programming after hours in the library

Making Space in the Library

Beginning new maker programming in the library can be a daunting task, and it can be difficult to know where to start. The following recommendations can help librarians best utilize the space in the library to provide youth with STEM-rich making activities.

First, some librarians find it helpful to create a "makerspace" cart for patrons to use.[18] The makerspace then becomes any space that the cart occupies. Often a cart contains common maker supplies such as Legos, K'Nex, knitting supplies and yarn, Makey Makey kits, and various craft

---

18. Dana Gierdowski and Daniel Reis, "The MobileMaker: An Experiment with a Mobile Makerspace," *Library Hi Tech* 33, no. 4 (2015): 480-496.

supplies for creative construction.[19] Librarians can include whatever materials they would like on the cart, which is mobile and can be moved to create space when needed or put into storage when not in use.

Second, it is helpful to consider the flexibility of the space. Are there coffee tables, chairs, or couches that can be used or, if needed, moved out of the way to provide a temporary place for making? Are there tables and chairs available to create temporary workspaces? Can folding tables and folding chairs be brought into the space? Is there space adjacent to the library that is part of the civic complex that can be utilized for maker programming? As we begin to think creatively about library space, we can almost always find a way to create space for STEM-rich maker programming. A separate, dedicated makerspace is often unnecessary; instead, making can appear as a pop-up activity in existing space.

Another important consideration is how to create space to display the projects youth patrons have created. This act of sharing artifacts is an important motivator for youth. The tops of bookshelves or display cases are great locations for displaying projects.[20] Partner librarians often would temporarily move books on display to create a space to display youth maker projects. Another librarian provided a wall space for youth to display paper circuit creations. Other librarians used social media such as Instagram to display and promote youth making in the library by sharing images of the final projects.

Lastly, attention needs to be given to the rules of the space. What will the expectations be for noise levels? Making is a collaborative activity, and youth are excited to work together to create. This means that they most likely will not be whispering. In response, we found that many librarians who allow youth "permissive transgressions" such as taking their shoes off, sitting on the counters, or listening to music had higher attendance

---

19. Bronwyn Bevan, "The Promise and the Promises of Making in Science Education," *Studies in Science Education* 53, no. 1 (2017): 75-103.

20. Aubrey Rogowski, Abigail L. Phillips, Mimi Recker, and Victor R. Lee, "Design Capacity for Informal Learning within Schools: An Analysis of School Librarians and Maker Activities," (paper presented at the American Education Research Association Conference, Toronto, CA, April, 2019).

and more enthusiastic participation at youth programs than those who maintained traditional library norms.[21] Permitting transgressions allows many youth to feel ownership of the space and can boost creativity by offering more stimuli and the free flow of ideas for program attendees. When serving neurodiverse youth populations, those extra stimuli can be exchanged for other permitted transgressions that provide a novel experience for all, such as doing maker activities with dimmed lights.

Conclusion

Rural libraries serving youth do not need to be excluded from the Maker Movement because they do not have the budget for costly digital fabrication equipment. We also maintain that rural libraries need not succumb to any apparent pressure to create and house dedicated makerspaces. Rather, rural libraries can democratize making by providing inclusive, low-cost maker programming for youth in existing spaces. These can be a form of pop-up activity for patrons and reduce implied barriers and the need for permission to participate in making. Libraries need not purchase laser cutters and CNC mills and can instead involve race car tracks and assembly kits. The products of these maker programs can go home with the patrons or go on display for the duration of the program or longer.

By reconfiguring existing spaces for maker programming and resisting the urge to create dedicated makerspaces, librarians are implicitly challenging the dominant image of making as requiring access to special spaces. It can cultivate more inclusive and accessible spaces for youth to learn and create that allows all to participate regardless of gender, race, or socioeconomic status. It changes the image of making from one that is highly technical and requiring specialized knowledge to one that is playful, creative, and accessible to all ages. We believe that the approach of focusing on inexpensive programs is more consistent with the spirit of the Maker Movement. It is also an approach that is more sensitive to the realities and constraints faced by small town and rural

---

21. Rogowski, Phillips, Recker, and Lee, "Design Capacity."

libraries that can still yield, in our experience, a very positive reception from youth patrons.

Acknowledgements

More information and resources about these activities is available via our website: library-making.usu.edu.

This work was supported by the Institute of Museum and Library Services grant number RE-31-16-0013-16. We thank Jenny Hansen, Whitney Lewis, and Abigail Phillips for their invaluable help, as well as our partnering librarians and their libraries.

Bibliography

Calabrese Barton, Angela, and Edna Tan. "A Longitudinal Study of Equity-Oriented STEM-Rich Making among Youth from Historically Marginalized Communities." *American Educational Research Journal* 55, no. 4 (2018): 761-800. https://doi.org/10.3102/0002831218758668.

Bevan, Bronwyn. "The Promise and the Promises of Making in Science Education." *Studies in Science Education* 53, no. 1 (2017): 75-103.

Blikstein, Paulo. "Digital Fabrication and 'Making' in Education: The Democratization of Invention." In *FabLabs: Of Machines, Makers and Inventors,* edited by J. Walter-Herrmann & C. Buching, 1-21. Bielefeld, DE: Transcript Publishers, 2013.

Braun, Linda W., Maureen L. Harman, Sandra Hughes-Hassell, and Kafi Kumasi. "The Future of Library Services for and with Teens: A Call to Action." *Young Adult Library Services Association*, 2014.

Buechley, Leah. "A Critical Look at Making". Keynote address presented at the Annual FabLearn Conference, Stanford, CA, October 2013.

Buechley, Leah, Kylie Peppler, Michael Eisenberg, and Yasmin Kafai. *Textile Messages: Dispatches from the World of E-Textiles and Education. New Literacies and Digital Epistemologies. Volume 62*. New York: Peter Lang Publishing Group, 2013.

Gierdowski, Dana, and Daniel Reis. "The MobileMaker: An Experiment with a Mobile Makerspace." *Library Hi Tech* 33, no. 4 (2015): 480-496.

Lee, Victor R., Whitney Lewis, Kristin A. Searle, Mimi Recker, Jennifer Hansen, and Abigail L. Phillips. "Supporting Interactive Youth Maker Programs in Public and School Libraries: Design Hypotheses and First Implementations." In *Proceedings of the 2017 Conference on Interaction Design and Children*, pp. 310-315. ACM, 2017.

Lee, Victor R., and Mimi Recker. "Paper Circuits: A Tangible, Low Threshold, Low Cost Entry to Computational Thinking." *TechTrends* 62, no. 2 (2018): 197-203.

Lee, Victor R., Mimi Recker, and Abigail L. Phillips. 2018. "Conjecture Mapping the Library: Iterative Refinements Toward Supporting Maker Learning Activities in Small Community Spaces." In *Proceedings of the International Conference of the Learning Science, London*, 2018, 320-327.

Lee, Victor R., Mimi Recker, Abigail L. Phillips, and Aubrey Rogowski. 2018. "An Asset-Based Framework for Youth Maker Development in Libraries." Poster presented at the American Education Research Association, New York, 2018.

Moorefield-Lang, Heather. "Change in the Making: Makerspaces and the Ever-Changing Landscape of Libraries." *TechTrends* 59, no. 3 (2015): 107-112.

Preddy, Leslie B. *School Library Makerspaces: Grades 6–12*. Santa Barbara, CA: ABC-CLIO, 2013.

Resnick, Mitchel and Eric Rosenbaum. "Designing for Tinkerability" In *Design, Make, Play: Growing the Next Generation of STEM Innovators*, edited by Margaret Honey and David E. Kanter, 163-181. New York: Routledge, 2013.

Rogowski, Aubrey, Abigail L. Phillips, Mimi Recker, and Victor R. Lee. 2019. "Design Capacity for Informal Learning within Schools: An Analysis of School Librarians and Maker Activities." *Paper presented at the American Educational Research Association Conference, Toronto, 2019*.

Schrock, Andrew Richard. "Education in Disguise: Culture of a Hacker and Maker Space." *InterActions: UCLA Journal of Education and Information Studies* 10, no. 1 (2014).

Subramaniam, Mega, Ligaya Scaff, Saba Kawas, Kelly M. Hoffman, and Katie Davis. "Using Technology to Support Equity and Inclusion in Youth Library Programming: Current Practices and Future Opportunities." *Library Quarterly* 88, no. 4 (2018): 315-331.

Williams, Beth Filar and Michelle Folkman. "Librarians as Makers." *Journal of Library Administration* 57, no.1 (2017): 17-35.

Chapter 10

THE FEMINIST MAKERSPACE: SMASHING THE PATRIARCHY WITH CRAFTING, MENTORSHIP, AND CONNECTION

Meaghan Moody and Chava Spivak-Birndorf

Penn Libraries' Education Commons (EC) is not what most people picture when they think of a library; it is located in the stadium alongside the gym, and it has no books. The EC opened in 2012 and largely functioned as a study and meeting space. Patrons frequently did not realize they were in the library, and many students believed the space was for athletes only. As a library without a clear identity, we saw an opportunity to reimagine how the library can serve our students through making. Makerspaces are primarily occupied by male makers.[1] Left unchecked, this is a self-perpetuating trend. Makerspaces, and the Maker Movement as a whole, are failing women due to a lack of visible and accessible female mentors and an unofficial narrowing of what it means to make that focuses primarily on high-technology maker activities. This is a disservice to women makers who typically "identify with arts and creation, and describe themselves as coming to making via arts. Technology is a means, not an end, for them."[2] This chapter will explore the erasure of women in the Maker Movement and discuss the values and strategies

---

1. Vanessa Bean, Nicole M. Farmer, and Barbara A. Kerr, "An Exploration of Women's Engagement in Makerspaces," *Gifted and Talented International* 30, no. 1–2 (July 3, 2015): 61–67.

2. Intel Corporation, "MakeHers: Engaging Girls and Women in Technology through Making, Creating, and Inventing," 2014, 7.

we are applying to engage and elevate women as we create and grow the EC TinkerLab. We begin by examining the barriers women face in participating in the Maker Movement, followed by a discussion of the burgeoning feminist makerspace movement and our endeavors to establish the EC TinkerLab as one.

Is Everyone Who Makes a *Maker?*
Nonlinear Pathways and High-Tech Privilege

We interpret making broadly to intentionally push back against the misconception that making must involve a technological aspect. We use "making" to describe any do-it-yourself projects that involve creating, modifying, or repairing something. Makers "range from traditional artisans to computer hackers and encompass crafters, musicians, artists, cooks, students, welders, scientists, engineers, software developers, and circuit benders."[3] While half of all makers come from a technology background, the rest follow a non-technical path, often coming to making through craft, art, and design-oriented projects. Any makers may "follow this non-technical path, but women are more likely than men to come to making this way."[4] These makers share a different perspective, process, and focus; they are knitting, sewing, bookmaking, and creating jewelry and e-textiles. Despite the fact that these activities are generally understood and accepted as forms of making,[5] a culture of privileging high-technology over low-tech, crafting, and art projects prevails in makerspaces. In 2005, Maker Media's *MAKE* magazine gave the "Maker" community its name,[6] and the popular brand continues to serve as a barometer of what it means to belong in the "capital-M" Maker Movement. Leah Buechley—creator of the LilyPad Arduino

---

3. Intel, "MakeHers," 10.

4. Susan Faulkner and Anne McClard, "Making Change: Can Ethnographic Research about Women Makers Change the Future of Computing?" in *American Anthropological Association and Ethnographic Praxis in Industry Conference Proceedings* (New York, NY: American Anthropological Association, 2014), 187.

5. Intel, "MakeHers," 10.

6. "About Us," Maker Media, accessed May 15, 2019, https://makermedia.com/.

sewable microcontroller—examined *MAKE*'s entire archive to see how the magazine represents making. Of 36 covers, 53% focused on electronics, 31% on vehicles, and 22% on robotics, providing a "narrow" and "branded" impression of what making is.[7] This sends a message not only about the kinds of activities valued in the Maker Movement, but also about the kinds of people; while crafting, low-tech, and art are often coded as feminine, more complicated forms of technology are typically coded as masculine "despite women's early involvement in computing, engineering, and computer science."[8]

When less technical projects are taken less seriously, nonlinear pathways to making such as making activities founded in crafting and the arts are dismissed. With technical projects as the default, we fail to recognize the diversity of strengths makers from different backgrounds bring to the table. Makers' abilities are measured primarily by their technical skills, creating the assumption that those coming from technical backgrounds are naturally suited for making and those coming from non-technical backgrounds need to catch up. This false dichotomy persists in which crafters craft but makers innovate, in spite of the reality that many maker projects integrate both low and high technologies. This attitude translates to the way in which these makers create: "Makers with a less technical background find their work styles are often undervalued and misunderstood—sketching and thinking are taken as signs that a person needs help when he or she is actually just using a different work process."[9] The motivation for making is also often different for women. A 2014 Intel/Harris Poll report indicates that "female makers are particularly motivated by social-service aspects of making...[and] are more likely

---

7. Leah Buechley, "Thinking about Making" (keynote address, FabLearn Conference at Stanford University, Palo Alto, CA, October 28, 2013), http://edstream.stanford.edu/Video/Play/883b61dd951d4d3f90abeec65eead2911d.

8. Kristen A. Searle, Deborah A. Fields, and Yasmin B. Kafai, "Is Sewing A 'Girl's Sport' Addressing Gender Issues in Making with Electronic Textiles," in *Makeology*, eds. Kylie A. Peppler, Erica Rosenfeld Halverson, and Yasmin B. Kafai, vol. 2 (New York: Routledge, 2016), 74.

9. Susan Faulkner, "Women Who Make: Undercounted as Makers and Underwhelmed by Makerspaces," *Computer* 47, no. 12 (December 2014): 30.

than males to be motivated to make because they want 'to help or to give.'"[10] For women, making is often grounded in advocacy or resistance to oppression: the tools remain a means to an end.

Nonlinear pathways that comprise a difference in the choice of making activity, workstyle, and motivation lead to a unique maker identity that does not fit the makerspace mold: women makers see themselves reflected neither in makerspaces nor in the larger Maker Movement.

Male-Dominated Spaces

Most spaces for making are dominated by men.[11] In claiming these spaces, men establish norms and influence the space's culture, which permeates into the type of making activities, the tools used, the workflows, and the ways information is created and disseminated. Women frequently report feeling intimidated, unwelcome, unsure, and challenged in these spaces.

Established makerspaces, in particular, include major hurdles for women to overcome when they want to join as new members. Learning how to navigate these spaces often poses a problem since entry points for new members—such as signage or available mentors—remain unarticulated. A "tough love" ethos to learning pervades, particularly in university makerspaces, which frequently alienates female students. In interviews with undergraduate women in engineering makerspaces, Roldan, Hui, and Gerber found that novice makers often feel intimidated by these environments that provide little informational signage and few accessible, welcoming mentors. In many cases, novice makers must be assertive and seek help from these mentors who balance multiple responsibilities and focuses—including managing the space, supporting many other makers, and working on their own projects—and may appear unavailable. Harried interactions and a figure-it-out-yourself mentality leads to "female participants [feeling] that this way of initiation [was] particularly abrasive, turning them off from asking questions and

---

10. Intel, "MakeHers," 7-8.

11. Intel, "MakeHers," 43.

participating in the future."¹² Doubting the legitimacy of their inquiries, women frequently fear their questions will be poorly received and that the onus of learning to negotiate these spaces is on them.

The physical appearance of makerspaces can also deter women's engagement. One study of student preferences for makerspace environments in higher education found that most women surveyed preferred "a tidier, less complex looking space as they initiate participation in Makerspaces."¹³ Of the eight makerspace photos displayed to women in the study, four exhibited chaotic spaces filled with tables overladen with supplies, tools, and technologies. Little-to-no informational signage can be seen, and three of the eight photos prominently feature men working. The authors noted that most women surveyed had a preference for space that resembled a high school classroom, suggesting that women prefer an environment that is familiar and relatable.¹⁴

Further, many women describe the makerspace environment as overbearing and sometimes even openly hostile. Faulkner found that women overwhelmingly felt repulsed by the toxic machismo of makerspaces: "One woman told us her local makerspace is 'all guys, it's just a sweaty, dirty fraternity. I think that's the best way to describe it. It's just not friendly.'"¹⁵ Many women find their presence in makerspaces questioned and feel compelled to prove themselves. Liz Henry, one of the creators of the San Francisco-based feminist hackerspace, Double Union, explains, "Our geek cred is constantly challenged or belittled. You might be there coding, and you want to stop for a while and draw in your notebook and think, but if you're not staring at a black and green screen, or, like, melding your brain with an Arduino every second,

---

12. Wendy Roldan, Julie Hui, and Elizabeth M. Gerber, "University Makerspaces: Opportunities to Support Equitable Participation for Women in Engineering," *International Journal of Engineering Education* 34, no. 2 (2018): 764.

13. Morgan M. Hynes and Wendy J. Hynes, "If You Build It, Will They Come? Student Preferences for Makerspace Environments in Higher Education," *International Journal of Technology and Design Education* 28, no. 3 (2018): 880.

14. Hynes and Hynes, 880.

15. Faulkner, "Women Who Make," 31.

some dude is going to come up to you and act like you need his expert lessons in how to hack."[16] This form of men "helping" is common in the stories of experienced women makers, serving in most cases as an annoyance but in others leading to insidious self-doubt, confusion, and a lack of confidence. The participants in Roldan, Hui, and Gerber's study, for example, expressed doubt about whether their ideas qualified as "legitimate" projects.[17] One woman described abandoning her project idea to improve the way college students wash their dishes to join a male friend's group, only to realize later that her original project "was advanced enough to be accepted in the makerspace."[18]

Male-Dominated Movement

Conversations around making often ask, "Where are the women makers?" Women are making, but their projects and processes are not as respected in the maker community; indeed, their very presence is unwelcome and questioned. In her analysis of *MAKE* magazine, Leah Buechley found that 85% of the people featured on *MAKE* covers have been men or boys, and none were people of color. Representation within each issue was similarly distributed. Unsurprisingly, Buechley also found that *MAKE*'s editorial staff reflected this same skewed demographic with 87% men and, again, no people of color.[19] The emphasis on high-tech, high-cost making activities reflects and reinforces a privileged definition of making that is open primarily to affluent, educated, white men.

A 2012 exploration of popular online Do-It-Yourself (DIY) communities helps illuminate where the women makers are (and where they aren't). Researchers found that followers of crafting sites (e.g., textile arts) are predominantly women, whereas websites more commonly associated with the Maker Movement (e.g., *MAKE*), which primarily

---

16. Liz Henry, "The Rise of Feminist Hackerspaces and How to Make Your Own," *Model View Culture*, February 3, 2014, https://modelviewculture.com/pieces/the-rise-of-feminist-hackerspaces-and-how-to-make-your-own.

17. Roldan, Hui, and Gerber, "University Makerspaces," 755.

18. Roldan, Hui, and Gerber, 755.

19. Buechley, "Thinking about Making."

focus on electronics and technology, are dominated by men, particularly white men.[20] The Maker Movement is occupied and shaped by white men; it is no wonder that most women engaged in "making" activities do not identify with the term *maker* but rather see themselves in "terms related to creation and art."[21]

This lack of representation has contributed to the widespread misconception that women are simply uninterested in making. For instance, Henry describes a "long and infuriating thread on the hackerspaces.org mailing list [that] outlined many sexist and misogynist misconceptions, including that women are just not interested enough in 'hacking' to be a large part of DIY, hacker or maker culture."[22] Again, *MAKE* magazine reaffirms this false impression. A 2012 study commissioned by *MAKE* and Intel claimed that 81% of makers were men, with a median age of forty-four and a median income of $106,000, 73% were homeowners, 97% had attended or graduated from college, and more than 80% had some level of post-graduate education.[23] However, the study's methodology reveals its narrow perspective: the survey respondents were randomly selected from among exhibitors at Maker Media's Maker Faire and subscribers of either *MAKE* magazine or *MAKE* newsletter.[24] Although the report calls this sample a "cross-section of the 'maker universe,'" it's important to recognize the limitations of defining makers as followers of *MAKE* products, considering *MAKE* magazine does little to draw women makers. Based on responses from the survey, *MAKE* concludes that "Makers have a strong affinity for MAKE media properties and its online destinations," noting that 95% of respondents reported looking

---

20. Leah Buechley, Jennifer Jacobs, and Benjamin Mako Hill, "LilyPad in the Wild: Technology DIY, E-Textiles, and Gender," in *Textile Messages: Dispatches from the World of E-Textiles and Education*, eds. Leah Buechley et al., (New York: Peter Lang Publishing, Inc., 2013), 147.

21. Intel, "MakeHers," 30.

22. Henry, "The Rise of Feminist Hackerspaces."

23. *MAKE* and Intel, "Maker Market Study and Media Report: An In-Depth Profile of Makers at the Forefront of Hardware Innovation," 2012, 24.

24. *MAKE* and Intel, 8.

at or reading at least one *MAKE* print product in the past year, and nearly 80% had visited the website in the past three months.[25] Interestingly, they don't seem to draw a connection between these responses and their method of sample selection. *MAKE's* market study paints a picture of the participants in the *MAKE*-defined "Maker" community, but in doing so, it highlights the extent to which Maker Media and the Maker Movement consistently ignore a huge portion of people who are making. In turn, women's lack of presence in makerspaces and representation in the movement bolsters the status quo, as a majority of women cite lack of community and supportive female mentors to be among the main deterrents to their continued engagement in the maker community.[26]

Disrupting the Maker Movement with "Lowercase-m making"

A Feminist Makerspace

While the concept of an intentionally feminist makerspace is not a new one, the feminist makerspace movement is still in its infancy. Feminist makerspaces remain few in number, and scholarship surrounding them is scarce. However, feminist "hacker, maker and geek initiatives have existed, in the USA and elsewhere, under different shapes and forms— both physical and virtual — for more than a decade."[27] These initiatives have ranged from women-only nights in makerspaces, to projects involving e-textiles, to feminist wikis and blogs for makers. Recognizing a growing need for more enduring solutions, several uniquely feminist makerspaces have cropped up in recent years. Noting both the development of feminist makerspaces in the US and the lack of

---

25. *MAKE* and Intel, 32-34.

26. Intel, "MakeHers," 8.

27. Sophie Toupin, "Feminist Hackerspaces: The Synthesis of Feminist and Hacker Cultures," *Journal of Peer Production* no. 5 (October 2014): 1, http://peer-production.net/issues/issue-5-shared-machine-shops/peer-reviewed-articles/feminist-hackerspaces-the-synthesis-of-feminist-and-hacker-cultures/.

current literature on the subject, Sophie Toupin interviewed individuals involved in the feminist makerspace movement. She writes, "[Feminist hackers, makers, and geeks] want spaces responsive to their desired boundaries — that they may hack in peace without encountering the everyday sexism prevalent today both online and off. This recursive aspect reveals the true significance of feminist hackerspaces, demonstrating how these individuals work to shape the very institutions which make them hackers: they hack hackerspaces."[28] Feminist makerspaces allow underrepresented users the space to focus on simply making rather than learning to navigate male-dominated spaces, defending and justifying their projects and workflows, and thwarting off overbearing male makers. While some of these spaces are reserved for women and gender diverse users, and others are open to cisgender men as well, the common thread among them is the commitment to relieving members of marginalized communities from the mental and emotional burden of carving out a space for themselves in an unwelcoming environment. Feminist makerspaces are designed and operated with intention and awareness of the systemic and individual barriers that frequently prevent members of marginalized communities from engaging in these spaces. Sophie Toupin writes:

> When feminist and anti-oppression politics are not explicitly part of the ethos of a space, whether virtual or physical, the burden of education will often be placed upon the people who are living with these oppressions. The burden of education about white supremacy will be placed upon indigenous or people of colour, while the burden of education about gender analysis will be put upon women and queers. Having to explain the pertinence of working on gender issues in and of themselves all the time, and meeting resistance and defensiveness when trying to build such analysis in a space, can be a constant struggle for feminist and anti-oppression activists.[29]

---

28. Toupin, "Feminist Hackerspaces," 4.

29. Sophie Toupin, "Feminist Hackerspaces as Safer Spaces?" .*dpi* no. 27 (April 2013), https://dpi.studioxx.org/en/feminist-hackerspaces-safer-spaces.

Working within the confines set by non-feminist makerspaces can prove especially demanding when having to advocate for oneself. Instead, if makerspaces from their inception not only reinforce but celebrate feminist ideals, share an understanding of the marginalization many makers face, and work to push back against all forms of oppression, makers can not only focus on making but find allyship and form communities.

EC TinkerLab

Conceived as a comfortable, state-of-the-art space for collaborative learning, the EC has always been a popular study space, but defining its role in the larger University of Pennsylvania Libraries system has been a journey of trial and error. Due to its location in the stadium and next to the School of Engineering, athletes and engineering students represent a large portion of our users, but historically, the EC's relationship with these groups has primarily been as a host for their tutors and study groups. As we are on the outer edge of campus and have no book collection, even our fellow librarians frequently forgot about the space or viewed it as something of an annex study area rather than a true library.

We both started working in the EC as LIS graduate interns and now manage the space and programming as its librarians. When we stepped into our roles as the EC's librarians, we were determined to build an identity and solidify the EC as one of Penn's libraries. One of the EC's most successful and long-lasting endeavors is the 3D printing service, which was started in early 2015 by the librarian who previously ran the space. Several other campus locations have 3D printers, but they are exclusively for academic purposes and most are accessible only to students in specific programs. The EC is the only location to offer free 3D printing to all members of the Penn community and to welcome both academic and personal projects. As we collected information to guide our plans for the EC's future, we noticed that many of the university's other fabrication and emerging technology resources also served a limited population.

Building off the success of the 3D printing service, we saw an opportunity to broaden the EC's reach by developing a user-directed makerspace where everyone at Penn can explore technology and expand their knowledge and skills in a supportive, low-stakes environment. In spring 2018, we started researching and planning for the creation of the EC TinkerLab. As teaching librarians, we wanted to create a welcoming, dynamic, learning space that reflects the full and diverse spectrum of our students. We prioritized bringing women into the space and creating a safe and comfortable environment for them.

Over the course of our tenure at the EC, we have gained insight into its user base through our work developing and shaping pedagogical practices around a range of technologies; much of our work encompasses thinking critically and creatively about integrating technology into coursework. We teach workshops, meet with classes, and develop new resources. When we began developing programming for the EC TinkerLab, we took a critical eye to the EC's services and past offerings. Although women makers are more likely than men to use 3D printers in their projects (52% vs. 36%),[30] a review of our 3D printing service revealed that nearly 70% of its users were male. While the service was ostensibly available to everyone, it was primarily used by engineering students hoping to avoid the line for their school's dedicated 3D printers. Students who didn't need the technology for classes were often fascinated by the printers, but struggled to visualize what they could do with them and how to get started.

Feminist Pedagogy as a Framework

In the EC TinkerLab, we envisioned a new type of makerspace at the University of Pennsylvania. One that made tech, tools, and other resources accessible to the entire Penn community, valued and elevated the voices of women, and resulted in the formation of a strong and supportive maker community. Feminist pedagogy guides our efforts. Shrewsbury defines feminist pedagogy as "engaged teaching/learning— engaged with self in a continuing reflective process; engaged actively with the material being studied; engaged with others in a struggle to get

---

30. Intel, "MakeHers," 30.

beyond our sexism and racism and classism and homophobia and other destructive hatreds and to work together to enhance our knowledge; engaged with the community, with traditional organizations, and with movements for social change."[31] While we acknowledge that creating a space that is immune to hateful beliefs and behaviors is an unrealistic goal, by centering the EC TinkerLab around a feminist pedagogy we are committing to continually work to recognize, engage with, and confront oppression in its many forms.

Makerspaces and making activities are naturally suited for this teaching and learning framework due to their "ability to disrupt notions of who can do programming, engineering, or science and for what aims."[32] Making promotes experiential learning, offering an alternative to traditional learning methods. As respected institutions with a long history of fighting for equitable access to knowledge and disrupting cultural norms, libraries provide an ideal setting for exploring making as a powerful educational tool. Engaging in making in the library legitimizes it within the academic culture while also creating a space where students can develop their own learning priorities outside the demands of their coursework. The library provides a supported learning environment where it is safe to fail, empowering students to experiment with new skills outside their comfort zone. The EC has an added advantage as an independent library not beholden to any specific department, which allows us the freedom to serve all members of the Penn community equally.

Critical and feminist pedagogies have long informed our teaching philosophies, shaping our workshops and interactions with students. Our workshops are hands-on, collaborative, and experimental. We sit around communal tables and strive to cultivate a teaching and learning environment that dismantles the teacher/student binary: we are all teachers and learners. We endeavor to meet students where they are, both in terms of their interests and their skill level, and to see and value the

---

31. Carolyn M. Shrewsbury, "What Is Feminist Pedagogy?" *Women's Studies Quarterly* 21, no. 3/4 (1993): 8, http://www.jstor.org/stable/40022001.

32. Fields and Lee, "Craft Technologies 101," 121.

whole student. An ethic of care as articulated by bell hooks is crucial to our approach to teaching: "To teach in a manner that respects and cares for the souls of our students is essential if we are to provide the necessary conditions where learning can most deeply and intimately begin."[33] We want to honor our students' insights and creativity. By creating a feminist makerspace that challenges the marginalization that women face in makerspaces, we tell our makers that what they bring to the table is already valuable and does not need to be changed or adapted to fit. Like the feminist hackerspaces Toupin describes, we're attempting to open up the concept of making to be shaped by how women currently make.[34] These feminist tenets underlie our approach to shaping the EC TinkerLab and share a natural relationship that supports the creation of an inclusive feminist makerspace.

Learning in the TinkerLab

The EC Tinkerlab's first workshop, "3D Jewelry Design and Printing" embodies the feminist pedagogy we hoped to build this project around and has been one of our most popular workshops, both in the TinkerLab and in our time at Penn Libraries. In the first few years of the EC's 3D printing service, library staff occasionally held "Intro to 3D Printing" workshops, but these were rarely well-attended. We noted that these workshops lacked an obvious goal and hands-on aspects were minimal. Library workshops face stiff competition when vying for the attention of busy, overwhelmed students; 3D printing on its own may pique their interest, but without a meaningful project attached, it hasn't been enough to get them in the door. This is especially true for women, who are less likely to engage with technology as an end in itself.[35]

Promotional materials for "3D Jewelry Design and Printing" were designed to highlight the workshop as welcoming to women and students new to the technology: the workshop flyers featured a woman's

---

33. bell hooks, *Teaching to Transgress* (New York: Routledge, 1994), 13.
34. Toupin, "Feminist Hackerspaces," 4.
35. Intel, "MakeHers," 7; Whelan, "We Are Not All Makers," 78.

hand wearing a 3D-printed bracelet, emphasized the hands-on nature of the session, and stated prominently that all learning levels are welcome. While past workshops had been held in the EC's Seminar Room with the instructor at the head of the table, this workshop took place in the open space of the TinkerLab with participants and instructors sitting together around a large table. This removed the formal classroom atmosphere and encouraged collaborative participation, with students and instructors working together toward common goals.

We asked students to use the free, web-based 3D modeling software Tinkercad to design a custom accessory or piece of jewelry, but our central goal was to create a space where students felt both comfortable exploring and safe to fail. To ensure all students were supported, we had three instructors, including the two of us and an MLIS graduate student intern. We try to always have two to three instructors available during workshops, as having multiple instructors—each with their own personal experiences, background, and expertise—helps lessen the divide between teacher and student and builds a sense of community and mentorship. Roldan, Hui, and Gerber found that "having female leaders provides an alternative way for members, who may feel uncomfortable approaching a predominantly male leadership, to seek advice and help."[36] Once students began work on their designs, we were free to walk around and offer individual support to students who asked for it. This can be a relief for students who prefer not to announce their question to the full group: asking for help puts students in a vulnerable position, and instructors can ease this discomfort by showing approachability and taking the initiative to invite questions.[37] With students working around a communal table, they also had the opportunity to help each other and build community as they explored the software and discovered new features.

Throughout the workshop we emphasized a message important not only in making but across all aspects of our lives: even the "experts" went through a time when they did not know. A common struggle among

---

36. Roldan, Hui, and Gerber, "University Makerspaces," 757.

37. Roldan, Hui, and Gerber, 758.

teaching librarians is the fear of not knowing; nobody enjoys the feeling of standing in front of a classroom caught like a deer in the headlights because someone has asked a question beyond their expertise. Part of creating a feminist teaching space that flips traditional concepts of who belongs required getting over ourselves. Sometimes you don't know; admitting that can be a relief for everyone. Several students interviewed by Roldan, Hui, and Gerber expressed discomfort about asking for help, particularly as women in a male-dominated space. One student said, "I don't want to be that freshman but even more that girl that doesn't know what she's doing in the lab."[38] Another noted that she hesitates before asking for help with tools, because she fears her competence will be questioned.[39] We combat this insecurity by speaking openly about our own mistakes and mishaps. For instance, Meaghan often reminds students to use a ruler for reference to get a sense of how large their final creation will be. She shows the first piece of jewelry she designed and printed—a laughably tiny charm for a necklace with her name barely legible—and recounts that before seeing her completed miniature print, she was surprised about how quickly it printed. Chava shows students how to use the "TEXT" shape in Tinkercad to add text without adding each letter one at a time, and admits that it took her a surprisingly long time to realize you could edit the word. The takeaway is that it's okay to be "that girl that doesn't know what she's doing."

We kept time spent on instruction to a minimum, reserving the majority of the time for students to get to know the software and create their designs. Studies show that attempts to engage women and girls in tech projects benefit from "hands-on, authentic science explorations tied to personal experiences and allowing them to co-create curriculum based on their interests and strengths."[40] Students were given a step-by-step tutorial but were also told they should feel free to adapt the project or even throw it away and start blank. For students who get bogged down

---

38. Roldan, Hui, and Gerber, 758.
39. Roldan, Hui, and Gerber, 759.
40. Intel, "MakeHers," 46-47.

in initial planning or felt nervous about the tech, the suggested projects provided the structure they needed to feel confident about trying something new. For others, the freedom to follow their own direction helped hold their attention, "[enabling] them to tie their work to their personal interests, experiences and strengths."[41] Some students followed the outlined project faithfully, while others played around with the software, creating something new or exploring what they could do by importing and adapting free models from sites such as Thingiverse.com. By the end, every student created something that was uniquely theirs.

Reflections on the EC TinkerLab and Beyond

Since the EC TinkerLab's inception, our user base has started to transform in exciting ways. Use of the 3D printing service has nearly tripled, and the ratio of male to female users has shifted. The EC Tinkerlab's new programming, resources, and outreach strategies have changed the composition of its users dramatically: in the spring 2019 semester, more than 50% of users were women. Of the fifteen patrons who attended an orientation for our self-serve 3D printer, nearly half (7) were women, several of whom learned about the service through the "3D Jewelry Design and Printing" workshop.

The nature of our workshops lends itself to collaboration and sharing; we often see attendees showing their work to one another excitedly, asking for feedback, and troubleshooting together. We have also started to see several repeat participants, engaging in new services and programming. A small community of women makers is beginning to form and seek out additional resources on their own. Several groups, such as the English Language Program and the Wharton Tech Club, have reached out to us for custom workshops. Our workshops often serve as a gateway to deeper engagement. We hope to continue reinforcing this growing community by forging connections and establishing mentors and a support system through authentic engagement. As mentors in

---

41. Intel, 47.

the EC TinkerLab, we feel a responsibility to share our experiences and align them with those of our students/fellow makers. The presence of compassionate and supportive female role models plays an essential role in helping other makers feel a sense of belonging, thereby increasing continued engagement.[42] We hope to continue to develop the space as a nurturing environment that fosters new mentors.

As we have developed programming and started to build an identity for the EC TinkerLab, we also have recognized the importance of creating a welcoming physical space that reflects our feminist and anti-oppressive ideals. We have taken small steps to demonstrate that the EC TinkerLab is a safer space where we value and affirm our users' identities, such as displaying inclusive artwork and placing a basket of assorted pronoun buttons at the front desk with a sign inviting visitors to take one. Going forward, we plan to redesign the space further to establish a space that will appeal to and inspire women. Taking into consideration women's design preferences as outlined in Hyne's and Hyne's study, we envision a newly renovated EC TinkerLab as an organized, welcoming, and relatable space with clear visual cues for patrons.[43] These cues will provide information about how to get started, how to seek out guidance, and how to find supplies. Women indicate that they appreciate seeing "physical indicators that reduced barriers to female participation, such as providing smocks to protect certain clothing or hair ties for long hair."[44] At the same time, we believe it is essential that our feminism be trans-inclusive, anti-racist, and anti-oppression, recognizing that we still have work to do to ensure that we understand and meet the needs of all of our students. We are committed to continuing to educate ourselves and to furthering our efforts to center the voices of people of color and confront the particular barriers faced by non-white women and trans and gender nonconforming students.

---

42. Roldan, Hui, and Gerber, "University Makerspaces," 753.
43. Hynes and Hynes, "If You Build It, Will They Come?," 880.
44. Roldan, Hui, and Gerber, "University Makerspaces," 757.

Conclusion

Discussions about engaging more women in STEM fields often revolve around the concept of "unlocking the clubhouse": transforming the "boys' club" atmosphere in traditional STEM spaces to make them friendlier to women.[45] Diversifying the engineering profession is a worthy goal, and it is important for women who wish to participate in traditional STEM spaces to feel welcomed and supported. However, one implication of this mindset is that getting into the traditional clubhouse is the only valid way to be involved in STEM. This tracks with a common theme in some "empowerment" movements — that women should demand respect and success by taking on traditionally masculine traits, an idea that undervalues traditionally feminine traits. Leah Buechley believes "the best way to increase diversity in STEM is to seed new subcultures where STEM can happen, and a person can keep her own identity as artsy, outdoorsy, a people-person, or feminine."[46] Rather than focusing on unlocking the clubhouse, Buechley advocates for "building new clubhouses."[47] Instead of pushing women to embrace traditional STEM activities, push the STEM world to expand and make room for traditionally female-dominated activities, resulting in "more widespread appreciation for the relevance, complexity, and importance of [these] pursuits."[48] The EC TinkerLab celebrates maker activities that broaden what it means to make, emphasizing purpose-driven and accessible projects. These projects disrupt the purist view of making that requires excitement about tech for tech's sake and embrace the varied passions of potential makers.

Bibliography

"About Us." Maker Media. Accessed May 15, 2019. https://makermedia.com/.

---

45. Buechley, Jacobs, and Hill, "LilyPad in the Wild," 156.
46. Intel, "MakeHers," 54.
47. Buechley, Jacobs, and Hill, "LilyPad in the Wild," 156.
48. Buechley, Jacobs, and Hill, 156.

Bean, Vanessa, Nicole M. Farmer, and Barbara A. Kerr. "An Exploration of Women's Engagement in Makerspaces." *Gifted and Talented International* 30, no. 1–2 (July 3, 2015): 61–67.

Buechley, Leah. "Thinking about Making." Keynote Address, FabLearn Conference at Stanford University, Palo Alto, CA, October 28, 2013. http://edstream.stanford.edu/Video/Play/883b61dd951d4d3f90abeec65eead2911d.

Buechley, Leah, Jennifer Jacobs, and Benjamin Mako Hill. "LilyPad in the Wild: Technology DIY, E-Textiles, and Gender." In *Textile Messages: Dispatches from the World of E-Textiles and Education*, edited by Leah Buechley, Kylie Peppler, Michael Eisenberg, and Yasmin Kafai, 147–57. New York: Peter Lang Publishing, Inc., 2013.

Faulkner, Susan. "Women Who Make: Undercounted as Makers and Underwhelmed by Makerspaces." *Computer* 47, no. 12 (December 2014): 30-31.

Faulkner, Susan and Anne McClard. "Making Change: Can Ethnographic Research about Women Makers Change the Future of Computing?" in *American Anthropological Association and Ethnographic Praxis in Industry Conference Proceedings*, 187-198. New York: American Anthropological Association, 2014.

Fields, Deborah A. and Victor R. Lee. "Craft Technologies 101: Bringing Making to Higher Education." In *Makeology*. Vol. 1, *Makerspaces as Learning Environments*, edited by Kylie Peppler, Erica Rosenfeld Halverson, and Yasmin B. Kafai, 120–37. New York: Routledge, 2016.

Henry, Liz. "The Rise of Feminist Hackerspaces and How to Make Your Own." *Model View Culture*. February 3, 2014. https://modelviewculture.com/pieces/the-rise-of-feminist-hackerspaces-and-how-to-make-your-own.

hooks, bell. *Teaching to Transgress*. New York: Routledge, 1994.

Hynes, Morgan M. and Wendy J. Hynes. "If You Build It, Will They Come? Student Preferences for Makerspace Environments in Higher Education," *International Journal of Technology and Design Education* 28, no. 3 (2018): 867-883.

Intel Corporation. "MakeHers: Engaging Girls and Women in Technology through Making, Creating, and Inventing." 2014.

Make Magazine, and Intel. "Maker Market Study and Media Report: An In-Depth Profile of Makers at the Forefront of Hardware Innovation." MAKE, 2012.

Quattrocchi, Christina. "MAKE'ing More Diverse Makers," Last modified October 29, 2013, https://www.edsurge.com/news/2013-10-29-make-ing-more-diverse-makers.

Roldan, Wendy, Julie Hui, and Elizabeth M. Gerber. "University Makerspaces: Opportunities to Support Equitable Participation for Women in Engineering," *International Journal of Engineering Education* 34, no. 2 (2018): 751-768.

Searle, Kristen A., Deborah A. Fields, and Yasmin B. Kafai. "Is Sewing A 'Girl's Sport'? Addressing Gender Issues in Making with Electronic Textiles." In *Makeology*. Vol. 2, *Makers as Learners*, edited by Kylie A. Peppler, Yasmin B. Kafai, and Erica Rosenfeld Halverson, 72-84. New York: Routledge, 2016.

Shrewsbury, Carolyn M. "What Is Feminist Pedagogy?" *Women's Studies Quarterly* 21, no. 3/4 (1993): 8-16. http://www.jstor.org/stable/40022001.

Toupin, Sophie. "Feminist Hackerspaces as Safer Spaces?" *.dpi* no. 27 (April 2013). https://dpi.studioxx.org/en/feminist-hackerspaces-safer-spaces.

Toupin, Sophie. "Feminist Hackerspaces: The Synthesis of Feminist and Hacker Cultures." *Journal of Peer Production* 5 (October 2014). http://peerproduction.net/issues/issue-5-shared-machine-shops/peer-reviewed-articles/feminist-hackerspaces-the-synthesis-of-feminist-and-hacker-cultures/.

Webb, Lynne M., Myria W. Allen, and Kandi L. Walker. "Feminist Pedagogy: Identifying Basic Principles." *Academic Exchange Quarterly* (Spring 2002): 67-72.

Whelan, Tara. "We Are Not All Makers: The Paradox of Plurality in the Maker Movement." In *Proceedings of the 19th International ACM SIGACCESS Conference on Computers and Accessibility - DIS '18*, 75–80. Hong Kong, China: ACM Press, 2018. https://doi.org/10.1145/3197391.3205415.

Chapter 11

INTERROGATING WHAT WE MEAN BY "MAKING": STORIES FROM WOMEN WHO MAKE IN COMMUNITY

Bibhushana Poudyal, Tetyana Zhyvotovska, Estefania Castillo, Nora Rivera, Ann Shivers-McNair, Joy Robinson, and Laura Gonzales

Introduction

In recent years, innovation, entrepreneurship, and globalization have become popular concepts in relation to technology design. While some major corporations and other entities continue pushing for globalization through the design and dissemination of digital technologies, researchers also caution against the biases and oppression that can be embedded in US culture's "near-ubiquitous use of algorithmically driven software."[1] Countering some previously established orientations to globalization and entrepreneurship, this chapter highlights the importance of building technological innovation with (rather than just for or about) historically, structurally, and systematically marginalized and underrepresented communities. The overall purpose of this chapter is to showcase how technological innovation, when it is made and developed through reciprocal mentorship networks,[2] can disrupt a chain of signifiers of a

---

1. Safiya Umoja Noble, *Algorithms of Oppression: How Search Engines Reinforce Racism* (New York, NY: New York University Press, 2018), 1.

2. Angela Haas, Christine Tulley, and Kristine Blair, "Mentors versus Masters: Women's and Girls' Narratives of (Re) Negotiation in Web-Based Writing Spaces," *Computers and Composition* 19, no. 3 (2002): 231-249.

privileged structure and create makerspaces for and with community knowledge and information.

Multilingual User-Experience

In November of 2017, we—a team of students, researchers, practitioners, and teachers interested in writing and technology—designed and/or participated in the "Multilingual User-Experience Research Symposium." This event brought together over one hundred researchers, technology designers, translators, community organizers, students, teachers, and other attendees to engage in conversations about the challenges and affordances of creating tools and technologies in multiple languages, including, but not limited to, English. In developing the Multilingual User-Experience Research Symposium and the emerging Multilingual User Experience Research Consortium[3] that stemmed from this initial event, we seek to develop a "space where community engagement, professional development, translation practices, and technological design converge, and where professionals and community members with different types of expertise collaborate in reciprocal ways that highlight linguistic and cultural diversity as assets in the design process."[4] In short, the purpose of this consortium is to bring together diverse stakeholders who can influence the design and usability of tools and technologies that are developed for and by multilingual communities and, predominantly, multilingual communities of color.

This chapter is written by a team of women currently collaborating on several technology-design projects through the Multilingual User-Experience Research Consortium and through a mentorship project for women funded by the Coalition of Women of Color in Computing and the Kapor Center. The purpose of the project that we describe in this chapter is to increase the representation of women of color in the technology industry, specifically by establishing relational mentorship

---

3. Multilingual User Experience, https://www.multilingualux.com/.

4. Ann Shivers-McNair, Laura Gonzales, and Tetyana Zhyvotovska, "An Intersectional Technofeminist Framework for Community-Driven Technology Innovation," *Computers and Composition* 51 (2019): 5.

networks that support women and women of color who are interested in technology design, but who may or may not have had previous opportunities to benefit from infrastructures that support training and curiosity in technology. Structured as a year-long mentorship project that consisted of weekly meetings and workshops to discuss ongoing projects and learn new techniques in technology design, this project allowed us, as a team of researchers, teachers, makers, and students, to pursue individual projects related to technology design while also coming together to discuss our ideas and share our progress along the way. At the end of the Spring 2019 semester, we took a trip to Seattle, Washington, where we met with professionals in the tech industry who gifted us with their time and provided more feedback on our projects and interests.

Stemming from our experiences of building and participating in the spaces of Multilingual User-Experience Research Consortium and the Women of Color in Computing project, this chapter describes our own orientations to, and relationships with, "making" broadly defined. In this chapter, our goal is to make space for multiple ways of participating in a Maker Movement without privileging or settling on one formulaic approach or definition. As we illustrate, our approach to community-driven, multilingual making and design is anything but linear. Rather, it is rhizomatic, meaning it "has no beginning or end; it is always in the middle, between things, interbeing, intermezzo" and "is alliance, uniquely alliance."[5] Thus, in the sections that follow, we offer re/definitions of "making," specifically through the perspectives of women and women of color who seek to disturb the linearity of makerspaces as male-centered and/or as spaces of whiteness.

Re-defining Making

While conversations about designing, building, and making have been taking center stage in multiple disciplines and professional contexts and

---

5. Gilles Deleuze and Felix Guattari, *A Thousand Plateaus: Capitalism and Schizophrenia* (Minneapolis, MN: University of Minnesota Press, 1987), 25.

since "everyone is a cheerleader for the Maker Movement these days, from President Obama to the Pittsburgh Pirates,"[6] we recognize, as the purpose of this edited collection makes clear, that not everyone has equal access to, investment in, or interest in making tools and technologies. There are vast and expansive reasons for a cited lack of diversity in many areas of the technology industry. For example, according to Maker Media's press fact sheet, of the readers of *MAKE: Magazine*, 81% identify as male. And of attendees at the 2014 Bay Area Maker Faire, 70% identified as male.[7] Similarly, in Hackster.io's survey (done in partnership with tech giants such as Intel, Microsoft, Google, Amazon, and Arm) of more than 3,000 makers across 104 countries, fewer than 7% of respondents identified as women.[8] Interestingly, neither Maker Media nor Hackster.io reported on race/ethnicity.

While the Maker Movement positions itself as both an economic and an educational resource, Vossoughi, Hooper, and Escudé are wary of the "uncritical adoption of branded versions of making, particularly with regard to their implications for education equity,"[9] because as Barton, Tan, and Greenberg argue, "[t]here is little evidence that the maker movement has been broadly successful at involving a diverse audience, especially over a sustained period of time."[10] While some see makerspaces and maker practices as opportunities to bring underrepresented groups, such as women, into STEM fields,[11] others point to women's

---

6. Remake Learning, "The Maker Movement Gets a Dose of Critique," February 23, 2015, https://remakelearning.org/blog/2015/02/23/the-maker-movement-gets-a-dose-of-critique/.

7. Maker Media, "Fact Sheet," 2015, http://makermedia.com/press/fact-sheet/.

8. Hackster.io, "Hackster.io Maker Survey," 2016, https://www.hackster.io/survey.

9. Shirin Voussoughi, Paula K. Hooper, and Meg Escudé, "Making through the Lens of Culture and Power: Toward Transformative Visions for Educational Equity," *Harvard Educational Review* 86, no. 2 (2016): 210

10. Angela Calabrese Barton, Edna Tan, and Day Greenberg, "The Makerspace Movement: Sites of Possibilities for Equitable Opportunities to Engage Underrepresented Youth in STEM," *Teachers College Record* 119, no. 7 (2017): 5.

11. Susan Blackley, Rachel Sheffield, Nicoleta Maynard, Koul Rekha, and Rebecca Walker, "'Makerspace' and Reflective Practice: Advancing Pre-Service Teachers in STEM Education," *Australian Journal of Teacher Education* 42, no. 3 (2017): 22-37.

exodus from male-dominated makerspaces and hackerspaces to form women-centric spaces that promote feminist ways of making and collaborating.[12] Stemming from our experiences as women and women of color who are in the process of developing feminist ways of making and collaborating, we employ storytelling method/ologies in the sections that follow to highlight the importance of critical engagement with conceptions of "making" in both academic and non-academic contexts. Through reflective sections that draw on Royster and Kirsch's notion of "strategic contemplation,"[13] we showcase our varied but connected experiences with making in our communities. As Royster and Kirsch explain, strategic contemplation "allows scholars to observe and notice, to listen to and hear voices often neglected or silenced, and to notice more overtly their own responses to what they are seeing, reading, reflecting on, and encountering during their research processes."[14] By engaging in strategic contemplation, both in the written elements of this chapter and in our processes of collaborating on this project, we highlight the importance of experience and relationality in establishing spaces and opportunities for technological making.

Joy Robinson—Making to Break the Expert/Novice Binary

I am an Assistant Professor of Technical Writing and New Media in the English department at the University of Alabama in Huntsville (UAH). For me, making has always been the idea of exposing technology to those who might otherwise not encounter technology or digital processes in other ways. For example, exposing high school students to robotics technology and allowing them to explore the building of these machines as part of a broader digital learning process. But, as I worked

---

12. Sara Fox, Rachel Rose Ulgado, and Daniela Rosner, "Hacking Culture, Not Devices: Access and Recognition in Feminist Hackerspaces," in *Proceedings of CSCW '15, Vancouver, BC, Canada, March 14-18, 2015*, http://dx.doi.org/10.1145/2675133.2675223.

13. Jacqueline Jones Royster and Gesa E. Kirsch, *Feminist Rhetorical Practices: New Horizons for Rhetoric, Composition, and Literacy Studies* (Carbondale, IL: SIU Press, 2012).

14. Royster and Kirsch, *Feminist Rhetorical Practices*, 86.

with the talented young women in the Multilingual User Experience Research Consortium and through the Women of Color in Computing project, the idea of making took shape in the form of concepts and ideas extracted from user experience.

Every day, people struggle with painful user experiences that prevent them from completing their work and enjoying leisure activities. For example, a Facebook user might get frustrated trying to change her privacy settings, or a student in an online biology class could get overwhelmed using the course website and supplemental materials. In these cases, the user is having problems with User Experience (UX). UX research helps us effectively design products, technologies, and services to fit people's needs, facilitate intuitive and productive use, and evoke positive emotions. UX researchers use both qualitative and quantitative methods to study multiple, complex human behaviors and responses. According to ISO 9241-210, which provides standards concerning human-centered design for interactive systems, "User experience includes all the users' emotions, beliefs, preferences, perceptions, physical and psychological responses, behaviours and accomplishments that occur before, during and after use."[15]

To evaluate UX, researchers deploy several methods, such as interviewing likely users, generating product prototypes, mapping user journeys, and conducting focus groups. User Experience (UX) can be approached using a number of methods, based on whether you are exploring projects, services, or processes. For this reason, using UX methods (such as the classic framework of discover, decide, make, and validate from 18F) has guided our exploration and collaboration in the Women of Color in Computing project. UX methods allowed us to establish a space where we could ask the right questions and break the binaries between who is a novice or an expert in technology design. After taking time to learn about the students' ideas and projects, we (the authors of this chapter) set up a schedule to discuss the various methods

---

15. The International Organization for Standardization, "Ergonomics of Human-system Interaction—Part 210: Human-Centred Design for Interactive Systems," 2015, https://www.iso.org/obp/ui/#iso:std:iso:9241:-210:ed-1:v1:en.

under the broad banners of the framework, leading us to learn about each other's ideas and to build on them throughout our collaboration.

For example, Estefania's project explores ways to improve the graduate school application process for international students. The process for applying and getting accepted has a number of known issues, including understanding the requirements, tracking the application, and getting an update on the progress of the application process. Beginning with interviews of users (i.e., students), Estefania will attempt to map the pain points for students undertaking this process. Although Estefania's project may not have been initially conceived as a "maker" project, making graduate school application processes more accessible to international students not only improves individual platforms, but also makes for a more inclusive and diverse student pool across universities.

Estefania Castillo—Making as Meaningful Collaboration

I am a Master's student in the Rhetoric and Writing Program at the University of Texas at El Paso, a university located on the Mexico/US border. I live in the neighboring city of Ciudad Juarez, Chihuahua, Mexico, and I commute to school in El Paso. To me, making and building can only be achieved through meaningful collaborations. Being a *transfronteriza* student who crosses borders on a daily basis to pursue an education has made me conscious of the need for social justice work within my own community as well as other marginalized communities. I was first introduced to UX as an undergraduate student, when I took a course in rhetoric and writing. This course was eye opening for me, because it made me pay closer attention to the way the projects I produced and worked on would be utilized by users. As I pursued my graduate education at an institution on the Mexico/U.S. border and gained more interest in technical communication and UX, I began to notice the importance of collaborations between academia and the border community.

The Multilingual User Experience Research Consortium and the Women of Color in Computing project gave me an opportunity to keep building on my personal collaboration with my transnational community and to build new relationships in the process. I am looking at the usability of graduate school applications for international students and trying to find ways to make these types of websites easier to navigate for students. I believe that making and building websites that will ultimately be more user friendly for international students can only be achieved through a close collaboration with this community. These collaborations become meaningful through the practice of empathy and listening, which helps designers understand where users come from and what experiences they bring to any new interaction with technology.[16] When we practice listening with empathy in our work with communities, we can begin to understand users' unique needs and use that information to build more accessible platforms. Engaging in conversations and listening with empathy will help me as a researcher to work alongside international students so that together we can localize graduate school application platforms and make the process of applying easier for future international students.[17] Through these important collaborations, we can make and build alongside communities.

Laura Gonzales—Making as a Community-Driven Practice

Currently, I am an Assistant Professor of Digital Writing and Cultural Rhetorics at the University of Florida. In my previous position, I was an Assistant Professor of Rhetoric and Writing Studies at The University of Texas at El Paso, where I had the opportunity to meet Estefania, Tetyana, Bibhushana, and Nora. In addition to my academic work, I'm also a technical translator who works with various organizations to translate information in Spanish and English.

I became interested in technology design during my Ph.D. program, where I worked with Dr. Liza Potts and the Writing, Information, and Digital Experience research center on several projects related to women

---

16. Indi Young, *Practical Empathy: For Collaboration and Creativity in Your Work* (Brooklyn, NY: Rosenfeld Media, 2015).

17. Huatong Sun, "The Triumph of Users: Achieving Cultural Usability Goals with User Localization," *Technical Communication Quarterly* 15, no. 4 (2006): 459-460.

in technology, social media research, and writing program development. During this time, I also had the opportunity to work with community organizations and contribute to community engagement projects, which included working as a translations coordinator for the Language Services Department at The Hispanic Center of Western Michigan, facilitating a technology summer camp for Indigenous and Latinx girls through the guidance of Dr. Estrella Torrez at Michigan State University, and working with youth to write, share, and publish stories through after-school programs and initiatives in both Lansing, Michigan and Orlando, Florida. Through these experiences, I understood making as a community-driven practice with a long and often-erased history in Indigenous communities who acknowledge and centralize relationships between people, land, tools, technologies, and our surrounding environments.[18] I then decided that after graduating and as I continued my career, I wanted to focus on building infrastructures and programs that threaded together my interests in community engagement and technology design, specifically within the linguistically and ethnically diverse communities that fuel both my history and my work.

It was at this time that I began working at the University of Texas at El Paso, which sits on the Mexico/US border and has a student population that is approximately 90% Latinx (largely Mexican and Mexican-American). The first thing I learned after moving to El Paso is that my new community already inhabits the connections between community engagement, language, and technology that I only imagined during my graduate study. In this community, I had the opportunity to meet brilliant students who navigate across physical, linguistic, and technological borders whenever they visit family and/or return home to Ciudad Juarez, Chihuahua, Mexico, communicate in multiple languages (including Spanishes and Englishes) through a wide range of apps like WhatsApp and Facebook Messenger, and, perhaps most emphatically in terms of seeking an education, as they navigate an academic institution

---

18. Gabriela Rìos, "Cultivating Land-Based Literacies and Rhetorics," *Literacy in Composition Studies* 3, no. 1 (2015): 60-70.

that is still largely driven by White, Western, English-dominant values. In this context, I also have had the privilege of working with many international graduate students who, having left their families and homes behind in countries like Ghana, Nepal, Ukraine, and Mexico, utilize various assets to navigate tremendous institutional challenges as they pursue their degrees in the U.S.

While the community and the students I have the privilege to work with have invaluable assets that they can bring to scholarship and practices in community engagement and technology design, due to institutionalized racism and oppression these students do not always have avenues to enact their skills and see themselves as technology designers who can and do influence the development of tools and technologies that can inform our contemporary international, multilingual, cross-cultural realities. For this reason, with the collaboration and wisdom of my colleagues, we decided to develop the Multilingual User Experience Research Consortium as well as to participate in the Women of Color in Computing Project. Our goal through this work is to establish a cross-institutional, transnational, and multilingual mentorship model that will allow students like Bibhushana, Estefania, Tetyana, and Nora to practice and connect with technology designers across and beyond the United States. By staying in touch with attendees of the inaugural Multilingual User Experience Research Symposium as they undertake various projects in their home contexts, I continue to note the ways in which reciprocal collaboration can lead to technological innovation that is both grounded in community expertise and developed for linguistically and ethnically diverse users. Drawing on lessons that I've learned from my collaborators (including the authors of this chapter and tech and community leaders such as Clarissa San Diego and Sara Proaño), I recognize that it's not enough for academics to critique or analyze the tech industry and the interfaces and technologies developed in corporate markets. Rather, my goal as a teacher, researcher, and practitioner invested in technological innovation is to co-develop design methods and practices that are successful, practical, effective, and grounded in ethical, social-justice-driven collaborations.

Ann Shivers-McNair—Relational Making

I am an Assistant Professor and Director of Professional and Technical Writing in the Department of English and Affiliated Faculty in the School of Information at the University of Arizona. When I first began studying makerspaces and the Maker Movement in 2015, I came to the research with assumptions about what "making" and "maker" meant that were informed by narratives of the Maker Movement (at least in the U.S.) as a white male-dominated culture. I learned from spending time with makers in Seattle that the people who make and the practices of making they draw upon are dynamic, varied, and nuanced. Specifically, I learned from my ongoing collaborations with Clarissa San Diego, Founder and CEO of Makerologist, that making is about relationships among people, communities, technologies, goals, and economies.

From Laura's wise framing and leadership of this project, to Joy's beautiful explication of agile and lean workflows as they intersect with design, to Clarissa's brilliant strategies for facilitating and managing remote collaboration, I have learned about good design, collaboration, and project management. And from the interns, Estefania, Bibhushana, Tetyana, and Nora, I have learned creative and innovative ways to engage and expand strategies for design and making to do social justice-driven work across borders, cultures, communities, and interfaces. I've come to understand this work as "relational making."

When I say "relational making," I'm drawing on Indigenous frameworks to emphasize accountability and to honor the onto-epistemologies of the land on which I am an uninvited settler. As Shawn Wilson explains, "The shared aspect of an Indigenous axiology and methodology is accountability to relationships."[19] Certainly, these relationships are among humans, but they are also among humans and non-humans, as Angela Haas argues in her decolonizing work on race, rhetoric, and technology: "Technology is not what does the work, it is the work—and that

---

19. Shawn Wilson, *Research is Ceremony: Indigenous Research Methods* (Black Point, Nova Scotia, Canada: Fernwood Publishing, 2008), 7.

work relies on an ongoing relationship between bodies and things."[20] This accountability to relationships is at the core of the work I see my colleagues in our group doing, and it's why I'm excited for the practices of making that my colleagues are modeling.

Tetyana Zhyvotovska—Making Space for Social Justice Work

I am a Ph.D. candidate in the Rhetoric and Writing Studies Program at the University of Texas at El Paso. I am also a trained translator and linguist from Ukraine. As a person interested in the intersections of technical communication, user experience, and translation, making for me means creating a space where social justice-driven work is taking place for and with diverse communities. Multilingual communities are often overlooked and marginalized in various contexts, particularly in relation to technology design, where translation is often positioned as a problem to be fixed after a product has been designed and developed. Technical communication scholars argue that the quality of translation and localization in documentation affects the lives of people in vulnerable communities and in some cases might even put the health of users at risk.[21,22]

My participation in the Multilingual User Experience Research Consortium and the Women of Color in Computing project allowed me to focus on the intersections of technical communication, user experience, and translation through a UX project. Specifically, I designed a usability study where users engaged with the translated content of a website, which provided an opportunity for me as a researcher to examine how

---

20. Angela M. Haas, "Race, Rhetoric, and Technology: A Case Study of Decolonial Technical Communication Theory, Methodology, and Pedagogy," *Journal of Business and Technical Communication* 26, no. 3 (2012): 212.

21. Godwin Y. Agboka, "Decolonial Methodologies: Social Justice Perspectives in Intercultural Technical Communication Research," *Journal of Technical Writing and Communication* 44, no. 3 (2014): 316.

22. Tatiana Batova, "Writing for the Participants of International Clinical Trials: Law, Ethics, and Culture," *Technical Communication* 57, no. 3 (2010): 276.

translation functions in multilingual UX, considering the verbal, visual, and cultural elements of usability in conjunction with issues of localization and internationalization. In addition to conducting multilingual usability studies, I also interviewed researchers and practitioners across the country who attended the inaugural Multilingual User-Experience Research Symposium. In these interviews, I asked participants to define what Multilingual User Experience means to them and how this work engages their own interests and backgrounds.

One of the important aspects of space making for multilingual communities in technology design is through a focus on empathy. Indi Young sees empathy as a mindset with a focus on people and with the goal of understanding people's diverse thinking processes and perspectives.[23] Gathering, comparing, and analyzing patterns allows designers to make better decisions about their services and products. This approach helps me view a usability session as a space where a multilingual user produces reactions, formulates reasoning, and takes actions while navigating a website with multilingual content.

Developing empathy happens through listening. In this case, moreover, empathy means listening to understand one's thinking patterns, perspectives, and emotions while using a product, but also listening to one's voice in general. Listening can contribute to greater inclusion, and multilingual UX cannot exist without good listening. Multilingual users must be a part of the technology design processes, and the only way to see their impact on designed products is to include their reactions and experiences through usability research conducted with empathy and listening as essential and vital strategies. Thus, making to me means creating an inclusive space and a place for social justice work for and with diverse communities to amplify agency and to promote more just and equitable social practices.

---

23. Indi Young, *Practical Empathy: For Collaboration and Creativity in Your Work* (Brooklyn, NY: Rosenfeld Media, 2015), 18.

Nora Rivera—Making as an Intercultural and Interlingual Experience

I am a Ph.D. student in the Rhetoric and Writing Studies Program at the University of Texas at El Paso. My story with computers began decades ago, when my dad purchased our family's first IBM PC back in the 80s. As dull and bare as this archaic artifact may seem to us today, I was immediately captivated by it. Computer classes were far from being available at schools in Juárez, Chihuahua, Mexico; therefore, besides the crash course on MS-DOS and Lotus 1-2-3 given by the company which sold the PC to my dad, it was on us—my siblings and I—to learn to navigate the interface, together. Then, in the late 1990s, when I attended business school, the talk gravitated towards the customer experience when walking into a brick and mortar retail store. This was also known as "feeling" the branding. And shortly after, information technology departments, dominated by computer engineers, shifted their attention to transferring this "feeling" of branding to online stores. It was during this time that I became interested in desktop and digital publishing, which I also learned by experimenting and collaborating. Technology has taken remarkable leaps since my first computer, yet the way I interact with digital interfaces has not changed. I dive in and learn by collaborating with others.

When Dr. Laura Gonzales invited me to join the Multilingual User Experience Research Consortium, I was thrilled to work in projects right at the intersection of rhetoric, language, culture, and technology. From Dr. Gonzales, I have learned to give a multidimensional contextual meaning to UX. Her leadership and innovative work teach me day in and day out that UX researchers have a responsibility to be the users' allies. Furthermore, collaborating with talented interns and researchers from different institutions is an invaluable undertaking that teaches me to appreciate research through various lenses.

While searching for a deeper commitment to non-Western discourses, I became involved in a community-driven project centered on Indigenous language interpreters in collaboration with colleagues from the University of British Columbia in Canada, the Universidad de Veracruz in Mexico, the Centro Profesional Indígena de Asesoría Defensa y Traducción (CEPIADET) in Oaxaca, Mexico, and Dr. Gonzales. Together, we organized a conference for Indigenous language interpreters in Oaxaca, a state where more than one million people speak an Indigenous language. The purpose of this project is to gather professional and academic resources that will help create a collection of ideas and strategies to assist in the professionalization of Indigenous language interpreters, and the ultimate goal is to publish this collection digitally. Our team "makes" by collaborating via videoconferencing from three different countries: Canada, the United States, and Mexico. We embody various cultures and languages, becoming a microcosm of the kaleidoscopic array of cultures and languages that were represented in the makerspace of the conference.

My story with technology has taken me to makerspaces of cultural and linguistic fluidity in both the physical and the digital realms; hence, my understanding of making is an intercultural and interlingual experience that allows us to learn from the making practices of others who offer views which we might have not considered. Through this journey, I have learned to collaborate with gifted colleagues who make communities by means of technologies as new as video conferencing in English or Spanish and as old as translating and interpreting in Mixe or Zapotec.

Bibhushana Poudyal—Making as an Endless Deconstruction of Epistemes

I am a Ph.D. candidate in the Rhetoric and Writing Studies Program at the University of Texas at El Paso and an Honorary Overseas Digital Humanities Consultant at the Center for Advanced Studies in South Asia (CASSA). My doctoral research combines South Asian Studies and Critical Digital Humanities. I define Critical Digital Humanities as the development, use, and reflection of and on digital tools and methods to address and engage in old and new critical questions in Humanities by consciously bringing in rigorous, radical, and relentless conversations among these tools and methods, these questions, and Cultural Criticism. With this interpretation, I am building an online, open-access digital archive of my street photography in Kathmandu Valley, Nepal, while also documenting and theorizing the process of building this archive. This archival project is available at http://cassacda.com and is titled, *Rethinking South Asia via Critical Digital A(na)rchiving: Politics, Im/possible Ethics, and Anti/Aesthetics* (RSA-CDA). Through the Multilingual Research Consortium and the Women of Color in Computing project, I worked with our team to develop the usability testing processes and protocols that I am implementing in the development of my archive.

To work through this project, I am studying various theories and praxes of digital archiving via postcolonial and feminist orientations, arguing that archives, even when grounded in benevolent intentions, cannot entirely *represent* the complexities of any phenomena, including, in the case of my project, South Asian societies and peoples. As Ellen Cushman clarifies, "[S]cholars need to understand the troubled and troubling roots of archives if they're to understand the instrumental, historical, and cultural significance of the pieces therein."[24] I argue that as post/de/anticolonial and/or feminist archival theorists and DH practitioners, we should always seek alternatives to representation, rather than only developing alternative representations. Making archives, however ethical they try to be, are never entirely free from the matrix of power structures. The simple way to understand this limitation is by asking a question: Who does and does not have access to building archives, and to making in general?

Through these questions, my digital archiving project attempts to showcase the political, ethical, philosophical, and aesthetic journeys that push toward decolonizing and depatriarchalizing the archives, digital archives, digitalism, and meaning-making performances. The goal of this project is to offer a multidimensional contingent of narratives regarding Nepal and South Asia, to challenge linear digital representations of Nepal, and to critique the claims that one can "truly" represent Other(ed) worlds (i.e., the discursive and material spaces that

---

24. Ellen Cushman, "Wampum, Sequoyan, and Story: Decolonizing the Digital Archive," *College English* 76, no. 2 (2013): 116.

are sometimes categorized as "Third" world countries, the Global South, Non-Western worlds, etc.). Through my project, I invite my audiences to rethink these Other(ed) worlds and their representations.

Overall, my project hopes "to further illustrate how issues of access, innovation, and cultural training intersect in the design and dissemination of contemporary digital archives and archiving practices, and how collaboration and participatory research, which have always been at the heart of DH, can also be critical components of building CDH infrastructures in perceivably 'non-traditional' spaces."[25] Therefore, through my internship with the Women of Color in Computing Project and the UX techniques planned and designed with this project team, I am regularly conducting user-experience (UX) research related to my digital archive with different non/academic non/South Asian audiences to bring out multiple contingent narratives and to build an archive with my community. Recently, I conducted a UX study in Nepal with participants in a workshop titled, "Critical Digital Humanities and Participatory Design: A Workshop Series in Kathmandu." Through an invitation from the South Asian Foundation for Academic Research (SAFAR), I co-facilitated this workshop with Dr. Laura Gonzales. The purpose of my UX study was multifaceted: to help me select banner images for my archive; to get feedback on my homepage text; to help me decide on the themes for various exhibitions in the archive; to experiment with the nature of metadata; and most importantly, to build the archive together with different users and stakeholders in the project. Through this study, I seek to develop an antenarrative of Nepal and South Asia. Natasha J. Jones et al. delineate antenarrative as: "part methodology and part practice, an antenarrative allows the work of the field to be reseen, forges new paths forward, and emboldens the field's objectives to unabashedly embrace social justice and inclusivity as part of its core (rather than

---

25. Bibhushana Poudyal and Laura Gonzales, "'So You Want to Build a Digital Archive?' A Dialogue on Critical Digital Humanities Graduate Pedagogy," *JITP Pedagogy*, 15 (2019), https://jitp.commons.gc.cuny.edu/so-you-want-to-build-a-digital-archive-a-dialogue-on-critical-digital-humanities-graduate-pedagogy/.

marginal or optional) narrative."[26] My WOC in Computing internship helped me in finding ways of performing an ethical collaboration with community in technological design and archive building. The reflection fostered through my UX research, as well as my journey of conducting street photography and building the archive itself, made evident (to me) that making is an endless deconstruction of epistemes. This means a relentless construction of meanings/knowledge/archives and at the same time, never stopping to critically examine these constructions however ethical they might sound, look, or feel. This rigorous construction and questioning of epistemes is what making is.

Implications and Conclusion

Through our layered and relational reflections, our research team orients to making as a *techne*—"a heterogeneous history of practices performed in the interstices between intention and subjection, choice and necessity, activity and passivity."[27] There is no singular definition of making, makers, and makerspaces. Instead, aligned with the goal of this collection, which emphasizes "the critical work that is being done to cultivate anti-oppressive, inclusive and equitable making environments,"[28] this chapter provides story-driven illustrations of what making means for us as women in technology design.

The understanding of makers that we are pushing for is related to how Sara Ahmed defines feminism. She says that there is no definition of feminism as such, as "not all feminist movement is so easily detected. A feminist movement is not always registered in public. A feminist movement might be happening the moment a woman snaps, that moment when she does not take it anymore... the violence that

---

26. Natasha N. Jones, Kristen R. Moore, and Rebecca Walton, "Disrupting the Past to Disrupt the Future: An Antenarrative of Technical Communication," *Technical Communication Quarterly* 25, no. 4 (2016): 212.

27. Barbara Beisecker, "Coming to Terms with Recent Attempts to Write Women into the History of Rhetoric," *Philosophy & Rhetoric* 25, no. 2 (1992): 156.

28. Maggie Melo and Jennifer Nichols, *Re-Making the Library Makerspace Critical Theories, Reflections, and Practices* (Forthcoming), https://litwinbooks.com/books/re-making-the-library-makerspace/.

saturates her world, a world."[29] Similarly, the work that we share in this chapter, while grounded in ongoing projects such as the Multilingual User Experience Research Consortium and the Women of Color in Computing project, is at the core a work of often-invisible relationship building and collaboration. As researchers and practitioners, such as the contributors to this collection, continue pushing for diverse representations of makers and makerspaces, we argue that listening to stories of feminist collaboration and relationality in technology innovation can help us continue valuing, welcoming, and sustaining diverse perspectives to making. Paying attention to not only the products, but also the processes and relationships that shape maker initiatives can help us continue expanding the boundaries of perceivably monolithic movements. As our projects demonstrate, marginalized communities (e.g., multilingual communities of color) have always been makers and have always led Maker Movements. Thus, the goal of pushing back against traditionally-held notions of making as a male, Western-oriented practice, is largely reliant on learning to listen to the work that our communities have been engaging in and sustaining for centuries.

Bibliography

Agboka, Godwin Y. "Decolonial Methodologies: Social Justice Perspectives in Intercultural Technical Communication Research." *Journal of Technical Writing and Communication* 44, no. 3 (2014): 297-327.

Ahmed, Sara. *Living a Feminist Life*. Durham, NC: Duke University Press, 2017.

Barton, Angela Calabrese, Edna Tan, and Day Greenberg. "The Makerspace Movement: Sites of Possibilities for Equitable Opportunities to Engage Underrepresented Youth in STEM." *Teachers College Record* 119, no. 7 (2017): 1-30.

Batova, Tatiana. "Writing for the Participants of International Clinical Trials: Law, Ethics, and Culture." *Technical Communication* 57, no. 3 (2010): 266-281.

---

29. Sara Ahmed, *Living a Feminist Life* (Durham, NC: Duke University Press, 2017), 3.

Beisecker, Barbara. "Coming to Terms with Recent Attempts to Write Women into the History of Rhetoric." *Philosophy & Rhetoric* 25, no. 2 (1992): 140-161.

Blackley, Susan, Rachel Sheffield, Nicoleta Maynard, Koul Rekha, and Rebecca Walker. "'Makerspace' and Reflective Practice: Advancing Pre-Service Teachers in STEM Education." *Australian Journal of Teacher Education* 42, no. 3 (2017): 22-37.

Cushman, Ellen. "Wampum, Sequoyan, and Story: Decolonizing the Digital Archive." *College English* 76, no. 2 (2013): 115-135.

Deleuze, Gilles, and Felix Guattari. *A Thousand Plateaus: Capitalism and Schizophrenia.* Minneapolis, MN: University of Minnesota Press, 1987.

Fox, Sara, Rachel Rose Ulgado, and Daniela Rosner. "Hacking Culture, Not Devices: Access and Recognition in Feminist Hackerspaces." In *Proceedings of CSCW '15,* Vancouver, BC, Canada, March 14-18, 2015. http://dx.doi.org/10.1145/2675133.2675223.

Haas, Angela. M. "Race, Rhetoric, and Technology: A Case Study of Decolonial Technical Communication Theory, Methodology, and Pedagogy." *Journal of Business and Technical Communication* 26, no. 3 (2012): 277-310.

Haas, Angela, Christine Tulley, and Kristine Blair. "Mentors versus Masters: Women's and Girls' Narratives of (Re) Negotiation in Web-Based Writing Spaces." *Computers and Composition* 19, no. 3 (2002): 231-249.

Hackster.io. "Hackster.io Maker Survey." 2016. https://www.hackster.io/survey.

Jones, Natasha N., Kristen R. Moore, and Rebecca Walton. "Disrupting the Past to Disrupt the Future: An Antenarrative of Technical Communication." *Technical Communication Quarterly* 25, no.4 (2016): 211-229.

Maker Media. "Fact Sheet." 2015. http://makermedia.com/press/fact-sheet/.

Melo, Maggie, and Jennifer Nichols. *Re-Making the Library Makerspace Critical Theories, Reflections, and Practices.* (Forthcoming). https://litwinbooks.com/books/re-making-the-library-makerspace/.

Multilingual User Experience. https://www.multilingualux.com/.

Noble, Safiya Umoja. *Algorithms of Oppression: How Search Engines Reinforce Racism*. New York, NY: New York University Press, 2018.

Poudyal, Bibhushana, and Laura Gonzales. "'So You Want to Build a Digital Archive?' A Dialogue on Critical Digital Humanities Graduate Pedagogy." *JITP Pedagogy*, 15 (2019). https://jitp.commons.gc.cuny.edu/so-you-want-to-build-a-digital-archive-a-dialogue-on-critical-digital-humanities-graduate-pedagogy/.

Remake Learning. "The Maker Movement Gets a Dose of Critique." February 23, 2015. https://remakelearning.org/blog/2015/02/23/the-maker-movement-gets-a-dose-of-critique/.

Rethinking South Asia via Critical Digital A(na)rchiving. http://cassacda.com/.

Rios, Gabriela. "Cultivating Land-Based Literacies and Rhetorics." *Literacy in Composition Studies* 3, no. 1 (2015): 60-70.

Royster, Jacqueline Jones, and Gesa E. Kirsch. *Feminist Rhetorical Practices: New Horizons for Rhetoric, Composition, and Literacy Studies*. Carbondale, IL: SIU Press, 2012.

Shivers-McNair, Ann, Laura Gonzales, and Tetyana Zhyvotovska. "An Intersectional Technofeminist Framework for Community-Driven Technology Innovation." *Computers and Composition* 51 (2019): 43-54.

Sun, Huatong. "The Triumph of Users: Achieving Cultural Usability Goals with User Localization." *Technical Communication Quarterly* 15, no. 4 (2006): 457-481.

The International Organization for Standardization. "Ergonomics of Human-System Interaction—Part 210: Human-Centred Design for Interactive Systems." 2015. https://www.iso.org/obp/ui/#iso:std:iso:9241:-210:ed-1:v1:en.

Voussoughi, Shirin, Paula K. Hooper, and Meg Escudé. "Making through the Lens of Culture and Power: Toward Transformative Visions for Educational Equity." *Harvard Educational Review* 86, no. 2 (2016): 206-232.

Wilson, Shawn. *Research is Ceremony: Indigenous Research Methods.* Black Point, Nova Scotia, Canada: Fernwood Publishing, 2008.

Young, Indi. *Practical Empathy: For Collaboration and Creativity in Your Work.* Brooklyn, NY: Rosenfeld Media, 2015.

RE-IMAGINED MAKERSPACES: POLICIES, PROCEDURES, AND CULTURE

Chapter 12

MAKERSPACE COLLABORATION AS DIALOGUE AND RESISTANCE

Sanjeet Mann

In this chapter, I claim that librarians need to adopt a purposeful and strategic approach to collaboration in order to create inclusive learning spaces. Makerspaces typically come into existence through collaboration, and the space's identity is shaped by the nature of these partnerships and by partners' views on making. While the Maker Movement typically celebrates making as a means of individual empowerment with the potential to transform contemporary education and address inequality, other observers have criticized the movement for upholding business and military interests and universalizing experiences of middle-class whiteness.[1] Uncritical approaches to making risk deepening socio-technical divides along lines of race, class and gender. Librarians who want to create spaces that resist forces of social oppression must create space for critical reflection in their collaborative work.

Newell and Bain define collaboration as autonomous, voluntary work undertaken by multiple participants who agree on their goals, the benefits of working together, their understanding of the problem

---

1. Evgeny Morozov, "Making It," *The New Yorker*, January 13, 2014; Sharona Ginsberg, "Diversity in Making," *MakerBridge*, August 16, 2016, http://makerbridge.si.umich.edu/2016/08/from-archives-diversity-making; Shirin Vossoughi, Paula K. Hooper, and Meg Escudè, "Making Through the Lens of Culture and Power: Toward Transformative Visions for Educational Equity," *Harvard Educational Review* 86, no. 2 (2016), 212-14.

domain, the decision-making systems they will use, and the processes that will structure their interaction.[2] Collaboration is seen to enable partners to efficiently meet the demands of complex work undertaken amid constrained resources.[3] Library professional discourse frequently embraces this view of collaboration founded on values of rationality, choice, and agreement and affirms collaboration as intrinsic to successful librarianship.[4] However, models of collaboration based on agreement and efficiency fail to foster meaningful dialogue between divergent perspectives, navigate institutional power divides, and resist forces of oppression. Rather, makerspace collaborators should represent a diverse range of constituencies faithfully in decisions where lower-status stakeholders (such as students) may not be invited to the table. And they need to be able to communicate broadly and inclusively amid environments characterized by information overload, where communications (such as email blasts and project charges) run the risk of narrowing a range of opinions and viewpoints down to a single authoritative narrative.

My recent experience as a systems librarian and interim co-leader of an academic library pursuing a makerspace collaboration with an academic computing unit has compelled me to reflect more deeply on collaboration and to question my assumptions. In 2016, my colleagues developed a vision of teaching information and media literacy (IML) lessons through a library makerspace and introduced the concept into

---

2. Catherine Newell and Alan Bain, *Team-Based Collaboration in Higher Education Learning and Teaching: A Review of the Literature* (Singapore: Springer, 2018), 17.

3. Adrianna J. Kezar and Jaime Lester, *Organizing Higher Education for Collaboration: A Guide for Campus Leaders* (San Francisco, Jossey-Bass, 2009), 8-13; Lorraine Walsh and Peter Kahn, *Collaborative Working in Higher Education: The Social Academy* (New York: Routledge, 2010), 4.

4. Dick Raspa and Dane Ward, "Listening for Collaboration: Faculty and Librarians Working Together," in *The Collaborative Imperative: Librarians and Faculty Working Together in the Information Universe*, ed. Dick Raspa and Dane Ward (Chicago: Association of College and Research Libraries, 2000), 4; Walsh and Kahn, *Collaborative Working in Higher Education*, xvii; R. David Lankes, *The Atlas of New Librarianship* (Cambridge, MA: MIT Press, 2011), 170; Joseph Fennewald, "The 'Commons' Manager: Coordinator and Collaborator of New Learning Spaces in Academic Libraries," in *Partnerships and New Roles in the 21st-Century Academic Library*, ed. Bradford Lee Eden (Lanham, MD: Rowman & Littlefield, 2015), 126.

university-wide strategic planning documents. Subsequently, academic computing moved forward with a project plan for a makerspace hub in the computer center focused exclusively on digital technologies, and when leaders of the two units met to reconcile the diverging plans, we realized we had different visions of making. Librarians spoke of initial user-needs assessment, critical evaluation of technology, and analog forms of making such as zines, buttons, and sewables, while computing staff spoke of leveraging the Substitution, Augmentation, Modification and Redefinition (SAMR) framework[5] to convince faculty to adopt digital technologies including augmented/virtual reality (AR/VR), 3D printing, and Arduinos. We eventually agreed that we would each pursue our own goals, giving the campus makerspace a decentralized, multi-hub structure. Our library went on to establish a zine collection, teach IML sessions involving zine-making, and deploy our button maker at various events with some success. However, our campus understands making primarily in terms of computer-mediated interactions with digital tools, and when people talk about the campus makerspace, they mean the room in the computer center–staffed, funded, marketed and assessed by academic computing. Academic computing has secured grant funding to purchase equipment and repurpose existing space, hosted events to raise the visibility of digital making, and funded competitive technology grants to incentivize faculty to use the space, applying institutional resources to shape campus conversations about making in a way that our library simply could not match.

Critical scholarship is the best way to probe into points of tension and contradiction in our work, such as the feeling of disillusionment that comes when collaborators discover that the outcomes of their partnership don't match the ideals that initially motivated them to seek an alliance. Critical scholarship is a process of "denaturalization" enabling us to examine things that would normally go unseen because they are

---

5. Ruben Puentedura, "Transformation, Technology and Education," (Strengthening Your District Through Technology Workshop, August 18, 2006), http://hippasus.com/resources/tte.

assumed to be unexceptional or inevitable.[6] Critical scholarship also bears responsibility for proposing a better alternative to replace what is being critiqued.[7] In this chapter, I denaturalize makerspace collaboration by proposing that technology projects in libraries are influenced by neoliberal ideologies and a Western tendency to view technology as objects to be exploited. As an alternative, technology can be treated as relational and grounded in the needs of human communities, and collaboration can be understood as a process centered around Freirean dialogue. My goal is to inspire approaches for creating and re-creating technology-infused learning spaces on terms that empower our users—and our colleagues—to better realize their aspirations.

Collaboration as Neoliberal Instrument

This section explores the ideological foundations of the common understanding of collaboration as a process involving reason, choice and agreement. It is important to explore the philosophical basis for collaboration because ideology and practice are reciprocally related: what we believe as librarians shapes what we do in libraries and how we experience our environment, while what we do and experience also influences what we believe to be true. I propose that makerspace collaboration often takes place under common understandings of technology as objects to be exploited, and partnerships as processes of aligning and realizing self-interest, in an environment of resource scarcity where the goal is to maximize efficiencies. These understandings were developed through the historical interaction of multiple ideologies and have reached their present state under the influence of neoliberalism, a defining ideology of contemporary Western society.

Neoliberalism as a philosophical movement draws on multiple historical developments and other Western philosophical traditions to redefine

---

6. Christopher Grey and Hugh Willmott, *Critical Management Studies: A Reader* (Oxford, U.K.: Oxford University Press, 2005), 5.

7. Jonathan Cope, "Four Theses for Critical Library and Information Studies: A Manifesto." *Journal of Critical Library and Information Studies* 1, no. 1 (2017), 7, https://doi.org/10.24242/jclis.v1i1.30.

the notions of property, markets, common welfare, and political-legal frameworks.[8] Neoliberalism holds that human well-being arises from ownership of private property, participation in free markets and trade, and individual entrepreneurship, and that government intervention should be limited to only what is necessary to secure these conditions for individuals.[9] When put into practice through economic policy and governance, neoliberalism acts as a conserving force to support existing power relations and orients human behavior around economic principles of rational choice, optimization of self-interest, and competition over scarce resources. This results in "a logic of ruthless individualism which forces individuals to be primarily responsible for their own well-being."[10] Neoliberalism leads to a view of education as job training to enable participation in labor markets; this is necessary protection for individuals in an economy oriented around maximizing financial return to capital owners and market investors. The work of schools, libraries, and other institutions of learning is thus valuable only insofar as it helps fulfill the demands of the economy.

Neoliberalism carries three implications for technology collaborations. First, the view that the common good is best realized through private sector activity results in policies that underfund public institutions, such as governments and schools, creating an environment of perpetual resource constraint and pressure to innovate quickly. Kezar and Lester thus describe collaboration as an "intuitively good idea" given mandates from funders, governments and accrediting bodies to show immediate results.[11]

---

8. Rachel S. Turner, *Neo-Liberal Ideology: History, Concepts and Policies* (Edinburgh, U.K.: Edinburgh University Press, 2008), 247.

9. David Harvey, *A Brief History of Neoliberalism* (Oxford, U.K.: Oxford University Press, 2005), 5.

10. Nathaniel Enright, "The Violence of Information Literacy: Neoliberalism and the Human as Capital," in *Information Literacy and Social Justice: Radical Professional Praxis*, ed. Lua Gregory and Shana Higgins (Sacramento, CA: Library Juice Press, 2013), 31.

11. Kezar and Lester, *Organizing Higher Education for Collaboration*, 3.

Second, collaboration comes to be viewed as a strategy that may provide an advantage in this environment of scarcity. Actors who manage to sufficiently align their interests to reach agreement on the terms of their alliance can pool their financial, intellectual, and experiential capital and improve their outcomes, while still holding on to their defining attribute—the ability to choose, individually and autonomously. Here we see echoes of Newell and Bain's definition of collaboration, which emphasized rationality, choice, and agreement. Negotiation is key to collaboration under this model; for an alliance to move forward, each party must acknowledge it is in their self-interest to agree to the partnership. This requires delicate balancing acts to establish objective criteria for the negotiation and provide each side with enough "wins" to motivate agreement.[12] Under this model, when partners have different levels of power or access to resources, collaboration carries inherent risks—particularly for the less advantaged collaborator, who may be pressured to agree to an inequitable partnership or lose access to badly needed resources altogether because the stronger party decided the alliance offered insufficient benefit.

Finally, information technology is valued for its ability to optimize decisions through the accumulation, transfer, and analysis of data, and for its flexibility in adapting to all sectors of the economy. Information technology is thus seen as "the privileged technology of neoliberalism," an inherently beneficial force that should be applied wherever possible.[13] This view helps explain the popularity of technology-adoption frameworks in education, such as the SAMR model espoused by my collaborators in academic computing, which has been criticized as a prescriptive hierarchy focused on maximizing technology-mediated change.[14]

---

12. Roger Fisher, William Ury, and Bruce Patton, *Getting to Yes: Negotiating Agreement Without Giving In*, 2nd ed. (New York: Penguin Books, 1991), 13.

13. Harvey, *A Brief History of Neoliberalism*, 165; 159.

14. Erica R. Hamilton, Joshua M. Rosenberg, and Mete Akcaoglu, "The Substitution Augmentation Modification Redefinition (SAMR) Model: A Critical Review and Suggestions for its Use," *TechTrends: Linking Research and Practice to Improve Learning* 60, no. 5 (2016), 439, https://doi.org/10.1007/s11528-016-0091-y.

Harvey insightfully recognizes that neoliberalism could not become dominant without appealing to shared values and conforming to a pre-existing social environment, thus appearing to be "common sense."[15] Understanding technology and technical work as ways to maximize efficiency and realize one's interests should not be seen simply as a recent aberration in our thinking, but rather in the context of a Western epistemology centuries in the making. Popowich explains that ever since the Enlightenment, "technology [has been] thought of as an extension of the natural world...something to be dominated and controlled."[16] The formal project management (PM) techniques used to structure technology work in most industries, including libraries, are similarly concerned with controlling and ordering the surrounding environment. These techniques presume "a functionalist, instrumentalist view of projects and organizations, where the function of PM is taken to be the accomplishment of some finite piece of work in a specified period of time, within a certain budget, and to specifications...this possibility typically assumes rationality, universality, objectivity, and value-free decision making, and the possibility of generating law-like predictions in knowledge."[17] An understanding of technology as primarily a way to maximize efficiency thus rests on prior assumptions that the environment can be ordered, controlled, subjected to reason, and parsed as objective knowledge.

Critical scholars directly connect these presumptions to the ideologies responsible for structural inequality. Freire suggests that the root cause of oppression is an objectifying experience of power which creates "in the oppressor a strongly possessive consciousness—possessive of the world and of men and women...the oppressor consciousness tends

---

15. Harvey, *A Brief History of Neoliberalism*, 5.

16. Sam Popowich, "'Ruthless Criticism of All That Exists': Marxism, Technology, and Library Work," in *The Politics of Theory and the Practice of Critical Librarianship*, ed. Karen Nicholson and Maura Seale (Sacramento, CA: Library Juice Press, 2018), 52.

17. Damian Hodgson and Svetlana Cicmil, "The Other Side of Projects: The Case for Critical Project Studies," *International Journal of Managing Projects in Business* 1, no. 1 (2008), 145, http://dx.doi.org/10.1108/17538370810846487.

to transform everything surrounding it into an object of its domination. The earth, property, production, the creations of people, people themselves, time—everything is reduced to the status of objects at its disposal."[18] de jesus contends that historical patterns of objectification constitute the ideologies responsible for structural inequality in the United States, including racism, colonialism and Orientalism; these ideologies have been legitimized by democracy as the outcome of free elections and the impartial rule of law, and then perpetuated by institutions such as schools and libraries which claim to uphold democracy.[19] Once technology is seen as an object, it can easily be called upon to create prescriptive planning systems intended to maximize efficiency and effectiveness which serve to exclude people along categories of difference.[20] The work of these critical scholars demonstrates how neoliberalism endures as a structuring ideology because of an epistemology which regards one's environment as an external object and a resource to be exploited. This attitude of objectification has shaped Western understandings of technology and technological work and encourages us to view makerspace collaboration primarily as a way to maximize efficiency and realize our interests. However, adopting this perspective impairs our ability to imagine how we would orient makerspaces to advance social justice.

Collaboration as Relational Dialogue

Paulo Freire's *Pedagogy of the Oppressed* provides a lens through which collaboration can be understood differently—as a relational dialogue. Freire does not succinctly define dialogue; rather, he introduces it in relation to other concepts, beginning with the proposition that the opposite

---

18. Paulo Freire, *Pedagogy of the Oppressed* (New York: Continuum, 2000), 40.

19. nina de jesus, "Locating the Library in Institutional Oppression," *In the Library with the Lead Pipe*, September 24, 2014, https://www.inthelibrarywithaleadpipe.org/2014/locating-the-library-in-institutional-oppression.

20. Ursula M. Franklin, *The Real World of Technology* (Toronto: Anansi, 1999), 76; Angela Calabrese Barton and Edna Tan, *STEM-Rich Maker Learning: Designing for Equity with Youth of Color* (New York: Teachers College Press, 2018), 52.

of oppression is liberation. If oppression dehumanizes by objectifying the world, liberation humanizes as we strive for the right to live more freely alongside others also engaged in this struggle. Freire then amplifies his definition of liberation. He writes that liberation affirms human existence, and "to exist, humanly, is to name the world, to change it."[21] Naming is an exercise of power, a way of acting upon the outside world, but it does not necessarily give us the power to exploit the world so much as create the potential to be in relationship to it. Think of the difference in how we interact with people in, say, a meeting or classroom, when we do or do not know or remember their names. Since liberation is relational, to liberate is to dialogue. Dialogue refers to communication—people committing to talk and work together—but also suggests a longer-term alliance that goes beyond meeting immediate needs and transcends self-interest. Freire says dialogue both requires and produces critical "thinking which discerns an invisible solidarity between the world and the people and admits of no dichotomy between them—thinking which perceives reality as process, as transformation, rather than as a static entity."[22] The familiarity of our environment is disrupted when we encounter partners in dialogue and find that they perceive things differently. Each time we have this realization, our worldview changes in some way, however small, even though we may never fully understand or adopt our partners' distinct perspective. When partners are open to this dynamic of dialogue, they are able to display solidarity, "entering into the situation" of people experiencing oppression, which is "a radical posture" and a risky "act of love. True solidarity is found only in the plenitude of this act of love."[23] Liberation depends on recognizing that difference is an essential part of human nature and yet not an obstacle to our relatedness. Solidarity creates greater change: people who were once silenced now name the world; spaces once marked by dehumanization now affirm life. Freire is careful to point out that this is not the

---

21. Freire, *Pedagogy of the Oppressed*, 69.
22. Freire, 73.
23. Freire, 32.

privileged "saving" the oppressed, but rather distinct subjects meeting as equals to name and transform a shared world.[24] Dialogue ultimately creates mutual trust and the opportunity for participants to continue to learn and grow together, laying a foundation for future collaboration and a deeper engagement with each other's concerns.

The nature of collaboration looks quite different under dialogue than under neoliberalism: engaging in open-ended learning rather than meeting finite goals as efficiently as possible; entering into the concerns and situations of others rather than focusing on satisfying one's interests; occurring in conditions of abundance rather than scarcity. Some writers have reflected on the relational nature of collaboration and their statements take on new importance with Freire's concept of dialogue in mind. Partnerships succeed when collaborators adopt a position of humility and recognize the limits to what they can independently know and verify.[25] When aware of the limits of their knowledge, collaborators proceed with an other-centered mindset, acknowledge that they are accountable and interconnected, and open themselves to learning from their partners.[26] Knowledge created by these collaborations is not stable, rational, or predictable; it does not exist apart from participants but is created when they "wonder together": "we work together to bring into being dreams that would otherwise lie dormant in the imaginations of separate people."[27]

This mindset poses intriguing possibilities for makerspace creators. Instead of aligning individual interests at the start of a partnership in order to maximize efficiencies later on, what if we approached collaboration seeking to recognize our mutual interdependence with our

---

24. Freire, 148-49.

25. Rebecca Aanerud, "Humility and Whiteness: 'How Did I Look Without Seeing, Hear Without Listening?'" in *White Self-Criticality Beyond Anti-Racism: How Does it Feel to Be a White Problem?* ed. George Yancey (London: Lexington Books, 2016), 105.

26. Raspa and Ward, "Listening for Collaboration," 7; Donna Lanclos, "Embracing an Ethnographic Agenda: Context, Collaboration and Complexity" in *User Experience in Libraries: Applying Ethnography and Human-Centered Design*, ed. Andy Priestner and Matt Borg (New York: Routledge, 2016), 31.

27. Raspa and Ward, "Listening for Collaboration," 3.

partners? Instead of treating project work as a process of gathering and exploiting resources, what if we remained conscious that the materials we work with (ideas, people, natural and manmade resources, time) have inherent value unrelated to our ability to put them to work for us? Instead of making decisions only based on what seems certain and reasonable to imagine according to best practices and conventional wisdom, what if we also approached projects with openness and humility, seeking to learn alongside our partners and allowing the work to organically take shape through dialogue?

Implications for Makerspace Collaborators

I propose that librarians collaborating on a makerspace first examine the mindset with which we approach our work. We need to recognize how we are privileged as information professionals (particularly if we live and work in the Global North), as well as the ways in which our varying institutional situations can marginalize us with respect to likely partners (such as having lower pay or a contingent position, the historical gendering of librarianship as feminine, or the belief that library work is irrelevant now that information is "all online").[28] Intersectionality helps us achieve a clearer view of our relationships to the various groups affected by a collaboration, such as students, other library colleagues, IT collaborators, or administrators. We must approach our work with humility, particularly when seeking to enter into relationships of solidarity. Activists recognize they cannot claim the title of "ally" for themselves, but the people they work with will know when it is deserved.[29] Collaboration through dialogue is an ongoing process that requires patience, endurance, and the courage to embrace setbacks as part of the process of learning.

---

28. Shana Higgins, "Embracing the Feminization of Librarianship," in *Feminists Among Us: Resistance and Advocacy in Library Leadership* (Sacramento, CA: Library Juice Press, 2017), 70; 86.

29. Unsettling America, "Allyship & Solidarity Guidelines," *Unsettling America*, March 3, 2013, https://unsettlingamerica.wordpress.com/allyship/.

Second, we can use formal documents strategically to give voice to those with whom we are in solidarity by ensuring that process, structure, and user needs are considered at the start of a collaboration. Mission statements, strategic plans, and project plans are typically understood to legitimize the resource commitments needed to create and sustain a makerspace by appealing to institutional values and goals. However, these documents also render makerspace partners accountable to one another and mitigate some of the risk of conflict inherent in shared work. Formal documents are useful for these purposes insofar as they present a clear, authoritative perspective, but this comes at the cost of potentially erasing marginal voices and ideas that do not coexist easily with institutional norms. Walters and Van Gordon's suggestion that partners create memorandums of understanding (MOUs) at the start of a new partnership may be helpful here. Rather than signaling distrust of one's partners, these documents ensure that necessary conversations about structure and process take place and help those conversations to honestly acknowledge differences, leading to more balanced partnerships.[30] While Walters and Van Gordon do not discuss the potential for power imbalances in partnerships, MOUs can provide lower-status partners with a way to hold more powerful collaborators accountable – provided that the agreement is drafted equitably to begin with.

Insights from feminist writing collaborators may help address this caveat. O'Meara and MacKenzie demonstrate how different approaches to collaborative writing can affect the power dynamics within a partnership. They describe a method of collaboration called "compilation" which is reminiscent of the approach taken by my library and academic computing: here collaborators divide up responsibility for the work, with each partner working independently to complete "their" section. O'Meara and MacKenzie acknowledge this may be the best approach to take in some situations, but they also contrast compilation with another approach to joint authorship they call "melding." Here the authors each

---

30. Carolyn Walters and Elizabeth Ann Van Gordon, "Get it in Writing: MOUs and Library/IT Partnerships," *Reference Services Review* 35, no. 3 (2007), 392.

wrote a complete draft of their paper, then met to discuss the two drafts and create a third, hybrid version representative of each author's ideas. Melding proved an effective way to handle disagreement and represented "a double consideration of ideas," resulting in higher quality work.[31] It was less efficient than compiling work done independently, but more effective at pushing past the impulse to settle for "what could be agreed upon and not what was necessarily true."[32] Melding resists the temptation to foreclose on agreement and encourages partners to consider each other's ideas more deeply. This can give perspectives that aren't often heard the time and space needed to blossom into more convincing alternative visions to the status quo.

Finally, librarians can strengthen their ability to advocate with and for user communities by conducting ethnographic research about makerspace use. This suggestion follows from Freire's concept of dialogue as a participatory process that helps communities understand their own needs and resources, as well as O'Meara and MacKenzie's observation that melding worked best when they took time to discuss their audience before drafting their papers. Librarians are increasingly turning to ethnographic research to gain this sort of holistic understanding of user needs before designing new services and facilities. Lanclos explains that ethnography helps articulate the structural nature of complex problems and identify the diverse kinds of experience that must be brought together to solve these problems through collaborative work.[33] As a qualitative research method, ethnography shifts the focus of user research from "hard" data toward relationality and narrative and avoids objectifying the resulting knowledge. "There is a power in stories, in their relationships with one another, their resonance with a lived reality that is not effectively represented in spreadsheets and bar charts," Lanclos reasons. "Qualitative data gives us a chance to represent our patrons as

---

31. Anne O'Meara and Nancy R. MacKenzie, "Reflections on Scholarly Collaboration," in *Common Ground: Feminist Collaboration in the Academy* (Albany, NY: State University of New York Press, 1998), 218.

32. O'Meara and MacKenzie, "Reflections on Scholarly Collaboration," 219.

33. Lanclos, "Embracing an Ethnographic Agenda," 30-35.

people."[34] If my library had had user narratives documenting students' interest in analog making to refer to, our conversation with academic computing might have gone differently. When the discussion veered back toward objectified notions of making and tool-adoption strategies like SAMR, we could have put the focus back on students' needs and suggested participatory design work with students as a way forward for our campus makerspace.

Calabrese Barton and Tan demonstrate how participatory design contributes to inclusive experiences of making through their participatory action research conducted with students aged 11 to 16 as part of a summer maker camp. The youth studied what made makerspaces inclusive through interviews, photo diaries, and visits to local makerspaces. They prototyped ideas relevant to the needs of their communities, such as solar-powered scooters and light-up footballs for use in neighborhoods with infrequent public transit and few streetlights. They were encouraged to consider how their experiences with multi-generational poverty and social ties with extended family, churches, or neighborhood clubs were relevant to their making. As they applied this insider knowledge to their designs, they were motivated to learn science, technology, engineering, and math (STEM) concepts, but "digging more deeply into STEM took on local significance rather than reflecting a school and/or white male culture."[35] Calabrese Barton and Tan conclude that making undertaken in the context of community engagement does not simply meet vocational demands to learn STEM; rather, making amplifies the needs of communities, making them harder to ignore.[36] This project embodies the spirit and methods of collaboration I have been describing. Calabrese Barton and Tan's commitment to dialogue motivated their efforts to approach their students from a position of solidarity, their choice of participatory design methods, and their judgement about how much control to hand over to the students. The project intervened

---

34. Lanclos, "Embracing an Ethnographic Agenda," 25.
35. Calabrese Barton and Tan, *STEM-Rich Maker Learning*, 101.
36. Calabrese Barton and Tan, *STEM-Rich Maker Learning*, 103.

meaningfully in the lives of the student makers and resisted neoliberal understandings of making centered around acquiring job skills, adopting technology, and producing and consuming resources.

Librarians as Learners and Collaborators

Refuting neoliberal understandings of collaboration on technology projects is an ambitious undertaking that requires coordinated activity among librarians. The mindset of collaboration as dialogue that I have described in this chapter has to "scale up," with critical reflection by individual librarians leading to organizational learning undertaken by entire libraries that yields insights adopted by the library profession. David James Hudson has remarked on how hard it is for librarians to undertake this kind of collective action at scale. He contends that learning is a political activity and maintains that the structuring ideology of librarianship is a "practicality imperative" which channels librarians' professional growth toward incremental improvement and optimization of library workflows and away from constructing abstract or critical foundational knowledge. This discourages librarians from working collectively toward social justice, instead communicating that it is up to individual librarians or single libraries to solve problems with structural causes.[37] Clearly, we need to resist the notion that only readily applicable knowledge is worth pursuing, and instead support our colleagues in developing a holistic understanding of the problems facing our society and our profession's roles in working toward solutions. Librarians need supportive spaces in our libraries and in the broader professional world to engage in the difficult and often vulnerable process of learning through dialogue and critical reflection.

Systems and technology librarians have a crucial role in the process of initiating dialogue around makerspaces, since they are often tasked with leading makerspace initiatives and representing the library in collaborations. Observers have noticed how the "clashing cultures" of

---

37. David James Hudson, "On Critical Librarianship and Pedagogies of the Practical" (Critical Librarianship and Pedagogy Symposium keynote, February 25, 2016), https://repository.arizona.edu/handle/10150/612654.

libraries and technology centers complicate the efforts of their staff to work together, and have found a similarly unproductive dichotomy between "traditional" and "technological" librarianship.[38] Systems and technology librarians inherit both of these organizational cultures and may be able to use intersectionality to their advantage, helping translate a relational mindset regarding collaboration into terms that make sense to partners. Regardless of one's functional role, libraries need collaborators committed to long-term dialogue and trusted relationships of solidarity rather than short-term wins and temporary alliances of convenience. When our definitions of success, values, and methods diverge from those of our partners, we need to recognize these moments as the signals to foster dialogue. Hopefully, we will each learn something new in the process. Collaboration teaches us we are all interdependent, and we succeed or fail together, not on our own.

Bibliography

Aanerud, Rebecca. "Humility and Whiteness: 'How Did I Look Without Seeing, Hear Without Listening?'" In *White Self-Criticality Beyond Anti-Racism: How Does it Feel to Be a White Problem?* edited by George Yancey, 101-13. London: Lexington Books, 2016.

Askey, Dale, and Jennifer Askey. "One Library, Two Cultures." In *Feminists Among Us: Resistance and Advocacy in Library Leadership*, edited by Shirley Lew and Baharak Yousefi, 127-46. Sacramento, CA: Library Juice Press, 2017.

Calabrese Barton, Angela, and Edna Tan. *STEM-Rich Maker Learning: Designing for Equity with Youth of Color.* New York: Teachers College Press, 2018.

---

38. Edward D. Garten and Delmus E. Williams, "Clashing Cultures: Cohabitation of Libraries and Computing Centers in Information Abundance," in *Books, Bytes and Bridges: Libraries and Computer Centers in Academic Institutions*, ed. Larry Hardesty (Chicago: American Library Association: 2000), 61; Dale Askey and Jennifer Askey, "One Library, Two Cultures," in *Feminists Among Us: Resistance and Advocacy in Library Leadership*, ed. Shirley Lew and Baharak Yousefi (Sacramento, CA: Library Juice Press, 2017), 128.

Cope, Jonathan. "Four Theses for Critical Library and Information Studies: A Manifesto." *Journal of Critical Library and Information Studies* 1, no. 1 (2017): 1-7. https://doi.org/10.24242/jclis.v1i1.30.

de jesus, nina. "Locating the Library in Institutional Oppression." *In the Library with the Lead Pipe*, September 24, 2014. https://www.inthelibrarywiththeleadpipe.org/2014/locating-the-library-in-institutional-oppression.

Enright, Nathaniel. "The Violence of Information Literacy: Neoliberalism and the Human as Capital." In *Information Literacy and Social Justice*, edited by Lua Gregory and Shana Higgins, 15-38. Sacramento, CA: Library Juice Press, 2013.

Fennewald, Joseph. "The 'Commons' Manager: Coordinator and Collaborator of New Learning Spaces in Academic Libraries." In *Partnerships and New Roles in the 21st-Century Academic Library*, edited by Bradford Lee Eden, 113-28. Lanham, MD: Rowman & Littlefield, 2015.

Fisher, Roger, William Ury, and Bruce Patton. *Getting to Yes: Negotiating Agreement Without Giving In.* 2nd ed. New York: Penguin Books, 1991.

Franklin, Ursula M. *The Real World of Technology*. Toronto: Anansi, 1999.

Freire, Paulo. *Pedagogy of the Oppressed*. New York: Continuum, 2000.

Garten, Edward, and Delmus Williams. "Clashing Cultures: Cohabitation of Libraries and Computing Centers in Information Abundance." In *Books, Bytes and Bridges: Libraries and Computer Centers in Academic Institutions*, edited by Larry Hardesty, 61-72. Chicago: American Library Association, 2000.

Ginsberg, Sharona. "Diversity in Making." *MakerBridge*, August 16, 2016. http://makerbridge.si.umich.edu/2016/08/from-archives-diversity-making.

Grey, Christopher, and Hugh Willmott. *Critical Management Studies: A Reader*. Oxford, U.K.: Oxford University Press, 2005.

Hamilton, Erica R., Joshua M. Rosenberg, and Mete Akcaoglu. "The Substitution Augmentation Modification Redefinition (SAMR) Model: A Critical Review and Suggestions for its Use." *TechTrends: Linking Research and Practice to Improve Learning* 60, no. 5 (2016): 433-41. https://doi.org/10.1007/s11528-016-0091-y.

Harvey, David. *A Brief History of Neoliberalism*. Oxford: Oxford University Press, 2005.

Higgins, Shana. "Embracing the Feminization of Librarianship." In *Feminists Among Us: Resistance and Advocacy in Library Leadership*, edited by Shirley Lew and Baharak Yousefi, 66-89. Sacramento, CA: Library Juice Press, 2017.

Hodgson, Damian, and Svetlana Cicmil. "The Other Side of Projects: The Case for Critical Project Studies." *International Journal of Managing Projects in Business* 1, no. 1 (2008): 142-52. http://dx.doi.org/10.1108/17538370810846487.

Kezar, Adrianna J. and Jaime Lester. *Organizing Higher Education for Collaboration: A Guide for Campus Leaders*. San Francisco: Jossey-Bass, 2009.

Lanclos, Donna. "Embracing an Ethnographic Agenda: Context, Collaboration and Complexity." In *User Experience in Libraries: Applying Ethnography and Human-Centered Design*, edited by Andy Priestner and Matt Borg, 21-37. New York: Routledge, 2016.

Lankes, R. David. *The Atlas of New Librarianship*. Cambridge, MA: MIT Press, 2011.

Morozov, Evgeny. "Making It." *The New Yorker*, January 13, 2014.

Newell, Catherine, and Alan Bain. *Team-Based Collaboration in Higher Education Learning and Teaching: A Review of the Literature*. Singapore: Springer, 2018.

O'Meara, Anne, and Nancy R. MacKenzie. "Reflections on Scholarly Collaboration." In *Common Ground: Feminist Collaboration in the Academy*, edited by Elizabeth G. Peck and JoAnna Stephens Mink, 209-26. Albany, NY: State University of New York Press, 1998.

Popowich, Sam. "'Ruthless Criticism of All That Exists': Marxism, Technology, and Library Work." In *The Politics of Theory and the Practice of Critical Librarianship*, edited by Karen Nicholson and Maura Seale, 39-68. Sacramento, CA: Library Juice Press, 2018.

Puentedura, Ruben. "Transformation, Technology and Education." Strengthening Your District Through Technology Workshop, August 18, 2006. http://hippasus.com/resources/tte.

Raspa, Dick, and Dane Ward. "Listening for Collaboration: Faculty and Librarians Working Together." In *The Collaborative Imperative: Librarians and Faculty Working Together in the Information Universe*, edited by Dick Raspa and Dane Ward, 1-18. Chicago: Association of College and Research Libraries, 2000.

Turner, Rachel. *Neo-Liberal Ideology: History, Concepts and Policies.* Edinburgh, U.K.: Edinburgh University Press, 2008.

Unsettling America. "Allyship & Solidarity Guidelines." *Unsettling America*, March 3, 2013. https://unsettlingamerica.wordpress.com/allyship/.

Vossoughi, Shirin, Paula K. Hooper, and Meg Escudè. "Making Through the Lens of Culture and Power: Toward Transformative Visions for Educational Equity." *Harvard Educational Review* 86, no. 2 (2016): 206-32. https://doi.org/10.17763/0017-8055.86.2.206.

Walsh, Lorraine, and Peter Kahn. *Collaborative Working in Higher Education: The Social Academy.* New York: Routledge, 2010.

Walters, Carolyn, and Elizabeth Ann Van Gordon. "Get it in Writing: MOUs and Library/IT Partnerships." *Reference Services Review* 35, no. 3 (2007): 388-394. https://doi.org/10.1108/00907320710774265.

Chapter 13

DIVERSITY BY DESIGN: HOW TO CREATE AND SUSTAIN AN INCLUSIVE ACADEMIC LIBRARY MAKERSPACE

Katie Musick Peery and Morgan Chivers

Introduction

When the University of Texas at Arlington Libraries first conceptualized the creation of a makerspace, our aspiration was first and foremost to establish an inclusive space supporting a diverse community of users. We envisioned the space as a microcosm of the broader university—a hub of creativity designed with an open layout on the first floor of the Central Library, one of the most highly-trafficked buildings on campus. Once the initial construction of the UTA FabLab was completed and people began utilizing the space, however, we soon recognized that, although the lab was "available to all" in policy, it was not overtly welcoming, encouraging, or attractive to many learners who were not natural tinkerers or early adopters of these technologies. While we provided technical expertise and access to technologies unfettered from any curricular or departmental limitations, we were not actively addressing the invisible barriers that can inhibit one's sense of belonging in a place. Upon realizing this distinction, the work to conscientiously and purposefully reexamine and restructure the FabLab began in earnest.

Over the past four years, we have identified and worked to amend our approaches in four areas that greatly impact the user demographics of our makerspace: space design & equipment selection; student staff hiring; student staff training; and the intentional integration of course curriculum.

This chapter will focus on: the methods we've developed in the UTA FabLab to conscientiously recruit, train, and employ a diverse set of student employees; how our practices and approaches to makerspace design, intent, and management have evolved over time; and how these changes have led to a more robust, inclusive learning community.

Space Design & Equipment Selection

Like many other makerspaces, the UTA FabLab's physical location was originally carved out of reallocated library space. What once had been a help desk area for the campus's Office of Information Technology was now, with minimal new construction needed, the first iteration of our makerspace. This 800-square-foot "beta space," as we called it, was comprised of 3D printers, 3D scanners, a vinyl cutter, laser cutter, cameo cutter, desktop CNC mill, electronics station, Oculus Rift headset, and a sewing machine, along with the requisite computers and software to operate each tool and various hand tools. The technologies were arranged on counter-height tables, visible to anyone passing by over the open half-walls that enclosed the area. We intentionally did not add a door to the space, encouraging students to freely flow through and ask questions by eliminating what could serve as both a physical and psychological barrier to entry; we simply secured the area after closing with a retractable gate. The student employees staffing the space were trained to greet everyone entering the space and were expected to be sufficiently knowledgeable about each piece of equipment to assist anyone with their design projects; we refer to all non-FabLab-staff as "learners" to emphasize the peer learning environment where students, faculty, and staff are all equally welcome to experiment and learn together. Within this initial test space, we attempted to incorporate and maximize as many inclusive design and equipment selection decisions as possible to create a space that was appealing to learners from all colleges and departments on campus.

While many learners enthusiastically embraced this new space immediately, over time we were able to identify several factors that were hindering the realization of the holistic, interdisciplinary community we were seeking to build. Although the space was unrestricted by the presence of physical doors, the half-wall that served to form the doorway still created a choke-point for learners approaching the space.[1] People would often approach the entrance, peer in, and when asked how we could assist them, would gently decline the offer and walk away without further questions. Looking into the FabLab, would-be learners primarily saw high-tech tools being operated by male engineering students; the one small sewing machine and cameo cutter sat woefully neglected; most example projects reflected a distinct and somewhat insular nerd culture; and primarily only engineering and architecture students worked on curricular projects. In later assessments, some students reported that, while the staff was very friendly, they still felt too intimidated to ask questions, didn't want to be perceived as "stupid," and thought they should already be familiar with the tools in order to come in to use them. These observations and assessments led us to rethink how we should structure, staff, and equip the expanding space in order to encourage widespread adoption of the FabLab by both current and conspicuously absent learner groups going forward.

In preparation for our second phase of construction, we conducted focus groups and surveys to garner feedback from users on how they would like to see the space grow. This feedback helped to guide our thinking around future equipment purchases, such as the inclusion of a second laser cutter, more (and more reliable) 3D printers, and the capability to work with metals in the expanded FabLab's shop room. We built out a textiles area with more capable sewing machines, as well as adding sergers and an industrial embroidery machine. Around the time the planning for our expansion was beginning, we also had the opportunity to bring on our third permanent technician who was tasked

---

1. Charles Forrest and Lisa Janicke Hinchliffe, "Beyond Classroom Construction and Design: Formulating a Vision for Learning Spaces in Libraries," *Reference & User Services Quarterly* 44, no. 4 (2005): 296-300.

with integrating more of the arts. We also budgeted for the addition of printmaking equipment, such as screen printing and paper making, and electric kilns to work with glass and ceramics. When determining which technologies to add to the space, we synthesized the advice garnered from our focus groups with the foresight of our technicians, who aimed to identify tools that could easily integrate and overlap with the technologies we already had, while still offering novel capabilities and the ability to facilitate a wide variety of potential project workflows.

For the physical renovation, we removed the half-wall entirely to create a completely entrance-free space and extended our footprint across the entire southern half of Central Library's first floor, replacing worn-out soft seating, outdated computer stations, and paper printing (which was relocated to upper floors in the building). While the workbenches remained along the perimeter of the space to hold equipment, we added a mix of other tables and chairs in the center of the area to invite students to sit, study, and relax, regardless of whether or not their work related in any way to the FabLab. The new seating consisted of custom butcher-block tables,[2] as well as commercial laminate and whiteboard tabletops at both standard and workbench heights, along with stools and chairs. All tables are on casters and are a variety of sizes to allow for the frequent reconfiguring of the space as needed by users.

The subliminally open layout of the reconstructed and expanded space not only allows learners to be exposed to FabLab technologies without even realizing they've entered a new and different area, it also allows FabLab learners to become examples themselves as they use, display, wear, and share the objects made in our space in their life on and around campus. People curious about the FabLab do not necessarily need to seek out staff members to inquire about the tools or projects that they see—we frequently observe learners talking with each other as peers to learn about what, how, and why they are making. These conversations are initiated both by new students to the space who are

---

2. Morgan Chivers, "Scaling the DIY Approach: Do-It-Together with Student Staff Service Learning," Paper presented at the 2nd International Symposium on Academic Makerspaces, Cleveland, OH, September 2017.

inquiring as well as by veteran learners who are excited about their work, recognize the curiosity of onlookers, and are eager to share. These organic exchanges encourage previously unfamiliar students to engage in the FabLab when they otherwise might not have self-identified as a maker or sought out such an environment. The broader equipment offerings also helped to transform the FabLab into an area that was more appealing and comfortable to use for a wider variety of learners. See **Figure 1** and **Figure 2** for views of the UTA FabLab Beta Space.

Figure 1. UTA FabLab Beta Space with Half Wall Beside Entry

Figure 2. View into UTA FabLab Beta Space Post-Renovation

Student Staff Hiring

In the midst of construction to expand the FabLab, members of Libraries administration and FabLab leadership also brainstormed solutions to address the issue of representation amongst our student employees. While we, like many other academic makerspaces, utilized a peer-based student staffing model, our staff initially was not hired with the intention of being reflective of the demographics we wanted to welcome into the space. When hiring the first round of students for the FabLab, we counterbalanced the absence of any permanent full-time staff (at the time) by employing technically competent student employees who were enthusiastically engaged with the FabLab technologies, all but one of whom came from the College of Engineering. These students could quickly and adeptly learn how to use and help maintain the equipment and assist others with learning how to use the tools, which was precisely what we needed when first launching the space. However, the assessments mentioned above also helped us to understand that staffing is an important aspect of encouraging use by people of all disciplines, which meant that we needed to look for more than just prior demonstrated technical expertise when hiring new students—we needed capable, though perhaps as yet inexperienced, students who could reflect our philosophy that every tool in the space is accessible, learnable, and usable to any individual who has the time and desire to commit to learning them. We needed to reduce the stigma of incompetence and shame associated with not knowing how to use the equipment and felt the best approach to amend this was to hire more students without strong technical backgrounds who, perhaps, also felt intimidated by the very tools they would be expected to teach.

To address this, we sought out applicants who represented a wide range of majors, ages, backgrounds, ethnicities, and skillsets, and who all shared the collaborative desire to share knowledge with others in a communal space. During interviews, we inquired about students' experience with FabLab tools, but also asked questions to glean how they would approach learning new skills, what methods they used to teach others new information and assess understanding, how they communicated and interacted in difficult situations, what motivated them, and what other creative endeavors they had been a part of. We screened for technical competence, interpersonal skills, philosophy of customer service, and enthusiasm about contributing to this community. This shift in focus deprioritized the emphasis on prior digital fabrication experience and instead gave the demonstrated ability to learn new technical skills equal weight along with the ability to care for and assist others.

We encouraged students to embrace a growth mindset, to not equate inexperience with stupidity or failure with incompetence, and to understand that, although they were not expected to know everything, they were expected to ask questions and to commit to the process of learning each day that they work in the FabLab. Though many of these new student employees were unfamiliar with FabLab technologies when hired, they were able to gain competence with the tools and then leverage those learning experiences as a means to empathize with and inspire other learners. We have continued to use this approach to hiring for several years with great success.

Student Staff Training

To create a strong student staff out of novices, we also needed to provide rigorous training. Though a bit daunting and time-intensive, we have worked to evolve an instructional model for new student staff that enables them, in turn, to effectively teach other learners in the space. In its current state, our training regimen encompasses: training on software, hardware, and soft skills such as customer service, tour giving, and handling conflict; "shadowing" hours to observe and ask questions in situ; and assignments to complete after trainings to reinforce concepts and accrue hours of practical machine use. This comprehensive approach instills the significance of the intertwined teaching and learning processes in our staff, which informs the basis of their interactions with learners.

As mentioned above, our initial hiring ethos was rooted in the well-intentioned hypothesis that the best people to staff a makerspace are those most familiar with the tools in the makerspace. This assumption tends to encourage a more casual approach to training, along with an expectation that if a student staff member did not already know how to use a particular piece of equipment when they were hired, they would naturally learn how to use it through a combination of internal motivation and proximity to those who were using that equipment to make interesting objects.

This laissez-faire approach succeeded in producing FabLab student staff who were broadly knowledgeable about how to use the equipment and enthusiastic in sharing that knowledge with others. Experience working in the space, however, also revealed the shortcomings of this style and the need to improve the efficacy of our training approach. The extraordinary student staff who "got it" carried the bulk of the workload of tutoring learners—albeit predominantly by assuming a position of expertise that dispensed information and unilaterally determined what settings were appropriate for learners' projects without involving the learner in either cooperative or collaborative decision making.[3] Staff with less-developed competencies were content to defer to others or stumble through until some incident brought their ignorance into stark contrast. The resulting inconsistency of service and lack of emphasis on helping learners fully understand how to prepare their files and operate the equipment frequently resulted in frustration and feelings of learner disempowerment. Rather than blaming those student staff for inadequately teaching themselves to use our equipment and/or failing to instinctively employ advanced pedagogical methodologies, we critically examined our system for implicit structural inequities and proactively initiated processes that would better enable more students to gain fluency in the wide range of skillsets required to effectively help learners make. We also recognized that our new student hires would be especially in need of more guidance and oversight than we initially provided, given that many would not be beginning their tenure with any prior equipment experience. These processes are still, and will likely always be, evolving to further close the narrowing gaps in our collective knowledge.

---

3. William Damon and Erin Phelps, "Critical Distinctions among Three Approaches to Peer Education," *International Journal of Educational Research* 13, no. 1 (1989): 9-19.

In the same way that the first step towards fixing a problem is recognizing that a problem exists, the primary obstacle in our initial system was the peer-pressure against admitting that there was an aspect of a machine's workflow that one was unfamiliar with. A subtler insight was that our staff had a tendency to frame knowledge of a machine as a binary (knowing/not knowing), rather than a persistent spectrum (the ongoing process of learning more about various features and techniques). The binary mindset put social stresses on all makerspace staff, preventing the more novice from seeing a path for themselves to achieve self-actualization, and inhibiting the more experienced from using downtime wisely to push their own boundaries and expand beyond what they were already familiar with. Seeking to shift this culture, we reiterated the central importance of inquiry-based learning amongst makerspace staff, insisted that our staff communicate to "navigate" learners through the steps required rather than simply taking control of the interface to "drive" for them, and started training all student staff on every piece of equipment as part of the onboarding process, regardless of any professed or perceived pre-existing competencies.

Coinciding with this recognition that even those staff members familiar with a piece of equipment would benefit from formal training in the details of the interface and strategies surrounding its use, the deliberate decision to hire students with little to no prior experience amplified the importance of providing thorough training to all staff. Adding more equipment and raising the standard of expected workflow fluency while simultaneously lowering the standard of expected pre-hire experience presents an earnest challenge for everyone involved. When we began training student staff, we had five training sessions; we now have every student staff member complete thirty in-depth trainings![4]

---

4. Phase One: Intro to FabApp (our homegrown, open-source makerspace management software - https://github.com/UTA-FabLab); 3D Modeling with TinkerCAD; Intro to Adobe Illustrator; 3D Printing and Slicing; Epilog Laser; Boss Laser; Vinyl Cutter; Screen Printing; CNC Embroidery; Heat Transfer Vinyl Press

Non-Equipment Based: Onboarding and Expectations; How to Give Engaging Tours; How To Handle Accidents and Injuries; Mavs Bystander Training; Customer Service and Code of Conduct; four trainings administered by campus Environmental

In the three years since mindfully reorienting our methods to cultivate inclusivity, we have experimented with several variations on our training strategies, fully including ourselves and this entire process under the umbrella of iterative design. With each round of hiring, we have adjusted our training techniques in response to our frustrations in the previous cycles. Looking back, we can group these strategies into three categories: formal trainings at a fast pace followed by open-ended assignments; primarily student-led/train-the-trainer with semi-autonomous follow-up; and formal trainings paced out over most of a semester, supplemented with guided assignments and group critique.

Formal/Fast/Open-Ended
Once hired, new student staff would go through training in small groups on our most commonly used equipment (3D printers, 3D scanners, laser cutter, vinyl cutter, electronics, and sewing). Trainings were typically two hours each and were led by either a full-time technician or two highly-trusted returning student employees; sessions were scheduled around students' classes and other commitments, with the intent of getting everyone through the trainings as soon as possible. After completing the full set of trainings, students were given an open-ended prompt to propose, design, and fabricate one project that made use of at least three technologies covered in the trainings.

To check for retention of information, we gave each student a cumulative written test and had them demonstrate their abilities and critical thinking skills with each trained technology through a series of case-study scenarios administered by full-time staff and our GRA. Those who struggled with certain areas were mentored individually until they were able to pass the test and demonstrate successful navigation of applied skills in further case-study example problems.

Health and Safety – Hazard Communication, Hand and Power Tool Safety, Laser Safety, Back Injury Prevention
 Phase Two: Desktop CNC Mill; Stratasys uPrint; 3D Scanning; Paper Making; Sewing Machines and Sergers; Electronics; Glass Fusing; 3D Modeling with Solidworks; Cameo Cutter; PCB Mill

This set of training tactics dramatically improved student staff capabilities in the use of our equipment compared to the laissez-faire approach and was instrumental in helping to focus on the facilitation of learner projects from an increasingly diverse array of majors. Training results were sufficiently successful as proof-of-concept that previously inexperienced students could be trained on the equipment and ethos of iterative design, make relatively interesting projects, and quickly demonstrate capacity to help learners with markedly improved customer service.

As it was, we were encouraged by these results, though dissatisfied with the time commitment required to get everyone through the trainings and testing, as it thoroughly dominated the schedules of all the trainers and thereby disrupted progress on all other projects. In this phase of our development, we were still building out a lot of the infrastructure of the lab, and once students completed their open assignment, many were incorporated into service-learning projects led by a full-time technician.[5] The intent of the prompted open-ended projects had been largely to gauge comprehension and design abilities, as well as to generate excitement about the possibilities of what could be made, though we generally felt that real fluency would be gained through participation in the service learning projects and by helping learners.

An unforeseen issue was that, when given the open-ended design assignment, several students were paralyzed by having to decide on a project to complete; many were somewhat overwhelmed with the flood of information and had never been faced with such an unstructured assignment. Some students were overly ambitious with the projects they attempted and went through numerous design cycles before completing a project satisfactorily. Other than scheduled trainings, students were generally given the freedom to determine for themselves when they would come in to work on their projects, though this did not lead to successes in the way we had envisioned, largely due to the students' underdeveloped time-management skills. Despite encouraging design

---

5. Morgan Chivers and Katie Musick Peery, "Walking the Walk: Iterative Design in Student Staff Service Learning Projects," Paper presented at the 2nd International Symposium on Academic Makerspaces, Cleveland, OH, September 2017.

consultations and assistance along the way, it felt as though some students were just going through the motions on their individual assignments, choosing projects that would require minimal effort to complete.

Train-the-Trainer/Semi-Autonomous

Responding to our perceived need for greater efficiency in the training process, and with an extension of trust in the ethos of peer-to-peer knowledge sharing, we shifted course with a subsequent round of hiring to feature student staff trainers, significantly curtailing the number of hours each week spent by full-time staff leading trainings. All of these student trainers were highly proficient in the use of the equipment they were leading trainings on and had performed admirably in both service learning and customer service contexts.

One of our most dedicated student staff members had been hired on as full-time staff after graduation and led the initiative to create a workbook to help guide new student staff in their journey through the trainings. Throughout the trainings, students were encouraged to take notes in their workbook, and to build knowledge by completing challenges in the workbook instead of endeavoring to build an actual project of their own. Students were encouraged to ask each other for help when they were flummoxed, and to let their supervisor know if they wanted more in-depth training or mentorship. The lab ran smoothly with the new student staff integrated into the schedule, and full-time staff were happy to have more time to continue working on machine maintenance, course integration, and other projects without the time commitment of the earlier approach to student staff training.

When it came time to test the students' comprehension and retention, we gave the same written test and an abridged version of the case-studies. Results were decidedly mixed: some students demonstrated clear competence while others were surprisingly unprepared to answer simple questions about the nature of the technologies. Digging deeper, we found that those students who were less competent had effectively memorized the most frequently encountered situations and the settings required to achieve good results for learners with common projects, asking for assistance from student shift leads when a learner's project went beyond their knowledge. Some of the students who had led the trainings evidently had stressed the "all you need to know" basics, rather than introducing trainees to the logic by which the technology actually works and the rationale behind the differing effects of various settings choices in obtaining certain results.

Formal/In-Depth/Paced/Cohort Critiques
Realizing that we had taken a step back in the effectiveness of the training, we put more effort into selecting and developing potential trainers, clearly outlining the content to be covered and observing training sessions more attentively. After multiple rounds of hiring and training with this approach, we now believe we have found a sustainable training solution. Rather than aiming to complete all trainings as quickly as possible, trainings are intentionally spaced out, with each new hire generally completing three two-hour trainings a week, with the trainings paced across at least two months to allow for practice time and make-up sessions for trainees. This also allows the full-time staff to balance the workload of conducting trainings with the need to continue making progress on existing projects, while also attending to the requirements of maintaining a busy makerspace. Training sessions are scheduled for small groups, since the training curriculum incorporates frequent hands-on experiences operating the equipment. Trainees are given an independent assignment after each equipment training; these are designed to give enough room for creative flexibility to be interesting, but balanced with enough structure that it reinforces the most important lessons learned in the training and provides guidance to those novices who are still adjusting to gaining so many new technical competencies.

Between training sessions, new hires are expected to practice their skills by completing the directed projects and to "shadow" already trained student staff as they help learners with their projects. Trainings are ordered to complete sessions on the most vital and frequently used equipment first, enabling these "shadow" students to quickly gain sufficient competence to be of real help to learners during their scheduled shadow shifts. This sense of contribution to the communal goal is empowering for new hires and provides them with myriad opportunities to absorb nuances from existing staff, flex their new skills, and rejuvenate their motivational endurance to stay engaged with the trainings.

A crucial component of our current training structure is the cohort critique, which occurs twice within the semester-long span of the trainings. This group showing of their individual projects to their whole training cohort and all full-time staff; it has proven to be an effective motivator for getting students to take their assignments seriously and reinforces our emphasis on the path to mastery through iterative design. Gathering and giving meaningful feedback on a project is an important facet of iterative design that we had not explicitly built into our process in previous training regimens. We have found that by establishing an official event during which constructive criticisms can be shared with peers, and modeling such behavior in our discussions during that meeting and beyond, students are more likely to share insights with each other along the way, as well as with future learners. This greater sense amongst our staff of being a learning community has contributed to the quality of the projects we help learners make, the thoroughness and resiliency with which our student staff seek answers to puzzling situations, and the greater collective strength arising from our diverse interdisciplinarity.

Makerspace Curriculum Integration

A founding vision of the global Fab Lab Network is to provide access to maker tools and know-how—to help anybody "make (almost) anything."[6] As a library department, the UTA FabLab proudly supports the democratized access to creative learning resources by facilitating projects across the spectrum of making, giving as much priority to personal or beginner projects as we do to academic or advanced ones. Since the FabLab first opened, we have welcomed professors to assign use of the FabLab for required course assignments; initially, these projects primarily came from

---

6. "The FabLab Charter," The Fab Foundation, 2019, https://fabfoundation.org/getting-started/#fablabs-full.

engineering faculty and did not necessarily involve any consultation or involvement with FabLab staff. As we further assessed how we might evolve our space to better incorporate more of campus, one natural solution was to increase the number of FabLab-integrated courses from the arts and humanities. We have done this through two methods: brainstorming, consultation, and instruction with interested faculty; and formal integration into our assessed Maker Literacies program.

When first seeking to increase course involvement, FabLab staff pursued those instructors whom we knew were already using the space, as well as those enthusiastic faculty who were open to experimenting with FabLab technologies within their assignments. Initial conversations allowed us to gain insight into their course objectives while also granting us time to discuss and navigate the policies and potential workflow issues around executing their projects. The success of these efforts has led naturally to faculty sharing about their experiences, garnering more interest and engagement from new faculty each semester with nominal effort required from FabLab staff.

In an effort to measure and assess how students learn in makerspaces, the Libraries formed the Maker Literacies taskforce as a combined effort between the Libraries' Experiential Learning and Undergraduate Research Department, the FabLab, and select faculty, gaining insights from professors in Engineering, English, Education, and Art about how each discipline's broad student learning outcomes might be germane to the resources in the FabLab. Together, we developed a beta-list of transdisciplinary Maker Competencies modeled on the Information Literacy Competency Standards for Higher Education.[7]

The following semester, we began formally working with professors from several different colleges across campus to integrate FabLab resources into their syllabi and to assess both student and faculty experiences in the project. The response has been overwhelmingly positive; in the past three years of building this program, we have worked with

---

7. Association for College and Research Libraries, *Information Literacy Competency Standards for Higher Education*, American Library Association, 2000, http://www.acrl.org/ala/mgrps/divs/acrl/standards/standards.pdf.

over two dozen faculty to run at least forty-four courses for hundreds students at UTA and have piloted this program in several more courses at four additional universities across the country as part of an Institute of Museum and Library Studies planning grant, including courses from sculpture, history, mathematics, education, geology, and beyond.[8] Other publications detail the competencies themselves, our assessment strategies, the experiences of faculty/librarians/makerspace staff, the resulting data, etc.;[9] for the purposes of this chapter, the Maker Literacies initiative is important to mention, as it has explicitly brought students into the FabLab who would never have come in if they weren't assigned to do so.

At the beginning of our course integration efforts, it seemed natural to formalize the extant curricular work being made in our lab, though we were not then conscious of how thoroughly this would alter the social dynamic by transforming a lab that had been a haven for self-motivated projects into a hybrid space where learners who are fervently working on passion projects are mixed with those who are there as a requirement for their expected coursework. Another unanticipated corollary, especially in classes where physical making is almost never required, was the presence of learners who simply didn't sign up for this; most students don't expect their writing course to assign 3D modeling and prototyping, haven't ever thought about how to approach that type of project, don't know where to start, and aren't entirely convinced how this could be related to their studies. While some learners never come to fully embrace the FabLab technologies, others have reported that, despite their initial hesitancy, being required to use the tools challenged them to think creatively and increased their self-confidence in a way that

---

8. Martin Wallace, Gretchen Trkay, Katie Musick Peery, Morgan Chivers, and Tara Radniecki, "Maker Competencies and the Undergraduate Curriculum," Paper presented at the 3rd International Symposium on Academic Makerspaces, Stanford, CA, August 2018.

9. Martin Wallace, "LG-97-17-0010-17," Institute of Museum and Library Services, May 16, 2017, https://www.imls.gov/grants/awarded/lg-97-17-0010-17; Martin Wallace, Gretchen Trkay, Morgan Chivers, and Katie Musick Peery, "Making Maker Literacies: Integrating Academic Library Makerspaces into the Undergraduate Curriculum," Paper presented at the 2nd International Symposium on Academic Makerspaces, Cleveland, OH, September 2017.

felt empowering and encouraging. Many returned to use the lab after their assignment was complete and admitted that they hadn't known about the FabLab and would not have used it independently if they hadn't been required to do so for class.

Conclusion

In analyzing the effectiveness of all our efforts to diversify our user base, we have seen a significant increase in the number of equipment uses by all learners from almost all colleges between 2015 and 2018, with some variability in later years, after many of these changes were implemented.

Additionally, the percentage of use by college has become more equitable over time. While engineering remains our largest user group, their percentage of use has decreased from 74.24% to 45.49% while Liberal Arts rose from 5% to almost 24%. Though the percentage of use for some colleges has decreased, the number of uses from these majors has increased; we are not losing some user demographics in favor of others, there are just more people coming to use the FabLab.[10]

Consciously evaluating our physical space and the ways we approach student staffing and training, and the intentional involvement of coursework have all contributed to fundamentally altering our learner demographics. This experiential learning through praxis, iteratively seeking transformative experiences for all learners, requires patience and time before the results can be observed and measured; our experience suggests that such efforts are effective and well worth any endeavor to adapt and implement at other institutions.

Bibliography

Association for College and Research Libraries. *Information Literacy Competency Standards for Higher Education.* American Library Association, 2000. http://www.acrl.org/ala/mgrps/divs/acrl/standards/standards.pdf.

---

10. Katie Musick Peery, and Morgan Chivers, "Intentionally Cultivating Diverse Community for Radically Open Access Makerspaces," Paper presented at the 3rd International Symposium on Academic Makerspaces, Stanford, CA, August 2018.

Chivers, Morgan. "Scaling the DIY Approach: Do-It-Together with Student Staff Service Learning." Paper presented at the 2nd International Symposium on Academic Makerspaces, Cleveland, OH, September 2017.

Chivers, Morgan and Katie Musick Peery. "Walking the Walk: Iterative Design in Student Staff Service Learning Projects." Paper presented at the 2nd International Symposium on Academic Makerspaces, Cleveland, OH, September 2017.

Damon, William and Erin Phelps. "Critical Distinctions among Three Approaches to Peer Education." *International Journal of Educational Research* 13, no. 1 (1989): 9-19.

Forrest, Charles, and Lisa Janicke Hinchliffe. "Beyond Classroom Construction and Design: Formulating a Vision for Learning Spaces in Libraries." *Reference & User Services Quarterly* 44, no. 4 (2005): 296-300.

"The FabLab Charter." The Fab Foundation. 2019. https://fabfoundation.org/getting-started/#fablabs-full.

Musick Peery, Katie and Morgan Chivers. "Intentionally Cultivating Diverse Community for Radically Open Access Makerspaces." Paper presented at the 3rd International Symposium on Academic Makerspaces, Stanford, CA, August 2018.

Wallace, Martin. "LG-97-17-0010-17." Institute of Museum and Library Services, May 16, 2017. https://www.imls.gov/grants/awarded/lg-97-17-0010-17.

Wallace, Martin, Gretchen Trkay, Morgan Chivers, and Katie Musick Peery. "Making Maker Literacies: Integrating Academic Library Makerspaces into the Undergraduate Curriculum." Paper presented at the 2nd International Symposium on Academic Makerspaces, Cleveland, OH, September 2017.

Wallace, Martin, Gretchen Trkay, Katie Musick Peery, Morgan Chivers, and Tara Radniecki. "Maker Competencies and the Undergraduate Curriculum." Paper presented at the 3rd International Symposium on Academic Makerspaces, Stanford, CA, August 2018.

Chapter 14

HIRING, TRAINING, DESIGNING, AND HOSTING: A CASE STUDY OF AN INCLUSIVE LIBRARY MAKERSPACE

John T. Sherrill

As many critiques of the so-called "Maker Movement" have pointed out, framing makerspaces in terms of economic growth, entrepreneurship, and job training tends to privilege digital technologies, and the spaces themselves tend to privilege white men. Given this broader context, I will describe The Lab[1] in this chapter. The Lab is particularly significant because it has successfully marketed itself by using the language of economic growth and job training, while simultaneously developing a diverse community. I argue that The Lab has helped welcome and engage a diverse community by foregrounding hospitality and equity through its policies and practices. That is, while The Lab does not actively market itself as a feminist space, or an activist space more broadly, it does foreground diversity, inclusion, and equity in practice. In short, one of the primary takeaways from my time at The Lab as a researcher is how small decisions and day-to-day practices, supported by policies and consistent training, contribute to building equitable and diverse communities. As such, I will discuss in this chapter how The Lab practices hospitality as well as its hiring and training practices and some of the outcomes of these practices.

---

1. A pseudonym.

I argue that within the context of makerspaces, things like greeting visitors, structured orientation processes, events, and even policies, can be considered forms of hospitality. Further, I argue that such hospitality is particularly important for building inclusive and sustainable communities within makerspaces. Hospitality is not limited to simply greeting people or helping them feel welcome, though. Drawing from Jacques Derrida's definition of hospitality in *Of Hospitality*, hospitality stems from differences in culture and being and, paradoxically, involves mutual understanding of differences. Derrida's understanding of hospitality is, admittedly, paradoxical, because if there was already understanding, there would cease to be any foreignness.[2] Policies, however, are also part of this definition of hospitality inasmuch as, Derrida argues, "the foreigner doesn't only have a right, he or she also has, reciprocally, obligations, as is often recalled, whenever there is a wish to reproach him for bad behavior."[3] Clarifying these rights and obligations to visitors, in turn, may also be considered part of hospitality. That is, spaces which clarify their expectations and community standards, as well as the obligations of visitors, make it easier for outsiders to enter an unfamiliar space and community.

Similarly, Michelle Eodice examines the reciprocity between hosts and visitors in the context of educational spaces and, more specifically, writing labs. She argues that ultimately, hospitality is about creating equitable access, writing: "the hospitality we enact derives from historical and cultural definitions and from its contemporary usage as a metaphor for a set of moves—moves made in service to values found in our mission statements: access and equity."[4] She further argues that, in the context of educational spaces, hospitality depends on understanding more than just the space itself, devices, and people; it rests on

---

2. Jacques Derrida and Anne Dufourmantelle, *Of Hospitality*, trans. Rachel Bowlby, 1st ed. (Stanford, CA: Stanford University Press, 2000), 15, 17.

3. Derrida and Dufourmantelle, *Of Hospitality*, 23.

4. Michele Eodice, "Participatory Hospitality and Writing Centers—Hospitable Spaces," in *The Rhetoric of Participation*, by Paige V. Banaji et al., 2019, 50, https://ccdigitalpress.org/book/rhetoric-of-participation/eodice/hospitable-spaces.html.

understanding reciprocity. Quoting Parker Palmer, Eodice argues that "[H]ospitality is always an act that benefits the host even more than the guest....By offering hospitality, one participates in an endless reweaving of a social fabric on which all can depend....thus the gift of sustenance for the guest becomes a gift of hope for the host."[5] Recognizing that, the benefit of hospitality seems clear to makerspaces: putting in effort to welcome visitors and guests, and having clear procedures in place for enculturing the values of the space in new members, ultimately serves the goal of creating accessible and equitable spaces.

To build this argument, I first describe my visits to The Lab in 2017 to conduct research on women's experiences in makerspaces for my dissertation. I describe my research methods in this first section below, including how I addressed challenges of studying makerspaces by using a DIY electronic survey device. I then describe the design of the lab and the individuals I encountered there. Afterward, I briefly discuss the structure of workshops within the space. I then discuss in more detail the hiring and training processes that The Lab follows. Finally, I conclude this chapter with a brief discussion of the origins of The Lab's hospitality practices and how these practices can benefit other spaces.

Methods

I visited The Lab in July 2017 for my dissertation research. To conduct this research, I followed a mixed methods approach. During my two-day visit, I observed instructional workshops in the space, interviewed workshop leaders and volunteers, and collected various documents from the space. I observed two workshops: the first covered how to use the 3D printer in the space and the second workshop covered how to use the laser cutter. The first workshop was led by a woman of color, and the second was led by a white man. Before and after each workshop, I spent time talking with each of the workshop leaders about their experiences in the space. From these semi-structured interviews, I also learned about the history of the space and how it operates. Additionally, before

---

5. Eodice, "Participatory Hospitality and Writing Centers—Hospitable Spaces," 50.

and after each workshop, I spent some time walking the area to better situate my questions and analysis locally during conversations with the workshop leaders. Further, in talking with staff and volunteers at The Lab, I was able to collect documents, including membership applications, volunteer applications, codes of conduct and policy agreements, and training materials. After my observations at the space, I conducted a follow-up phone interview with a manager of The Lab to get additional background about the space's policies and procedures, and about some of the documents I had gathered. Finally, after my initial visit, I triangulated my observation and interview results via an electronic survey device that collected quantitative user experience data over three weeks.

For the survey, I custom built a DIY survey device.[6] After a longer online survey had yielded fewer responses than I had expected (and none from The Lab), I decided to use a simple analog interface with digital data entry. In particular, this device responded to the unique constraints of conducting surveys in makerspaces: users frequently enter and exit throughout the day, they may not have the privacy required for traditional interviews, and they are unlikely to complete online surveys after leaving the space. Further, the electronic survey offered an advantage of paper surveys compared with a touch-screen device: no surprise questions or requests for contact information. The survey itself was a 4-button Likert Scale, ranging from a very frowny face to a very happy face, in response to the prompt, "Please rate your experience today!" When one of the four buttons was pushed, the device logged the response to a text file along with a timestamp. The survey device was placed in The Lab for three weeks, and I was able to collect a total of seventy time-stamped responses during that time. The time-stamped responses helped prevent anyone from skewing survey results by repeatedly responding, and also helped The Lab by identifying popular times for lab use. At

---

6. For a more detailed description of how and why I built this device from scratch for use in makerspaces, including step-by-step build instructions, please see John T. Sherrill, "A DIY Electronic Survey Device for Studying User Experience," *Kairos: A Journal of Rhetoric, Technology, Pedagogy*, 23 no. 3. (2020), http://praxis.technorhetoric.net/tiki-index.php?page=PraxisWiki%3A_%3ADIY+Survey+Device.

the conclusion of my study, I gifted this survey device to The Lab for their future use.

Lab Description

The Lab is a small makerspace within a large public library in a major metropolitan area of Minnesota. The library itself is part of a larger system of thirteen libraries in the area and is located downtown just blocks from a science museum, post-industrial power plant, performance halls, and other culturally significant sites and tourist destinations. Like other buildings in the area, the library is an historical site, having been around for over 100 years. More recently, though, The Lab and the library have become important spaces for job training and professional development for a changing workforce—particularly for people of color and historically marginalized groups, and those who are re-entering the job market and need to develop new literacies and skills.

Part of what makes The Lab particularly noteworthy is its emphasis on hospitality and the communities it serves. While I situate this hospitality in relation to Derrida's *Of Hospitality* and hospitality in educational spaces later in this chapter, one form of hospitality is immediately apparent upon entering the space. Compared with spaces where visitors simply walk into an empty room or crowd of strangers, anyone who enters The Lab is individually greeted by a staff member. Though seemingly a small gesture, based on the results of my dissertation research,[7] whether or not visitors were greeted at a makerspace makes a significant impact on how welcome they feel in unfamiliar makerspaces and communities. At The Lab, visitors are greeted with a smile by library staff at the main desk, just outside The Lab makerspace.

Upon entering The Lab, in addition to being greeted, one of the first things that struck me was the diversity of library staff, volunteers, and members who greeted me. Their diversity broadly reflects the local community in terms of race, gender, age, and expertise in

---

7. John T. Sherrill, "DIY Feminism in Post-Industrial Spaces" (PhD diss., Purdue University, 2019).

different industries and crafts (based on library demographic data, local census data, my observations in the space, and interviews). Not surprisingly, this library has been recognized by the city for its efforts towards racial and social equity, aligning with similar city-wide hiring and training initiatives. This diversity, as well as practices like greeting all members, helps distinguish The Lab from more homogenous makerspaces. Additionally, the space also promoted hospitality through clear signage, including a prominent "Refugees Welcome" sign made on the space's laser engraver, a sign on the door clearly identifying The Lab and its operating hours, and large stickers on each wall of the space labeling various pieces of equipment. Further, visitors are able to observe the space and any active members through a large window before even entering the room. Though these features are not entirely unique to The Lab, they contribute to its overall welcoming atmosphere.

Despite its small physical footprint, The Lab consists of approximately 383 members, and hosts more than 1,600 library patrons each year. Of those members, 52% are men, 41% women, two members identify as transgender, and the remainder didn't report their gender, based on an interview with a manager at The Lab. The average member is forty-five years old. In terms of race, 69% of members are White/Caucasian, 10% Black/African American, 7.3% didn't report, 6.8% Asian, 3.1% Multiracial, 1% Other, 1% Hispanic/Latino, and The Lab includes one American Indian/Alaska Native member (n=173). Generally, Lab members represented the broader demographics of the local area, with these percentages being within +/- 5% of American Community Survey data for the city, with the exception of Hispanic/Latino members who were underrepresented in The Lab by 7.9%. Of the eight total volunteers and staff members I observed, the majority were women. Only two were observed to be white, generally reflecting the library and city hiring initiatives.

The space itself consists of a main desk, a central room with a work area, a recording studio, and a conference room. The main work area consists of several tables and chairs, a whiteboard (with a wish list for the space as well as timely information), multiple bulletin boards, storage space, and counters. The main space provides access to a digitization station (for converting between analog and digital audio/video formats), vinyl cutter, laser cutter, 3D printer, laptops with design software, sewing machines, and a range of crafting materials. All devices and storage in the main lab space are clearly labeled and arranged so that no single technology takes precedent, and all are equally accessible within the space. That said, there is one major physical division in The Lab: the recording studio is just around the corner from the main lab space and has a separate entrance.

The recording studio is further subdivided into an observation room; a recording room with microphones, keyboard, additional recording equipment, and an editing station; and an isolation room. The recording studio, and its relation to the main lab space, is particularly significant for two reasons: it is the second most popular aspect of The Lab for homeless patrons, but it has also been a source of division between members in the space. That is because the recording studio particularly welcomes patrons who might otherwise not use The Lab (and who are often excluded from mainstream makerspaces). This physical and social division in The Lab also demonstrates that hospitality sometimes needs to take multiple forms to be most effective, which I discuss in more detail in the Orientation section.

Workshop Descriptions

In addition to serving as a multi-use workspace throughout the day, The Lab also offers weekly workshops throughout each month. These workshops serve as an introduction to the space and the community there, while also teaching technical skills. The Lab management is well aware of this dual purpose. This awareness is demonstrated in part through the naming conventions of workshops. Each workshop is titled as some variation on "Learn [Skill] with [Person]," emphasizing both technology and individual community members. As I learned from talking with workshop leaders at The Lab, the choice to promote events as "Learn [Skill] with [Person]" was a very intentional choice.

Very early in the development of The Lab, workshop leaders recognized that drop-in style workshops failed to attract participants, and that participants were more comfortable knowing specifically what they would do during a workshop. Further, associating individual leaders with the workshops helped build community. By reading a name in the event title, participants gained a sense of which volunteers had particular skills and expertise, even without attending events. Further, this decision also subtly conveys a sense of gender diversity within The Lab based on workshop leader names.

In addition to discussing the naming strategy for workshops, workshop leaders also discussed workshop and event attendance. Although some workshops are held regularly each month, and others less frequently, anywhere from two to five participants is considered "a good turnout." Although there doesn't seem to be a clear pattern or reason for the variation in workshop attendance, one thing that was clear was who the workshops served. One of the most surprising things about The Lab is that it regularly serves patrons from local homeless shelters. In particular, the recording studio is the second most popular feature of the lab with patrons experiencing homelessness, but workshop leaders were even more surprised at the popularity of sewing workshops.

When the sewing workshops began, they were intended to be accessible introductory workshops that helped familiarize new lab members with basic stitches, sewing machines, and how to sew on a button. That is, the workshops were intended to welcome a wide range of patrons, including those with no prior sewing experience. Furthermore, because makerspaces often focus on "high tech" workshops that cover digital tools and technologies, the sewing workshops were also designed to welcome visitors who might be intimidated by, or less interested in, workshops on laser cutting or 3D printing (not to mention the gendered histories of these different technologies as well). However, workshop leaders quickly realized that patrons from local homeless shelters were attending the workshops to learn how to mend clothes and make other repairs, and to gain access to essential sewing supplies available through The Lab. In response to the popularity of the sewing workshops, The

Lab now holds workshops on making bags, mittens, wool slippers, and pillows. As a result of these expanded workshops, patrons are able to make items for themselves and often donate the finished goods to local shelters. In other words, returning to Eodice, these expanded workshops have helped foster a literal "reweaving of a social fabric on which all can depend," in which "the gift of sustenance for the guest becomes a gift of hope for the host."[8]

In short, there are many different factors that make The Lab a welcoming space, some of which include having a designated welcome desk, nametags, signage, an informative website, and a diverse staff. But to reach a level of hospitality in which members report overwhelmingly positive experiences and also broadly reflect local populations in terms of diversity, I assert that makerspaces need consistency in training, orientation, and policies. In the remainder of this chapter, I focus on these structures of The Lab and their significance. To do so, I first briefly discuss the results of my user experience survey, which further support my argument that The Lab is an effective and welcoming space. I will then discuss the application, training, and orientation processes for staff, volunteers, and members.

Survey Results

While my observations, interviews, and experiences in the lab suggested that members and visitors generally had positive experiences, I was limited to observing just two workshops in total. Further, being a white, cis-gender man, I entered the space as a privileged researcher and outsider, and as such would be unlikely to encounter any issues based on my race or gender during my visit. Given this, to help triangulate my observations and interviews, I collected quantitative data about visitors' experiences in The Lab via a one-question push-button electronic survey. This survey asked participants to "Please rate [their] experience today!" on a 4-point Likert scale. Shockingly, of the seventy responses to the survey over a period of three weeks, 100% of the experiences were

---

8. Eodice, "Participatory Hospitality and Writing Centers - Hospitable Spaces," 50.

positive. Of these responses, 86% were very positive, and 14% positive. This result reinforced that the policies and practices of The Lab have had a positive impact on user experiences, and suggests that my observations and interviews generally aligned with the experiences of visitors to the space.[9] It is too early to say if these results are generalizable for other similar library makerspaces, but I plan to conduct a future survey across multiple spaces in order to provide a baseline quantitative comparison of user experiences. That said, one immediate purpose of this survey was to produce quick results for The Lab with minimal labor, while also triangulating my observations and interview data.

Of course, even with high ratings, no space is perfect, and The Lab has had to respond to members acting inappropriately in the past. Before The Lab had addressed issues of gender, sexual harassment, race, and using gendered pronouns during orientation for new members, there had been some issues related to gender and pronoun use. Although staff and volunteers at The Lab were uncomfortable sharing details about past incidents and did not clarify whether it was an issue of misgendering, using transphobic language, or something else, they did describe how they respond to individual incidents. Further, they explained Lab policies and how updated orientation procedures have prevented further incidents via explicit training.

In response to issues reported or observed in The Lab, staff and volunteers have been trained to have a conversation with individuals to address the issue (no matter how awkward), learn more about what happened, how each person involved interpreted the situation, and how to respond appropriately. Depending on the severity of the situation, staff/volunteers may use the recording booth or isolation room to mediate the situation privately, or may elect to address the situation

---

9. By comparison, a second similar space where I conducted the same survey over three weeks yielded only twenty-four responses. Of those experiences, 17% were very negative, 8% negative, 17% positive, and only 58% very positive. Comparatively, this second space had a less structured training process for managers and volunteers, as well as a less formal orientation process, less signage, and fewer workshops aside from events focused on digital technologies, among other differences.

in the main lab in order to model their response for newer members and volunteers. Furthermore, Lab staff and volunteers are supported in their responses by library policies that set clear criteria for banning members, temporarily and permanently, and revoking Lab and library membership. In other words, these policies and procedures help create hospitality by setting clear expectations, boundaries, and consequences for new visitors and current members—guests in the space are not simply expected to adapt on their own through trial and error, but are actively guided.

Toward transparency of community expectations, the Library Conduct Policy is available on the library's website and is also posted in several locations throughout each library building. All Lab members are required to read and agree to the general library policies in addition to the specific lab policies. The conduct policy first addresses issues of "discrimination, violence, harassment, and offensive behavior," outlining what constitutes each of these. It also clarifies that this policy applies not only to the library, but that the city does not tolerate such behavior "toward any city employee or visitors to city property." That is, the hospitality of The Lab is also anchored in local laws and policies. Policy violations within the library are divided into two major categories: one-week bans, and longer "one to six month" bans. Weeklong bans are for behaviors including "shouting, swearing," "interfering with others' use of the library," and eating. Longer bans are issued in response to things like damaging library property, harassment, discriminatory behavior, aggression, assault, or repeated violations of library policies. Although this conduct policy does not clearly state that library membership can be permanently revoked, that point is clarified on the library website and in The Lab's materials and policies.

As with the application and orientation materials described below, it is significant that The Lab has a written conduct policy in place at all, and one that explicitly addresses particular behaviors (rather than broad philosophies of "don't be a jerk" or "be excellent"). Although having a policy does not prevent issues,[10] it does make the work of staff and volunteers easier, in that they are able to fall back on written documents and have a clear rubric for assessing appropriate consequences. That is, the conduct policy is a document that many makerspaces feel is unnecessary, until issues arise. This is particularly problematic when spaces assume that "everyone's welcome" and "welcoming everyone" mean the same thing. In addition to having written policies, minimizing issues in the first place requires performing and modeling the policies as well. At The Lab, this modeling happens during the membership application process, orientation, and through day-to-day interactions in the space (i.e., at times when people are newest and least familiar, but also throughout their time in the space). To explain further, in the following sections, I will briefly describe the application materials used by The Lab, and will then detail the orientation process.

Application Processes

For every role in The Lab, whether it is filled by staff or members, there is a formal written application and/or agreement. Additionally, staff are interviewed and go through individual training with library staff. Both staff and volunteers also undergo a background check as part of the application process. As described below, the process also involves formal orientation.

Staff

In the opening job description for both Lab Assistants and Recording Studio Assistants at The Lab, the diverse community of patrons is foregrounded alongside the economic goals of the space. "Many patrons are disenfranchised, speak English as a second language, or have other barriers to employment. [The Lab] seeks to address those barriers by assisting all members of the public in their pursuit of career or technical skills acquisition." Although this audience is not represented in the

---

10. Maggie Zhou, Alex Clemmer, and Lindsey Kuper, "A Code of Conduct Is Not Enough," *Model View Culture* (blog), October 27, 2014, https://modelviewculture.com/pieces/a-code-of-conduct-is-not-enough.

technical skills required for the position, it matters that this context is the first thing on the page across different applications (i.e., it is the first thing that greets potential applicants). Further, this statement is consistent with, and reflects the content of, orientation materials for staff, volunteers, and members.

Volunteers
Similar to the job application format for staff, the volunteer application requests contact information, applicants' preferences for different types of volunteer work, availability, background and experience, and references. Additionally, the volunteer application form clarifies that volunteers within the broader library system can be younger than eighteen years old. Though I did not encounter any volunteers in The Lab who were under eighteen during my research, other makerspaces within the library system are youth focused, as are different library events, which explains why this information is part of the application. In part, these form fields help the space track its successes and failures at representing various communities over time, particularly in terms of skills and experiences. Such information is important in helping The Lab's managers decide who will welcome new members and who will lead workshops on particular technologies and techniques. Ideally, the information collected helps avoid creating a homogenous mix of technical expertise among volunteers and consequently fosters a wider range of members.

Lab Members
To become a member, applicants must be at least eighteen years old and have a library card. Beyond that, they are required to provide contact information and age. They are also asked to voluntarily provide demographic information about their race/ethnicity, gender, occupation, and emergency contact information. This is particularly important, as it allows The Lab to generate annual reports that include demographic information and makes it possible to track changes in membership over time. This is further reinforced by the equipment reservation system, which enables the space to track use over time and the popularity of

equipment for different groups, all of which help give The Lab insight into who uses the space and how. In other words, this information helps the community get to know new members and track trends over time.

Finally, members are asked if they are interested in joining an advisory board and whether they are willing to allow the library to use their photo for informational and promotional materials. Regardless of whether applicants are interested in joining the advisory board, all members are welcome to attend monthly Lab board meetings and offer feedback on the space. The form also includes a section for staff use that documents whether the applicant attended orientation and whether they provided a photo release.

Orientation

After completing the necessary paperwork, prospective members attend an informational orientation session. The orientation sessions are standardized via a PowerPoint presentation and a membership form. The orientation PowerPoint covers the process of how to become a member, how to acquire a library card, expectations of members, equipment reservations, lab conduct, maintaining the lab, the space's anti-harassment policy, copyright information, research initiatives the space participates in, how to donate to the library, and a detailed discussion of all lab equipment. Based on interviews with volunteers and the manager for The Lab, orientation also includes a tour of the space, demonstrations of how to use the various tools, safety training, and a review of how to reserve equipment. Significantly, orientation also covers topics of gendered language, pronoun use and gender identity, community standards, and how standards are enforced and sustained. As a final step, new members are required to attend workshops for the major technologies in the space (e.g., 3D printing, laser cutting, sewing machines, recording studio). These workshops not only reinforce how to operate equipment safely, but also cover how to keep the space clean, how to use various materials, what types of projects members in the space value, and in turn, what values are embedded in members' projects. That is, while the workshops do help ensure that neither members nor equipment are harmed, they also play an important role in enculturating new members to The Lab more broadly.

It is important to recognize here the significance of simply having standardized orientation materials and application processes, even in a relatively small makerspace. For many spaces, introductions are informal if they even happen, orientation processes and materials are overlooked, and both members and volunteers/staff are expected to individually figure out how to interact with the community. When issues do arise, if they are even reported, managers are often caught off guard and do not have clear policies to enforce. Further, many spaces neglect to track or report demographic information about their members, which hinders their ability to accurately assess diversity in the space and makes it harder to identify issues of exclusion with much nuance. In other words, when basic practices of hospitality are neglected, it is much harder to correct at a later date. By comparison, hospitality practiced from day one fosters further hospitality by cultivating a culture of welcoming guests, while at the same time recognizing that guests also share responsibilities to the existing community. As one final example of how The Lab has fostered hospitality and responded to unexpected community issues over time, I will describe the creation of a monthly event designed to help unite different groups within The Lab.

After opening, although The Lab was successfully attracting members with a range of interests and expanding its community as a result, a problem was encountered that is familiar to many makerspaces with distinct work areas: members who used the main lab and members who used the recording studio didn't interact very much. The Lab recognized this, in part, through observation, but also by looking at equipment reservations and the training workshops new members were opting for. Despite the best efforts of library staff, volunteers, and members to get folks using the full Lab, people crafted with the various tools available in the lab space, or they recorded, but rarely mixed. Coincidentally, a solution to this issue emerged in response to another common problem: limited hours of operation.

Because the library that houses The Lab is only open until 5 PM, some members' work schedules prevented them from visiting The Lab. Given the scale of the library itself, simply extending the regular hours of The Lab was impractical, since it would require keeping the whole library open (and secured). As a compromise, The Lab started hosting "After Dark" events once a month, mostly to be more hospitable to members who couldn't attend during regular operating hours. These monthly After Dark events are more social in nature than regular workshops and The Lab stays open for an extra hour. For each After Dark event, visitors can participate in a make-and-take tutorial (as well as normal equipment reservations), but there is also usually some type of live performance (by musicians, artists, guest speakers, performers, etc.) held in the main lab space. The performances and speakers helped draw in lab users; in fact, many of the performers in the lab were people who normally used the recording studio. This alone helped members mingle, but lab users also started helping performers think about promotion and branding, particularly how they could use the lab to produce things like promotional stickers or business cards. As a result, the After Dark events helped to bridge these two distinct groups within the broader Lab community through craft and performance centered on socializing. Additionally, following the After Dark events, the lab adjusted new member orientations to cover all areas of the space rather than focusing only on the areas new members were interested in, which helped to create a more unified community.

Conclusion

For makerspaces, the results of this case study suggest that it is important for spaces to not only have clear conduct policies, but that these policies are performed and enforced consistently across written applications and documents, orientation processes, workshops and training, events, and especially in day-to-day interactions within the space. Although The Lab is not directly identified in this chapter, many of the policies and practices of the space have been modeled after the hospitality of the YOUmedia space in the Chicago Public Library.[11] Further, The Lab shares many principles with the Ada Initiative.[12] In short, The Lab is a space that has foregrounded building an inclusive and accessible community first, while providing access to technology, training, and professional development opportunities to that community. In turn, this community has helped build an even more effective space for a wider range of community members. In other words, being welcomed in a structured and active way helped guests succeed in the existing Lab community, and eventually led to them practicing the same hospitality when welcoming new members. Hospitality, by Derrida's definition, requires distinguishing between hosts and visitors. As such, simply assuming that members will feel welcome, rather than actively welcoming them, often leads to homogeneity. Outsiders who feel welcome without any acts of hospitality are likely already familiar with the conventions of a given community, or assume that they are, until problems arise. By comparison, outsiders who feel unwelcome are unlikely to stay for long or suddenly feel welcome without active hospitality from hosts. Though this premise seems straightforward, as evidenced by the efforts of The Lab, succeeding at creating hospitable makerspaces takes considerable work, despite the work sometimes being a simple "Hello!"

Bibliography

"Ada Initiative." Ada Initiative. Accessed August 1, 2019. https://adainitiative.org/.

Derrida, Jacques, and Anne Dufourmantelle. *Of Hospitality*. Translated by Rachel Bowlby. 1st edition. Stanford, CA: Stanford University Press, 2000.

Eodice, Michele. "Participatory Hospitality and Writing Centers—Hospitable Spaces." In *The Rhetoric of Participation*, by Paige V. Banaji,

---

11. "YOUmedia," accessed August 1, 2019, https://www.chipublib.org/programs-and-partnerships/youmedia/.

12. "Ada Initiative," Ada Initiative, accessed August 1, 2019, https://adainitiative.org/.

Lisa Blankenship, Katherine DeLuca, Lauren Obermark, and Ryan Omizo, 2019. https://ccdigitalpress.org/book/rhetoric-of-participation/eodice/hospitable-spaces.html.

Sherrill, John T. "A DIY Electronic Survey Device for Studying User Experience," *Kairos: A Journal of Rhetoric, Technology, Pedagogy,* 23 no. 3. (2020). http://praxis.technorhetoric.net/tiki-index.php?page=PraxisWiki%3A_%3ADIY+Survey+Device.

Sherrill, John T. "DIY Feminism in Post-Industrial Spaces." Dissertation, Purdue University, 2019.

"YOUmedia." Accessed August 1, 2019. https://www.chipublib.org/programs-and-partnerships/youmedia/.

Zhou, Maggie, Alex Clemmer, and Lindsey Kuper. "A Code of Conduct Is Not Enough." *Model View Culture* (blog), October 27, 2014. https://modelviewculture.com/pieces/a-code-of-conduct-is-not-enough.

Chapter 15

CONFRONTING EXPECTATIONS: REFLECTIONS ON IMPOSTOR SYNDROME IN THE MAKER MOVEMENT

Leanne Nay

When I first learned of impostor syndrome, I immediately thought of my work with makerspaces. My institution is home to several makerspaces and I'm part of a group of campus makerspace partners. When I initially joined the group, I was fairly confident in my library bubble, but completely unprepared to engage in the broader Maker Movement beyond the library. After all, I didn't manage a physical space, I didn't have a 3D printer (gasp!), and I was the only woman in the group. Unlike my colleagues, my expertise was in areas like screen printing and sewable circuits, rather than digital fabrication. How could I talk about making light-up valentines alongside someone who had 3D printed a prosthetic arm? Because of my insecurities, I rarely spoke in meetings. It wasn't until I heard about impostor syndrome that I realized why I consistently dreaded these interactions.

To those who are unfamiliar with the term, impostor syndrome is "commonly understood as a false and sometimes crippling belief that one's successes are the product of luck or fraud rather than skill."[1] In other words, it's the sinking feeling that you're a phony and it's only a matter of time before people find out. After my self-diagnosis, I set out

---

1. "Where Does 'Impostor Syndrome' Come From?" *Merriam-Webster*, accessed April 13, 2019, https://www.merriam-webster.com/words-at-play/what-is-impostor-syndrome.

to find librarians to commiserate with and whenever I spoke of impostor syndrome, I was instantly met with enthusiastic nods of agreement or likes on Twitter. The most reassuring step in this process was the feeling that I wasn't alone. As I delved deeper into these interviews, I was pleasantly surprised to find that although many of my peers had experienced similar feelings of inadequacy, they somehow managed to keep moving forward.

Over the course of four months, I conducted formal interviews, had countless casual chats with my colleagues, and gave a local presentation about conquering impostor syndrome in academia. I also read and reread Dr. Valerie Young's book, "The Secret Thoughts of Successful Women" and consulted her work repeatedly.[2] For the interviews, I looked for individuals with a leadership role in a library makerspace and started with folks that I had interacted with online or at conferences. I developed a set of questions to kick off these interviews and then proceeded to email back and forth with follow-up questions. These discussions have convinced me that there's plenty more to say about this topic, but for the sake of brevity, I chose to include interviews from the individuals that touched on the themes I identified.

I should also note that I chose to only interview women, and the majority of my interviewees were white cisgender women. An often cited study from Intel and *Make* magazine found that 81% of American makers were men.[3] Given this gender gap, I was most interested in hearing about women's experiences, but I recognize that as a white woman at a large research institution, I've had opportunities that are not available to others. Much of the research suggests that women are more likely to experience impostor syndrome, but people of color and non-binary individuals are affected even more significantly.[4] This pub-

---

2. Valerie Young, *The Secret Thoughts of Successful Women* (New York: Crown Business, 2011).

3. Make/Intel, "Maker Market Study and Media Report," 2012, https://cdn.makezine.com/make/bootstrap/img/etc/Maker-Market-Study.pdf, 24.

4. Kristin Wong, "Dealing With Impostor Syndrome When You're Treated as an Impostor," *New York Times*, June 12, 2018, https://www.nytimes.com/2018/06/12/

lication is one of the first to truly investigate different perspectives in library makerspaces. As our community grows, I hope that we are able to hear from an even wider range of voices.

My intention is that any librarian who is actively engaging in makerspaces or has suddenly found a makerspace in their purview will recognize that impostor syndrome is real but can be overcome. As a result of my impostor journey, I determined four affirmations for working through self-doubt:

1. Embrace non-technical forms of making. Arts, crafts, and design have a place in the Maker Movement.
2. Take pride in your library. Libraries are a unique and fitting environment for makerspaces.
3. Find comfort in not knowing.
4. You are not alone! When in doubt, reach out to other librarians doing similar work for encouragement.

Interview #1: Camille Andrews

Camille Andrews is the Emerging Literacies Librarian at Cornell University's Mann Library, home of the mannUfactory makerspace.

Leanne: What's your role in the mannUfactory and how did you come to makerspaces?

Camille: I am currently responsible for instruction, curricular integration and outreach in the mannUfactory. My library career has led me, variously, into areas like instruction, information and digital media literacies, learning technologies, user studies, design thinking, and space assessment. I was co-chair for the original design and implementation team that re-started the library's investigation into 3D printing and makerspaces, which ultimately led to my current role. I'd actually never really done anything in makerspaces until I started on that team.

Do you consider yourself a maker? Have you ever experienced impostor syndrome when it comes to making?

---

smarter-living/dealing-with-impostor-syndrome-when-youre-treated-as-an-impostor.html.

I never considered myself a maker and that's slowly changing; impostor syndrome is real, as they say. Most of the infrequent making I do is digital (writing, video) and I've never considered myself crafty, handy, or mechanically inclined. I've been lucky enough to be part of communities that encourage amateur and participatory creation though, and also with new areas at work I've had to learn to jump in and try things out and play around, to get comfortable not knowing and also modeling what you do when you don't know and need to learn. This has definitely stretched that set of skills, and I often remind myself how much I do know, that it's OK not to know or be an expert or be perfect, and that I can learn so much that once seemed unattainable.

You mentioned that the mannUfactory hosted a couple of workshops about impostor syndrome early on. Can you tell me more about that?

One of the reasons we did the workshops about impostor syndrome was I experienced it myself and I knew if I did and if we wanted the space to be welcoming and inclusive, we'd probably better address it up front. Also, at an Ivy League school where there's a lot of stress around work and perfection, having an explicit place to address this and de-stress was a big goal. Luckily, we had a staff member who had done a session on impostor syndrome in tech for a couple of professional development events, so I had someone to call on as a presenter. She did a couple of those workshops and while we only had a small number of attendees, I think they really got something out of it, and we had people who couldn't make it express interest (and another group contact us to see if the speaker might be able to do something for their members).

The main thing that stands out to me about the mannUfactory is the range of activities you support. I see a 3D Modeling workshop and a Galentine's Day crafting event on your calendar this month (definitely stealing that idea for next year, by the way). Is it harder to justify supporting crafts compared to supporting digital fabrication? Do you get any administrative pushback or do you have the freedom to try different kinds of events?

Please do "steal" it! (I totally got it from somewhere else that I sadly forget now and I loved Parks and Rec). And we have no difficulty justifying doing crafts and get zero pushback. In fact, we got a request from our Communication department to help launch a yarnbombing project[5] to cover the library gates at our two biggest libraries on campus to make them less intimidating to students. Button making and then sewing and mending are two of our most popular activities besides 3D printing. We also did a Black Panther party around Black History Month last February and the release of Black Panther, and this year we did a Sheroes event around the beginning of March for Black and Women's History months and the release of Captain Marvel (I'm a Marvel fan and a black woman). For Earth Week this year we're doing snack container making/repurposing and T-shirt-making workshops. We pretty much have free rein.

And crafts and non-digital fabrication are an important part of our curricular integration as well. We've had classes, especially a lot of our first-year writing classes, do zines, artists' books, buttons, sculptures and dioramas, collages, a quilt, and papercraft for final projects. This semester we're working with a math class that has a creative final group project, and they can make anything related to the math concepts they're studying, whether it's 3D printing, origami, knitting, music, or anything else.

Do you see a difference between making and crafting?

I don't see a difference between the two. Somewhere in our initial investigation, I read an article[6] about the white, middle class, tech-focused biases of how the Maker Movement is framed and something else about how, traditionally, female or people of color-focused crafts or types of making were devalued or not counted.

I also noticed in your Galentine's Day event description that it says, "Gals and non-binary folks of all kinds especially welcome." This is such a small detail, but it speaks volumes about your space, particularly because makerspaces are often criticized for catering to white heterosexual male audiences. Are there other ways that the mannUfactory has tried to be more inclusive? Do you think the mannUfactory is a welcoming space?

---

5. "Give Our Gates a Yarnover," Mann Library, Cornell University, February 1, 2019, https://mannlib.cornell.edu/news-events/news/give-our-gates-a-yarnover.

6. Debbie Chachra, "Why I Am Not a Maker," *The Atlantic*, January 23, 2015, https://www.theatlantic.com/technology/archive/2015/01/why-i-am-not-a-maker/384767/.

We do try—from things like having pronoun buttons at the desk that we make in-house to diversifying the resources and examples we use to trying to hire a diverse student staff and bring in all kinds of presenters and do events that will appeal to a wide range of people. (For one zine workshop we pointed out the Queer Zine Archive Project,[7] and we had as an example to try folding a zine on trans activism.[8]) It's always a work in progress though.

Reflections on Camille's Interview: Crafting is Making

In a presentation about gender and makerspaces, Dr. Kim Martin shared the history of the short-lived *Craft* magazine, a companion publication to the notorious *Make* magazine.[9] At one point, actress and crafter-extraordinaire Amy Sedaris was featured on the cover surrounded by ribbons, cake, and lots and lots of pink. The cover is wonderful and certainly something I would pick up and read, but begs the question: why not put Amy on the cover of *Make* magazine? Are crafting and making not one and the same? Is crafting a female domain and making a male domain? *Craft* only lasted for ten issues, but its existence was enough to establish a distinction between making and crafting and raise questions about gender in the Maker Movement.

I've often wondered if crafting has a place in makerspaces and higher education. Over the past four years, I've taught more than thirty-five maker workshops with topics ranging from stop motion animation to screen printing. Whenever I teach something crafty, I can't help but feel like I'm getting away with something. While I would gladly tell our Dean about an Arduino workshop, I would think twice before sharing the results of an embroidery session. I'm not alone in thinking that crafting is generally perceived as a frivolous pursuit. In a 2014 article

---

7. Queer Zine Archive Project, https://www.qzap.org/v9/index.php.

8. Ramona is Online, https://ramonaisonline.tumblr.com/post/179600544894/looking-for-some-things-you-can-do-to-help-the?is_highlighted_post=1.

9. Kim Martin, "Centering Gender: A Feminist Analysis of Makerspaces and Digital Humanities Centers" (presentation, Indiana University, November 28, 2017) https://scholarworks.iu.edu/dspace/handle/2022/21827.

from Intel about women makers, the authors explain, "Art projects are not seen as being as serious as other, more technical, projects. There is a gendering of technology at play in these environments. Technology is construed as masculine and art as feminine."[10] These preconceptions haven't prevented me from offering non-technical workshops, but I've typically shied away from talking about them.

I reached out to Camille because I was impressed to see a blend of crafty and techie offerings on the mannUfactory events calendar. If a prestigious university like Cornell could support crafts, then why couldn't we? Everyone I spoke to was adamant that crafting is a form of making and should be treated as such. Hearing other women speak confidently about their choices to support crafting made me realize that I was perpetuating the artificial divide between making and crafting by only promoting our more technical offerings. When I look back at our workshop statistics, it's clear that crafting does have a place in our library. Light-up valentines and bullet journals have been our most well-attended workshops to date. Perhaps the best way to combat the gendering of technology is to stop belittling these pursuits.

Interview #2: Michele Potter

Michele is currently the Collection Strategist for Science, Technology, Engineering, and Math (STEM) at the University of California, Riverside. At the time of this interview, she was the Open Research Librarian and coordinated technology, 3D services, and daily operations for the Creat'R Lab makerspace.

Leanne: How do you define the term makerspace? Has your definition changed over time?

Michele: I think makerspaces are places that provide materials and equipment for making. I am not sure how or whether the definition has changed. It is such a new word, and such a flexible one, that it seems to accommodate a wide variety of types of making, accessibility, location

---

10. Susan Faulkner and Anne McClard, "Making Change: Can Ethnographic Research About Women Makers Change the Future of Computing?" *2014 Ethnographic Praxis in Industry Conference Proceedings*, 191.

etc. The available space and the organizational purpose play such an enormous role in the form a makerspace will take.

I like that you used the word "flexible" here. Sometimes when I tell people about makerspaces it seems like anything can be a makerspace and therefore the definition falls apart, but I think the fact that it's open-ended is a wonderful thing. It leaves room for new and different ideas. Do you consider yourself a maker?

Sort of. I am a bit of a lifehacker. I will typically learn how to use a tool or piece of equipment when I see a need for a thing that it could create, alter, or facilitate. I like to invent things, and sometimes the only way to get the prototype to exist is to make it myself. I most enjoy altering existing things to be more awesome. I don't excel at yarn arts, or painting, or other endeavors that require starting with a blank canvas. However, I love to thrift, and frequently find things that are almost awesome. I am way more likely to buy an existing scarf and sew pockets onto it than I am to crochet a scarf.

At the 2018 Makerspaces in Innovation and Research in Academics (MIRA) conference, you co-presented a talk about collaborating with faculty in the Creat'R Lab. How have faculty responded to your space? Is it challenging to bring them into this realm, or are they receptive?

I have had a cadre of faculty respond very positively to the space. Some are familiar with similar spaces and some are new to the concept, but wildly excited. I have not had any faculty respond negatively or even lukewarmly, but I don't necessarily have faculty beating down the door. This quarter, I am working with four instructors; one is new to the Lab this quarter and the other three I have worked with before.

I also work with a sometimes overlapping but sometimes completely different set of faculty as researchers rather than teachers. For faculty, I have scanned objects and printed teaching models, lab equipment, or something to showcase their research, or lent them media equipment, such as our 360 camera. If I did have faculty beating down the door, I don't know what I would do. We are almost at capacity as it is.

Have you experienced any skepticism from colleagues or other folks on campus who might not understand your space?

Yes. I could make a tidy list. The other people who run fabrication labs on campus, where they might have larger volume, are confused by our student focus and/or the fact that we are open to everyone. They are also confused, and sometimes rightly so, by the fact that we don't charge. I would say there are people in the library itself that are sometimes surprised by what we do, but many recognize the need for libraries to expand their roles in their communities. Students in engineering, sciences, and arts seem to get the space right away, but other students have to be drawn in. I hear, anecdotally, about administrators out there in the world that don't see the point of a makerspace or understand why it should be in the library, but we have been very well supported and people on campus seem so excited that such a space exists. They also seem to get that being in a library makes it accessible to everyone.

To your point about administrators not seeing the point of a makerspace, I also tend to hear these things secondhand, but I've never had someone say it to me directly. These comments always irk me a bit. How do you respond to criticism?

Since I have not generally been called on to respond to criticism but am frequently called upon to give my elevator speech, I definitely fall back on that quite a bit. The elevator speech is typically given in answer to someone who stumbles upon the room and has no idea what it is, or groups that come for tours, or classes that I wittingly or unwittingly wind up in delivering my elevator speech. I think it would be fascinating to role-play criticisms just so I can make sure I have ready answers. I would probably start with "I totally see where you are coming from, but...."

Salient points:
- There is nowhere else that is available to everyone on campus that has these technologies available to students.
- Not having to duplicate some types of equipment in many places is less expensive.
- We are fostering a lot of great work.
- Libraries have inventory management and organization pretty well down.
- Libraries are central and visible.

- The equipment here is available to students when their labs may not be open.
- This space is supervised for set hours, so people know when they can come in and work on projects.
- We have no theft and almost no breakage (not that we would be freaked out if we did.) So far, we have not had to replace any equipment that we paid for.
- Self-chosen, hands-on projects allow students to explore technologies in a low-stakes way, and possibly come up with new and awesome things.
- We can teach people how to sew/solder/3D print/use media equipment for them to use in their disciplines or just as useful life skills.
- We are giving our student employees experience with many new technical skills, as well as experience with public service, teaching, explaining, creating, etc.

These are excellent points! What's your general elevator pitch for the Creat'R Lab?

The Creat'R Lab is a space where students, faculty and staff from all over campus can come and be creative. We try to assemble the equipment, materials, and technical help so that people can play with the latest maker technologies and see where it takes them. The space is deliberately cross-disciplinary, so that people from different majors can share knowledge and enthusiasm. We are not attempting to replace any major-related labs, but rather to make a common space where people can work with people and technologies from outside of their majors.

Reflections on Michele's Interview: Library as Impostor

Young writes about uncovering your crusher, or "a core negative belief we hold about ourselves." She explains, "At its heart, your crusher has to do with a basic feeling of inadequacy and unworthiness."[11] According to Young, one way to determine your crusher is to imagine being publicly outed as a fraud. The thing you would most fear hearing aloud is your crusher.

---

11. Young, *The Secret Thoughts of Successful Women*, 83.

I imagined myself sitting amongst the group of campus makerspace partners and hearing, "You don't belong here." The image felt all too real, but I knew it was a lie. Michele's elevator pitch made me realize that the characteristics that differentiate us give us an advantage. Our space is open to everyone, including staff and community members. We've never charged for supplies or equipment use, and I have free rein to try out any workshop that folks might be interested in. Furthermore, when one of my faculty colleagues asked about our checkout system, I realized how lucky I was to exist within the library infrastructure, where we've been perfecting lending for decades.

I set out to learn how individuals were working through impostor syndrome in makerspaces but was surprised to find that often librarians were more uncertain about having a makerspace in the library in the first place. In a way, the library, not the librarian, was the impostor. A majority of my interviewees touched on their experiences defending their spaces and explaining why it made sense to put a makerspace in the library. I was frequently called upon to do the same, but I wasn't always prepared to sing our praises. Rather than let the differences weigh me down, I've tried to reframe my thinking and celebrate the sweet spot that is the library makerspace. We are a unique breed, but we enjoy support, resources, and freedom that other makerspaces will never know. We are not inferior to other spaces and we are every bit as real.

Interview #3: Diana Rendina

Diana is a media specialist/teacher-librarian at Tampa Preparatory School in Tampa, Florida, and creator of the Renovated Learning website.

Leanne: I'm a big fan of your site, Renovated Learning. Your blog post about defining makerspaces really resonated with me the first time I read it and I return to it often.[12] You describe an instance where someone said your space was not a "real" makerspace. This post is from 2015—have you encountered any skeptics since then?

---

12. Diana Rendina, "Defining Makerspaces: What the Research Says," Renovated Learning, April 2, 2015, http://www.renovatedlearning.com/2015/04/02/defining-makerspaces-part-1/.

How do you respond to criticism? Did you ever consider calling your space something other than a makerspace?

Diana: I haven't had anyone say directly that either of my makerspaces were not "real" makerspaces since 2015, but I have encountered criticism that's more subtle. I have had people tell me things like, "It must be so nice to let your students play with LEGOs in the library, but that wouldn't work at our school. We are very rigorous with our academics." Or things like, "Those craft projects look like so much fun, but how do you have time for 'extras' like that?" My response to criticism really depends on where and who it's coming from. Usually I will counter with stories of some of the learning experiences my students have had in our makerspace, or how I've collaborated with teachers on classroom projects, etc. I have considered other names—at Stewart, I started with the name Stewart Makerspace, because the concept was still so new (this was 2014), and I wanted teachers and students to have a clear understanding of what it was. After we'd had it going for a few months, I asked my students if they wanted to rename it, and they overwhelmingly chose to keep the makerspace name. I didn't get the final say for the name for my current space (the IDEAlab), since it was created before I was hired, which is why I tend to add "and Makerspace" to the end when talking about it. I think it's ultimately about what name works best for your school.

What was your first experience in a makerspace? Did you feel welcome?

I don't think I had actually visited any other makerspaces yet when I first started mine at Stewart in January 2014. I think the first makerspace I visited outside of my space was Tampa Hackerspace. They were amazingly welcoming and I immediately felt a part of the community. It was mostly made up of men who were older than me and who definitely had more of a hacker interest, but they were very supportive and excited about what I was working on at my school. I took a soldering class there and printed my first 3D print there. When we held our first maker faire at my school, they came as special guests and brought 3D printers and robots for my students to try out. In general, most makerspaces that I have visited have been very welcoming and inclusive.

Do you consider yourself a maker? Have you ever experienced impostor syndrome when it comes to making?

I've always considered myself a maker, even if I haven't always called myself that. As a kid, my room was filled with LEGOs and K'nex. I learned how to sew in high school, how to knit in college. I was always finding some sort of creative project to work on. I was always really into photography. The technology side honestly didn't really interest me until I got started creating the makerspace at Stewart. I had to learn alongside the kids—I had no idea at the time what conductive materials were, how to design a circuit, how to create a 3D file, etc. I've never really felt impostor syndrome with making—if I don't know how to do something, I teach myself or ask for help.

That's so refreshing to hear! Do you have any advice for people who do experience impostor syndrome in makerspaces?

I think that the main thing to remember is that we're all in this together. None of us are born expert makers. We are born creative, but we become makers. We all had to start somewhere, and we're all at different places in this journey. As an educator, I've always felt that it's important to admit that I don't know something. That's a part of the learning process, and it makes the experience so much richer. So, for those who feel a sense of impostor syndrome, try to embrace where you are in the process rather than worrying about how others might think of you.

You've also written about the distinction between making and crafting. Do you find that your students view crafting as "less than" other forms of making, or does this attitude mainly come from adults?

I think the view of crafting as less than tends to come more from adults. If the creative project doesn't have some sort of clear higher order thinking going on, it gets put down. The funny thing about this is that a student could 3D print out a project they'd worked on for five minutes, and these adults would be more impressed than with a student who spent hours designing an arcade game out of cardboard and recycled materials. To me, it's really all about creativity and supporting students to explore projects and try new things. And, frankly, sometimes it's okay to just make stuff for the sake of making it, without some greater academic purpose in mind.

What do you see as the biggest challenge for library makerspaces going forward?

I think the biggest challenge for library makerspaces is the one we've faced from the beginning—getting our communities to recognize how important it is to have these spaces in the library. I am all for creating multiple makerspaces in schools, and I think that classroom makerspaces are great. But the library is all about equitable access to resources for everyone. And I see makerspaces as a continuation of this—creating access for ALL our students to have creative experiences with a variety of tools and materials. If we take these spaces out of the library, it makes it much harder to level the playing field and give every student a chance to experience this.

Reflections on Diana's Interview: Embracing the Unknown

What stands out most to me about Diana's interview is her self-confidence. After following her blog, I was curious to hear if she had struggled with impostor syndrome, but if anything, she is a shining example of how to avoid self-doubt. As she points out, sometimes you're learning alongside your students or patrons, and that doesn't make you a fraud. The key is to find comfort in not knowing and be open to learning new things.

A majority of the women I spoke with expressed a similar sentiment as Diana, but this confidence might not come as easily for women as it does for men. Young describes a phenomenon called "male answer syndrome," where men are compelled to answer a question regardless of their knowledge of the subject rather than say "I don't know."[13] I've experienced this firsthand with male attendees at my workshops. Female participants are often quick to confess that they've never done something before, but men tend to keep that to themselves. When you consider the typical physical makeup of a makerspace, it's easy to get the impression

---

13. Young, *The Secret Thoughts of Successful Women*, 200-201.

that everyone in the room is an expert. This can be intimidating for newcomers, especially those from underrepresented groups.

Adopting a "fake it 'til you make it" approach might seem tempting, but I wouldn't recommend it. Instead, we should embrace our inexperience and let it fuel our curiosity and desire to learn. Fortunately, this is a basic principle of librarianship. When I was in grad school, a librarian with 40+ years of experience told me that one of the most important skills at the reference desk was to admit your ignorance. If someone approached the desk and wanted help with something you had never heard of, it was no reason to panic or pretend. Instead, you could simply say, "I'm not familiar with x, could you tell me more about that?" This attitude empowers us as librarians and can do the same in the makerspace.

Final Thoughts

The greatest lesson I learned was that support and encouragement are out there if you look for it. I wasn't necessarily going to find validation from my campus colleagues, because they work under different circumstances with different populations and different goals, but hearing from my library peers was much more significant. As I've reflected on my impostor syndrome, I've realized that a handful of women have encouraged me to keep going. Without this support system, I would have turned my back on makerspaces a long time ago. Connecting with other women has helped me to see myself in the Maker Movement. As Young explains, "the more people who look or sound like you, the more confident you feel. And conversely, the fewer people who look or sound like you, it can and does for many people impact their confidence."[14]

Gender imbalance in makerspaces is part of what motivated me to write this chapter, but I found it difficult to investigate this aspect of my impostor syndrome. In most of my interactions, I found that women weren't shy about saying they had experienced gender bias but

---

14. Valerie Young, "Yes, Impostor Syndrome is Real. Here's How to Deal with It," *Time*, June 20, 2018, https://time.com/5312483/how-to-deal-with-impostor-syndrome/.

seemed hesitant to put it in writing. It is evident there is much work to be done in this area.

At the end of Young's book [spoiler alert], she confesses that your impostor syndrome can lessen, but may never completely go away.[15] I won't pretend that this experience "cured" me, but these conversations have been instrumental in helping me find my voice and take ownership of my work. I hope it might inspire others to take a similar journey.

Acknowledgements

In addition to the interviews included here, I also spoke with the following individuals. Their thoughts and experiences were instrumental in shaping this chapter and I am incredibly grateful for their time and insight.

- Nicholae Cline, Scholarly Services Librarian at Indiana University Libraries and collection manager for Gender Studies, Media Studies, and Philosophy.
- Hailley Fargo, Student Engagement Coordinator at Penn State University Libraries.
- Laura Hohman, Production Manager for the Indiana University Press and an active member of the Bloominglabs makerspace in Bloomington, Indiana.
- Karen Jensen, Children's and YA Materials Selector at the Fort Worth Public Library and creator of the "Teen Librarian Toolbox," a *School Library Journal* blog.
- Dr. Kimberly Martin, Assistant Professor in History at the University of Guelph and co-founder of the Maker Bus, Canada's first mobile makerspace.

---

15. Young, *The Secret Thoughts of Successful Women*, 257.

Bibliography

Chachra, Debbie. "Why I Am Not a Maker." *The Atlantic*, January 23, 2015. https://www.theatlantic.com/technology/archive/2015/01/why-i-am-not-a-maker/384767/.

Faulkner, Susan, and Anne McClard. "Making Change: Can Ethnographic Research About Women Makers Change the Future of Computing?" *2014 Ethnographic Praxis in Industry Conference Proceedings*, 187-198.

"Give Our Gates a Yarnover." Mann Library, Cornell University. February 1, 2019. https://mannlib.cornell.edu/news-events/news/give-our-gates-a-yarnover.

Make/Intel, "Maker Market Study and Media Report," 2012, https://cdn.makezine.com/make/sales/Maker-Market-Study.pdf.

Martin, Kim. "Centering Gender: A Feminist Analysis of Makerspaces and Digital Humanities Centers." Presentation at Indiana University, November 28, 2017. https://scholarworks.iu.edu/dspace/handle/2022/21827.

Queer Zine Archive Project. https://www.qzap.org/v9/index.php.

Ramona is Online. https://ramonaisonline.tumblr.com/post/179600544894/looking-for-some-things-you-can-do-to-help-the?is_highlighted_post=1.

Rendina, Diana. "Defining Makerspaces: What the Research Says," Renovated Learning, April 2, 2015, http://www.renovatedlearning.com/2015/04/02/defining-makerspaces-part-1/.

"Where Does 'Impostor Syndrome' Come From?" *Merriam-Webster*, accessed April 13, 2019. https://www.merriam-webster.com/words-at-play/what-is-impostor-syndrome.

Wong, Kristin. "Dealing with Impostor Syndrome When You're Treated as an Impostor." *New York Times*, June 12, 2018. https://www.nytimes.com/2018/06/12/smarter-living/dealing-with-impostor-syndrome-when-youre-treated-as-an-impostor.html.

Young, Valerie. *The Secret Thoughts of Successful Women*. New York: Crown Business, 2011.

Young, Valerie. "Yes, Impostor Syndrome is Real. Here's How to Deal with It." *Time*, June 20, 2018. https://time.com/5312483/how-to-deal-with-impostor-syndrome/.

About the Contributors

Audrey Boklage is a research assistant in the Cockrell School of Engineering at the University of Texas at Austin. She is particularly interested in improving the culture and environment of the undergraduate education experience for all students, particularly those from underrepresented groups. Audrey has expertise in qualitative research methods, including exploratory case studies and narrative inquiry.

Jennifer Brown is an Undergraduate Learning and Research Librarian at the University of California, Berkeley, where she focuses on pedagogy and instruction rooted within anti-racist, critical pedagogies such as Critical Race Theory, visionary fiction, & speculative futuring. Previously, she was the Service Lead and Design & Technologies Librarian at Barnard College, where she focused on integrating critical maker praxis into the library's makerspace.

Estefania Castillo is a Master's student in the Rhetoric and Writing Program at the University of Texas at El Paso.

Morgan Chivers undertook extensive undergraduate studies at San Jose State University (2011), yielding four simultaneously conferred degrees: BA Global Studies, BFA Photography, BA History, and BFA Spatial Arts. He completed the MFA in Glass/Intermedia at the University of Texas, Arlington (2015), where he is now the FabLab Librarian and

Artist-in-Residence, collaborating with faculty to integrate critical making into curricula across a beautifully diverse campus.

Anna Montana Cirell. After earning her Ph.D. in Learning, Literacies, and Technology, Anna completed a postdoctoral appointment in Ira A. Fulton Schools of Engineering at Arizona State University. Her work as the Technology Lead for CATalyst Studios at the University of Arizona helps her to bridge the gap between research and practice.

Brooke Coley, Ph.D. is Assistant Professor of Engineering at the Polytechnic School in the Ira A. Fulton Schools of Engineering at Arizona State University. Dr. Coley is Principal Investigator of the Shifting Perceptions, Attitudes and Cultures in Engineering (SPACE) Lab that aspires to elevate the experiences of marginalized populations, dismantle systemic injustices, and transform the way inclusion is cultivated in engineering through the implementation of novel technologies and methodologies in engineering education. Intrigued by the intersections of engineering education, mental health, and social justice, Dr. Coley's primary research interest focuses on virtual reality as a tool for developing empathetic and inclusive mindsets among engineering faculty. She is also interested in hidden populations in engineering education and innovation for more inclusive pedagogies.

Anne Cong-Huyen is a Senior Associate Librarian and Digital Scholarship Strategist at the University of Michigan Library. She was previously the Digital Scholar and coordinator of the Digital Liberal Arts Program at Whittier College, and was a Mellon Visiting Assistant Professor of Asian American Studies at UCLA. She holds a PhD in English from the University of California, Santa Barbara. She is a co-founder of #transformDH, serves on the steering committee of HASTAC, and the American Studies Association Digital Humanities Caucus. She is also a director of the Situated Critical Race and Media (SCRAM) collective, which hosts the FemTechNet Network Gathering at the Allied Media Conference.

Danielle Dolan-Sanchez is a graduate student in Information Science at the University of Arizona. Her current research is focused on Human Computer Interaction (HCI) and ways that gender identities shape the use of interactive technologies and their design.

Xun Ge is Professor of Learning Sciences in the Department of Educational Psychology at the University of Oklahoma. Dr. Ge's scholarship focuses on the dimensions of cognition, metacognition, motivation, and assessment that intersect with each other in the design of technology-supported learning environments. Specifically, her research involves design scaffolding tools and learning environments to support complex problem solving and self-regulation in various learning environments, including Makerspace learning environments.

Laura Gonzales is an Assistant Professor of Digital Writing and Cultural Rhetorics and Associate Director of the TRACE Innovation Initiative at the University of Florida. Her research focuses on the intersections of language, technology, and community engagement.

DiMitri Higginbotham is a Makerspace Educator and Design Thinker at Good Shepherd Episcopal School in Dallas, Texas. DiMitri started his education career as a band director and later earned a Master's in Design and Innovation from Southern Methodist University's Lyle School of Engineering. His work is focused on maker education and design thinking for K-12 students, and consulting teachers to use these learning styles in the classroom.

Nadia Kellam is Associate Professor and Graduate Program Chair in the Polytechnic School of the Ira A. Fulton Schools of Engineering at Arizona State University. She is a qualitative researcher who primarily uses narrative research methods to develop critical understandings of the experiences of undergraduate engineering students and engineering educators. Her current research focuses on developing an understanding of makerspaces as potential spaces of empowerment for underrepresented engineering students.

Kyungwon Koh is Associate Professor in the School of Information Sciences at the University of Illinois at Urbana-Champaign. Her areas of expertise include the Maker Movement in libraries and education, learning and community engagement through libraries, youth information behavior/practice and information literacy, and competencies for information professionals.

Vicki Lázaro is a Librarian for Pima County Public Library at the Joel D. Valdez Main Library in Tucson, AZ, where she oversees the downtown Teen Lounge and 101 Space teen makerspace. Prior to Pima County, Vicki helped run and develop the CATalyst Studios, the Women's Hackathon, and the Emerging Technologies Experience for the Strategic Plan at the University of Arizona as an Emerging Technologies Librarian.

Lo Lee is a Ph.D. student in Library and Information Science at the University of Illinois at Urbana-Champaign. Her current research interest is on human information behavior, especially everyday information behavior of creative people, such as crafts hobbyists. She is also interested in the Maker Movement and how it influences library and museum programs.

Victor R. Lee is Associate Professor at Stanford University in the Graduate School of Education. He conducts research on learning with data in and out of school settings, the Maker Movement, and computer science education. He obtained his Ph.D. from Northwestern University in Learning Sciences.

Noah Lenstra is Assistant Professor of Library & Information Science in the School of Education at the University of North Carolina at Greensboro. He researches community engagement in public libraries, particularly as it relates to health & wellness, aging, and digital inclusion.

He obtained his Ph.D. from the University of Illinois in Library & Information Science.

Kathryn R. Lewis has served as the Director of Libraries and Instructional Technology for Norman Public Schools for nineteen years. Kathryn was the Project Director for an Institute of Museum and Library Services grant entitled, *Learning in Libraries: Guiding Inquiry Making and Learning in School Libraries.* She serves as the Immediate Past President of the American Association of School Librarians. Kathryn oversees school libraries and is interested in learner engagement and self-efficacy, the role of school librarians in inquiry and making, and collaboration and coteaching between school librarians and classroom educators.

Heather Lister is the Founder and Chief Education Officer at Construct Learning, a STEM and maker education consultancy and professional development provider. Formerly a school librarian, Heather now works with teachers and organizations around the globe in implementing hands-on learning.

Sanjeet Mann is Arts and Systems Librarian at the University of Redlands, where he coordinates library systems and technology and supports teaching and learning for faculty and students in music, studio art, creative writing, and theatre.

Brianna Marshall is Director of Research Services at the University of California Riverside Library, where she oversees the Creat'R Lab makerspace and initiatives to support the scholarly and academic activities of UCR faculty, researchers, and students.

Marijel (Maggie) Melo is an assistant professor in the School of Information and Library Science at the University of North Carolina at Chapel Hill. Her research specialization resides at the intersection of innovation, critical maker culture, and the development of equitable and inclusive collaborative learning spaces (i.e. makerspaces) in academic libraries. She co-founded the first interdisciplinary makerspace at the University of Arizona, and is the founder of the first women-only hackathon in the Southwest.

Meaghan Moody is the Teaching & Learning Librarian at the University of Pennsylvania Libraries. She supports instruction and programming around a range of technologies in the Libraries' collaborative learning commons, and is a co-founder of the Education Commons TinkerLab.

Heather Moorefield-Lang is an Assistant Professor of Library and Information Science in the School of Education at the University of North Carolina at Greensboro. She researches technology trends in education and libraries with a current focus on makerspaces in library settings.

Leanne Nay is Digital Engagement Librarian at Indiana University, Bloomington and founder of the Wells Library Mini Makerspace. Her research interests include digital media, design thinking, and makerspaces.

Lee B. Nelson has served as the Norman Public Schools' Technology Integration Specialist since 1998, providing district-wide staff professional development, developing curriculum and materials, analyzing data, and supporting technology initiatives. She holds a Masters and Ph.D. in Educational and Instructional Psychology and Technology from the University of Oklahoma. Her 2011 dissertation examined how teacher motivation and social responsibility related to classroom technology integration.

Jennifer T. Nichols is the Director of CATalyst Studios at the University of Arizona Libraries. She works with students, faculty, and campus and community partners to support digital scholarship, virtual and augmented reality, and critical making, both formally and informally. Jennifer's work is centered on supporting equitable practices within technology-rich spaces, and she continues to develop CATalyst Studios into a dynamic center of interdisciplinary learning communities.

Katie Musick Peery is the director of the UTA FabLab at the University of Texas at Arlington Libraries. Her research is focused on integrating maker literacies into higher education curricula and on diversifying makerspace student hiring and best practices for makerspace training to increase the impact and efficacy that makerspaces can have on a college campus.

Caitlin Pollock is the Digital Scholarship Specialist for University of Michigan Library, where she works with students and faculty on digital scholarship workshops, projects, and initiatives. Her work consists of coordinating workshops, programming, and facilitating digital exhibits for library staff, faculty, and students. She holds a Master of Science in Library and Information Science from Pratt Institute and a Master of Arts in Digital Humanities from Loyola University Chicago. Her research interests include Black digital humanities, critical race feminist data praxis, and DIY making pedagogy.

Bibhushana Poudyal is a Ph.D. student in the Rhetoric and Writing Studies Program at the University of Texas, El Paso and an Honorary Overseas DH Consultant at the Center for Advanced Studies in South Asia (CASSA). Her teaching and research interests emerge from the intersections of rhetorical theory, postcolonialism, feminism, and critical digital humanities.

Mimi Recker is Professor in the Department of Instructional Technology and Learning Sciences at Utah State University. She studies the role that emerging technologies can play in transforming education. She received her Ph.D. from the University of California, Berkeley.

Nora K. Rivera is a Ph.D. student in the program of Rhetoric and Composition at the University of Texas at El Paso. She holds a Masters in Business Administration with a concentration in Marketing and a Master of Arts in Spanish Literature. Her research interests are cultural and Borderland rhetorics, particularly the rhetorical practices that take place in the visual and oral realms.

Joy Robinson teaches user experience (UX) at the University of Alabama in Huntsville. Joy has 10+ years of experience in exploring user research. She holds a Ph.D. in Technical Communication and Masters and Bachelor degrees in Engineering. She currently manages UX teams at Northrop Grumman.

Aubrey Rogowski is a doctoral student in the Department of Instructional Technology and Learning Sciences at Utah State University. Her research interests include STEM-rich making and the various ways teachers and librarians interact with curricula resources to create learning experiences.

Rob Rouse is a Clinical Associate Professor in the Simmons School of Education at Southern Methodist University (SMU). In addition to teaching classes related to STEM education to pre-service and in-service teachers, Rob operated SMU's mobile makerspace, the MakerTruck, and is the past Interim Director of the SMU Maker Education Project.

Anthony Sanchez is an Assistant Librarian and liaison to the College of Social and Behavioral Sciences at the University of Arizona. He is a co-founder of the CATalyst Studios. His research interests include VR/AR applications in education, ethical archiving, peer learning models, and inclusive technology for underrepresented groups.

John T. Sherrill is an Assistant Professor of Professional Writing at Qatar University. His research interests include technical communication,

DIY communities, and digital rhetoric. He completed his Ph.D. at Purdue University.

Ann Shivers-McNair is an Assistant Professor and Director of Professional and Technical Writing in the Department of English and Affiliated Faculty in the School of Information at the University of Arizona. She is associate editor of *Technical Communication Quarterly* and co-organizer of UX@UA, a user experience professional community in Tucson, Arizona.

Shirley Simmons has worked as a district administrator for twelve years and is currently the Assistant Superintendent of Educational Services in Norman Public Schools. She also has 17 years' experience as an elementary and middle school principal. She earned her Ph.D. in Adult and Higher Education from the University of Oklahoma. She oversees all curriculum content areas and has great interest in the role of libraries in inquiry learning and making.

Chava Spivak-Birndorf is the Emerging Technologies Librarian at the University of Pennsylvania Libraries. She manages the Education Commons, a collaborative learning space, where she develops instruction surrounding a range of technologies, including 3D services, electronics, and makerspace activities. She is co-founder of the Education Commons TinkerLab.

Tetyana Zhyvotovska is a Ph.D. candidate and an assistant instructor in the Rhetoric and Writing Studies Program at the University of Texas at El Paso. She previously taught at universities in Ukraine and the United States. Her research and teaching interests are situated at the intersection of technical communication, translation, and user experience.

Index

3D printers, 19, 38, 47, 63, 88, 167, 192, 248-9, 256, 294

3D printing, 27, 86, 192-3, 195, 198, 229, 272, 278, 285, 287

A

AASL National School Library Standards, 141, 146-7

ableism, 15

accessibility, 73, 107, 289
  in makerspaces, 24, 91, 162, 168
  and "making the body", 107-8

accountability, 36, 213-4

Ada Initiative, 281

Adverse Childhood Experience Survey (ACE), 115-17

agency, 130, 215

Americans with Disabilities Act (ADA), 91

Anji Play Initiative, 107

Arduino, 67, 167, 184, 187, 288

B

Barnard Design Center, 19

barrier[s]
  to access, 40, 162
  to entry, 89, 92, 248
  to inclusivity, 161-64

Bike Kitchen program, 104

BIPOC (Black, Indigenous, and People of Color), 2, 12-14, 17-23, 83, 93

Blutrack racing system, 174

Buechley, Leah, 184, 188, 200

bullying, 5, 138-47; *see also* cyberbullying

C

card sort, 158-9

Center for Advanced Studies in South Asia (CASSA), 217

Centro Profesional Indigena de Asesoría Defensa y Traducción (CEPIADET), 217

Chicago Public Library, 281
Children's Art in Libraries (CAL) initiative, 103
circuit[s], 67, 172-5, 177, 283, 295
Coalition of Women of Color in Computing Project, 204, 208-9, 212, 214, 218-9, 221
code of conduct, 29, 90, 94
Code to Move program, 105
codeweaving, 60
coding, 29, 35, 47, 58-61
cohort critique, 259-60
collaboration, 213, 220-1, 227-32, 236-8, 240-2
communication, 38, 129, 131, 235
cortisol, 119, 122
counternarrative[s], 18-24
counter-storytelling, 16, 18
Craft magazine, 288
crafts, 39, 136, 140, 172, 270, 285-7, 289
Creat'R Lab, 86, 87, 289, 290, 292
Critical Race Theory (CRT), 11-8, 20, 23
cyberbullying, 142, 144; *see also* bullying

D
dance, 102-3, 109
Dance Dance Revolution mat, 175
Dance Mat Pacman, 103
Dedoose app, 59
deficit thinking, 72

democracy, 31, 234
democratization, 13, 153, 160
demographics, 76-7, 137, 158, 247, 252, 263, 270
denaturalization, 229
Derrida, Jacques, 266
downloading, 159-60
Drabinski, Emily, 85

E
EC TinkerLab, 184, 192-95, 198-200
empowerment, 21-2, 48, 50, 53-4, 200, 227
entrepreneurship, 86, 203, 231, 265
Eodice, Michelle, 266-7, 273
epistemes, 217, 220
epistemology, 55, 233, 234
equity, diversity, and inclusion (EDI), 84, 87-8, 96
E-textiles, 172, 184, 190
ethnography, 75, 239
exclusion, 11, 20, 66, 169, 279

F
Fab Lab Network, 260
Facebook, 208, 211
failure, 115, 127, 129, 155, 253
feminism, 15, 42, 199, 220-1
feminist making, 14-5, 34, 183-4, 187, 190-2, 195, 207
Firstspace, 52-3, 59, 62-3
focus group[s], 208, 249, 250
Freire, Paolo, 51, 233-35

G

gender, 30-32, 34, 37-8, 42, 54, 86-7, 90, 127, 178, 191, 199, 227, 269-70, 273-4, 277-8, 284, 288
gender bias, 28, 31-2, 36, 38, 168, 297
gendering, 237, 289
Grant Study, 124
grants, 148, 161, 229, 262
grounded theory, 35
Guided Inquiry Design (GID), 137

H

HackAZ, 29
hackerspace[s], 30, 135, 207
    feminist, 14-5, 21, 34, 187, 191, 195
Hackster.io, 206
HBCU (Historically Black Colleges and Universities), 14, 56, 63, 64, 77
Hispanic Serving Institution (HSI), 56, 66, 77
hooks, bell, 195
hospitality, 6, 265-67, 269-81
Human-Centered Design (HCD), 154-7, 160, 165, 208

I

ideology, 230, 234, 241
impostor syndrome, 6, 22, 36, 41, 283-86, 293, 295-98
inequality, 85, 227, 233-4
information and media literacy (IML), 228, 229
Information Literacy Competency Standards for Higher Education, 261
information technology, 216, 232
Instagram, 142, 144, 146, 177
intellectual property, 94-5
International Symposium on Makerspaces (ISAM), 11
intersectionality, 12, 237, 242
intimidation, 40
iSpace, 27-30, 34, 37-39, 41, 87, 88

J

job training, 231, 265, 269
Joint Council for Librarians of Color Conference (JCLC), 21-2
Jurek, Scott, 109

K

K'Nex, 173
knitting, 106, 176, 184, 287, 295

L

Latinx, 211, 270
Legos, 107, 176, 294-5
liberation, 20, 42, 235
Library Conduct Policy, 275
Likert Scale, 268, 273
localization, 214-5

M

machismo, 187
Make magazine, 3, 13, 30, 184, 188-9, 206, 284, 288
Maker Bus, 298
maker culture, 1, 3, 4, 92, 115, 19
maker education, 158, 160
Maker Faire, 189, 206, 294
Maker Literacies taskforce, 261
Maker Media, 190, 206
makerspace[s], 107, 285, 298
   academic, 19, 162-3, 252
   community, 153-4, 162-3
makerspace cart, 176-7
Makerspaces in Innovation and Research in Academics (MIRA), 290
Makey Makey, 103, 171-2, 174-76
making the body, 5, 101-04, 106-10
male answer syndrome, 296
male-dominated spaces, 186, 191
mansplaining, 73
melding, 238-9
mentorship[s], 5, 33, 42, 43, 183, 196, 203-05, 212, 258
microcontrollers, 126, 167, 185
mindset[s], 19, 48, 86, 129, 155, 200, 215, 236-7, 253, 255
   of collaboration, 241-2
   design, 49, 67, 71
   maker, 137, 148
   makerspace, 48-9, 54, 57, 59, 62, 163
   secondspace, 60, 64

multilingual usability studies, 215
Multilingual User Experience, 204, 215
Multilingual User-Experience Research Consortium, 204-5, 208-9, 212, 214, 216, 221
Multilingual User-Experience Research Symposium, 204, 212, 215

N

National Child Traumatic Stress Network, 119
National Survey of Children's Health, 117
neoliberalism, 29, 230-34, 236
Nepal and South Asia, 212, 218-9
Network Principles of Design Justice, 20
neuroplasticity of the brain, 122, 124

O

Obama, Barack, 13, 206
objectification, 233-5, 239

P

Palmer, Parker, 267
patriarchy, 34, 36, 38, 183
pedagogy[ies], 23, 51
   critical, 14, 19-20, 22, 24, 51, 194, 234
   feminist, 193-5
   maker, 147-8

Penn Libraries' Education Commons (EC), 183-4, 192-95, 198-200
positionality, 55-6, 86-7
power analysis framework, 83-85, 88, 95-6
Proaño, Sara, 212
programming, 116
    inclusive, 28, 33, 36, 41-2
    maker, 168, 170, 175-78
    race-conscious, 14, 18
    youth, 174-76
project management (PM), 213, 233
public health, 109, 131
punk rock, 70, 75
PWI (Primarily White Institutions), 13-4, 77

Q
Queer Zine Archive Project, 288

R
race, 11-6, 18-9, 21, 23-4, 29-30, 37-8, 127, 178, 206, 213, 227, 269-70, 273-4, 277
Racial Equity Institute, (REI), 85
robotics, 47, 66, 167, 185, 207

S
San Diego, Clarissa, 212
scaffolding, 73
Second Cycle Analysis, 60
Secondspace, 52, 53, 59, 60, 62, 64
Sedaris, Amy, 288

self-actualization, 255
sewing machine[s], 19, 47, 88, 248-9, 271-2, 278
sexism, 15, 33, 39, 191, 194
sexual harassment, 36, 38, 42, 138, 274
signage, 91-93, 186-7, 270, 273
skills, technical, 185, 253, 271, 276-7, 292
social capital, 125
social justice, 72, 146, 214-5, 219, 234, 241
solidarity, 235, 237-8, 240, 242
South Asian Foundation for Academic Research (SAFAR), 219
speculative futuring, 18-9
STEAM (Science, Technology, Engineering, Art, Math), 40, 107, 148
STEM (Science, Technology, Engineering, Math), 12, 31-2, 40, 49, 136, 168, 171, 200, 206, 240, 289
Stepanek, Mattie T. J., 137
StoryWalk program, 106
strategic contemplation, 207
Substitution, Augmentation, Modification and Redefinition (SAMR) framework, 229, 232, 240

T
Tampa Hackerspace, 294
TASK Parties, 104

The Lab, 265, 267-81
Thirdspace, 47, 53, 59-62, 65, 67-8, 71
Thirdspace theory, 52, 54, 60
TinkerCad, 106, 196-7
trauma informed education, 115

U
U.S. Centers for Disease Control and Prevention (CDC), 109
UA Women's Hackathon, 29
under-represented groups [URGs], 48-50, 53-59, 61-2, 67, 71, 73-4
User Experience (UX), 208-9, 214, 219-20
UTA FabLab, 247-8, 251, 260

V
virtual reality, 27, 229

W
white supremacy, 14, 32-3, 191
whiteness, 33, 205, 227
women of color (WOC), 27-29, 32-34, 37, 39, 41-43, 204
women-centric spaces, 207
workflows, 186, 191, 213, 241, 250
World Health Organization (WHO), 109

Y
yoga, 101, 103

Z
zines, 19, 229, 287
zone of proximal development, 73, 129

CPSIA information can be obtained
at www.ICGtesting.com
Printed in the USA
BVHW070144301020
592026BV00006B/88